POWER AND IDENTITY

The concepts of power and identity are vital to many areas of social research. In this edited collection, a prominent set of contributors explore the double relationship between power and group identity, focusing on two complementary lines of enquiry.

• In what ways can the powerful dictate the identities of the powerless?
• How can the powerless redefine their identity to challenge the powerful?

Each chapter is written by leading authorities in the field, and investigates a particular aspect of the interplay of identity and power via a range of empirical contexts such as colonialism, nationalism, collective action and electoral politics. The case studies include early modern Goa under Portuguese rule, the tribes of modern-day Jordan, the use of sexual stereotyping and objectification by female activists seeking to transform social systems, and a revisiting of the classic Stanford Prison Experiment. The chapters include contributions from a variety of social disciplines and research methodologies, and together provide a comprehensive overview of a subject at the cutting edge of social and political psychology.

Power and Identity will be of great interest to researchers, graduates and upper-level undergraduate students from across the social sciences.

Denis Sindic is Research Fellow at the Institute of Social Sciences, University of Lisbon, Portugal.

Manuela Barreto is Professor of Social and Organisational Psychology at the University of Exeter, UK.

Rui Costa-Lopes is Postdoctoral Research Fellow at the Institute of Social Sciences, University of Lisbon, Portugal.

CURRENT ISSUES IN SOCIAL PSYCHOLOGY
Series Editor: Arjan E. R. Bos

Current Issues in Social Psychology is a series of edited books that reflect the state-of-the-art of current and emerging topics of interest in basic and applied social psychology.

Each volume is tightly focused on a particular topic and consists of seven to ten chapters contributed by international experts. The editors of individual volumes are leading figures in their areas and provide an introductory overview.

Example topics include: self-esteem, evolutionary social psychology, minority groups, social neuroscience, cyberbullying and social stigma.

Self-Esteem
Edited by Virgil Zeigler-Hill

Social Conflict within and between Groups
Edited by Carsten K.W. De Dreu

Power and Identity
Edited by Denis Sindic, Manuela Barreto and Rui Costa-Lopes

POWER AND IDENTITY

*Edited by Denis Sindic, Manuela Barreto
and Rui Costa-Lopes*

Psychology Press
Taylor & Francis Group

LONDON AND NEW YORK

First published 2015
by Psychology Press
27 Church Road, Hove, East Sussex BN3 2FA

and by Psychology Press
711 Third Avenue, New York, NY 10017

Psychology Press is an imprint of the Taylor & Francis Group, an informa business

British Library Cataloguing in Publication Data
A catalogue record for this book is available from the British Library

Library of Congress Cataloging in Publication Data
Power and identity / edited by Denis Sindic, Manuela Barreto, and Rui Costa-Lopes.
1. Group identity. 2. Power (Social sciences) 3. Social psychology. I. Sindic, Denis. II. Barreto, Manuela da Costa. III. Costa-Lopes, Rui.
HM753.P69 2014
303.3--dc23
2014027137

ISBN: 978-1-84872-176-0 (hbk)
ISBN: 978-1-84872-177-7 (pbk)
ISBN: 978-0-20336-626-4 (ebk)

Typeset in Bembo
by Saxon Graphics Ltd, Derby

Printed and bound in the United States of America by Publishers Graphics, LLC on sustainably sourced paper.

CONTENTS

CONTRIBUTORS

Jill Allen, Department of Psychology, University of Minnesota, USA

Manuela Barreto, Department of Psychology, University of Exeter, UK and Centre for Social Research and Intervention, Lisbon University Institute, Portugal

Ângela Barreto Xavier, Institute of Social Sciences, University of Lisbon, Portugal

Philippe Bernard, Social Psychology Unit, Université Libre de Bruxelles, Belgium

Rui Costa-Lopes, Institute of Social Sciences, University of Lisbon, Portugal

John F. Dovidio, Department of Psychology, Yale University, USA

John Drury, School of Psychology, University of Sussex, UK

Atalanti Evripidou, School of Psychology, University of Sussex, UK

Eleanor Gao, Institute of Arab and Islamic Studies, University of Exeter, UK

Sarah J. Gervais, Department of Psychology, University of Nebraska-Lincoln, USA

S. Alexander Haslam, School of Psychology, University of Queensland, Australia

Olivier Klein, Social Psychology Unit, Université Libre de Bruxelles, Belgium

José Manuel Sobral, Institute of Social Sciences, University of Lisbon, Portugal

Stephen Reicher, School of Psychology, University of St Andrews, Scotland

Denis Sindic, Institute of Social Sciences, University of Lisbon, Portugal

Martijn van Zomeren, Department of Social Psychology, University of Groningen, The Netherlands

1

POWER AND IDENTITY

The multiple facets of a complex relationship

Denis Sindic, Manuela Barreto and Rui Costa-Lopes

Anyone who seriously contemplates a world map for the first time cannot help but notice a striking disparity in the way some national boundaries are drawn compared to others. Whereas many defy all geometrical logic, others seem to have been traced with a ruler. This disparity is so readily apparent that for many of us it forms the basis of the first geopolitical fact we learn. Indeed, even children are able to surmise that perfectly straight boundaries cannot possibly correspond to natural features but must result from human intervention, and if they enquire as to how the straight boundaries came to be as they are, they will be told by more informed adults that they are the result of colonisation and its aftermath.

However, the impact of colonisation on the current delimitation of some countries is only the proverbial tip of the iceberg. Not only the territorial boundaries of nations but also the contours of many of today's national identities are still bound up with the lines drawn by colonial powers. Many of the "unusually" straight borders originate from past arrangements between colonial powers or past internal administrative divisions within the territory of a single colonial power (Anderson, 1991). They were drawn with little to no regard for pre-existing groupings among the indigenous populations, and as a result, many who saw themselves as one people ended up on different sides of a divide, whereas others who saw themselves as different were joined together. In both cases, however, the end of colonisation did not necessarily entail a return to earlier patterns of group distinctions and group identifications. The sense of being one country (or of being different countries), fostered by living under arrangements created by colonial decision making, often persisted after colonisation. In time, many of the descendants of the first colonisers also came to see their particular colony as the prime focus of their sense of national loyalty (e.g. see Anderson, 1991). Colonisation, then, is responsible for the very creation of many of today's nations and their specific national identities. It also had dramatic effects on the specific nature and content of those identities, through the dissemination of the colonisers' languages, customs and religions in colonised lands. Once again, much of this colonial heritage has survived the end of colonisation, despite possible alterations. For instance, Christian faith is nowadays deeply ingrained in large parts of Africa and South America, and it is still on the rise despite its steady decline in Europe, the home of those who spread the faith to those continents in the first place (e.g. Bellofatto & Johnson, 2013; Jenkins, 2002).

With such considerations, we have left the realm of pure geopolitics to enter the domain of "psycho-politics" that defines the general theme of this volume. Identity is primarily a psychological construct, since it concerns the particular way in which human beings define their self-concept and since it draws its strength as an engine of human thought and action from its psychological existence. One may of course argue (as the very contributions in this volume exemplify) that identities are also inherently social or political, insofar as the specific way in which identities are defined is entirely dependent upon social and political relations, but making that argument is precisely to stress the social or political constitution of what is fundamentally a psychological reality. Power, on the other hand, is primarily a political concept. In very broad terms that are meant to encompass a variety of approaches, it can be defined as the ability to act upon the human world to change it or to maintain it. To enquire about the relationship between power and identity is therefore to enquire about the ways in which the psychology of identity interacts with the political dynamics of power.

Some scholars, such as Foucault, have argued that actually there is no identity without power—and the reverse could also be advocated. If that is the case (and even if it isn't), one can wonder why a joint consideration of power and identity (and of their relationship) has not been more pre-eminent in the social sciences, given their status as key concepts in many areas of social research. Of course, it is in the nature of social research to be selective and to isolate a few dimensions for analysis among the infinite number that compose the social world. However, one might nevertheless be surprised at the fact that power and identity have not been jointly selected for examination more frequently, and that the two issues have generally been compartmentalised by being the object of scrutiny of different disciplines and/or of different research traditions within the same discipline. This is the case even within the discipline of political psychology, which, if the above definitions hold, should in principle constitute the natural home for the consideration of the interplay between power and identity. Those hoping to find a long and strong tradition of coupling those two concepts together in the analysis of empirical phenomena within the domain of political psychology will soon be disappointed. Rather, they will find that each has generally occupied a central place in separate lines of research.

Fortunately, these claims are slowly becoming a thing of the past, for the last decade has seen an increased interest both in identity issues among those studying power and in issues of power within identity research. This volume seeks to contribute to moving the field forward by bringing together varied examples of these analyses in a single collection of essays. The leading role that political psychology would naturally be expected to play in this enterprise is reflected in the fact that the majority of the assembled contributions come from this field and/or from the sister discipline of social psychology. Nevertheless, as a way of resisting further compartmentalisation, they have been complemented by contributions from other highly relevant disciplines, namely history, anthropology and politics. Before outlining the details of these contributions, however, we will examine in more detail the general question addressed in this volume, i.e. what is entailed in an analysis of the intersection between power and identity within the perspective that is adopted here.

Power and identity: a two-way relationship

The questions raised by Foucault and Marx, as well as the limits in the scope of their enquiry, are helpful in circumscribing the general issues addressed in this volume. At the heart of Foucault's work, particularly in its later stages, is his pressing concern with the relationship between the self and power (Foucault, 1976/1998, 1982/2002a, 1984/1985, 1984/1986). For Foucault, the self is not constituted internally through the subject's own efforts, but externally by the multitude of social practices that are specifically dedicated to its moulding—practices that he coined the "technologies of the self" (Foucault, 1988/2002b). However, the Foucaldian self is more than just another variant on the idea of the social self, for the social practices that shape it are always the expression of strategies of power—they are always political, as well as social. As a result, the self is conceived as "a vital element in the networks of power that traverse modern societies" (Rose, 1999, p. 217); it is the fulcrum on which those networks rely to achieve their effects, defining people in particular ways in order to secure their alignment with dominant interests. The self is a political tool of subjection through "subjectification" (Foucault, 1976/1998), i.e. it turns people into subjects in the psychological sense for the purpose of ensuring their status as subjects in the political sense. What makes it such an effective tool in that regard is that the aspirations and imperatives of the self are generally deemed to come from "within", thereby hiding the power that presides over their constitution.

As our opening example suggests, the focus in this volume is on collective, social or group identities, i.e. identities that are derived from belonging to a particular segment of society, and are therefore both shared with others and limited in scope. At first sight this might appear to contrast with Foucault's approach. Indeed, as the title of one of his essays—"The political technology of individuals" (Foucault, 1988/2002b)—indicates, the practices on which he focuses often aim to construct human beings as individuals (e.g. through promoting the self-examination of one's sexual desires). At the same time, these practices are deemed to characterise Western society as a whole, rather than being specifically associated with any of its particular segments. Nevertheless, one of Foucault's important points is that the self-definitions engendered by the technologies of the self are also used to create, delimit and define particular social categories (e.g. sexual deviants). As such,

Foucault's insights into the relation between self and power can be, and have been, fruitfully applied to the analysis of group identities.

However, there is at least one fundamental way in which the questions raised in this volume go beyond a Foucaldian form of enquiry. Foucault's approach to the relationship between power and self is avowedly one-sided, with everything flowing from the former to the latter. By contrast, our goal is to consider the relationship between power and (group) identity as a two-way street, making room for the insight that the latter may constitute the basis through which human beings may, in turn, actively participate in the construction of power. In other words, identities can be more than the end result of strategies of power, and their effects on thoughts and actions can be more than a mere reflection of those strategies. Even when identities are initially imposed externally by dominant powers, those that are targeted by such impositions can actively reclaim the imposed identities by redefining their particular contours and content. What is more, they often do this precisely to regain power, at least over the definition of their own self. Foucault expressly denied that there was a single, coherent and dominant strategy of power in any society, suggesting instead that many diverse strategies are present as multiple vectors pushing in similar or opposite directions (Foucault, 1976/1998). However, his focus was definitely on the strategies that emerge as the winners in this interplay of power vectors. He did not provide a detailed account of how alternative strategies of resistance may develop, and in particular how they might develop around the very identities created by dominant powers. As a result, he failed to consider that identity might be a power resource (i.e. a source of power creation for the powerless) as well as a resource of power (i.e. a tool used by dominant powers).

In contrast, this dialogical relationship between power and identity can be found in Marxism with the twin concepts of "false consciousness" and "class consciousness"[1]—although the scope of these concepts is limited to one particular type of group identity, i.e. class identity (Marx & Engels, 1844, 1846/1978). In the exploitative relationship between the bourgeoisie and the workers, false consciousness is the means through which the submission of the latter is smoothly operated. Ideological and institutional resources are deployed by the bourgeoisie to shape the psychology of workers and mislead them into defining their wishes and wants in ways that do not correspond to their "real" interests. This operation creates a "false consciousness" that ensures the maintenance of the existing power structure based on economic differences. This includes promoting (illusory) group divisions among the workers. Achieving class consciousness, on the other hand, is one of the necessary steps in paving the way towards liberation from capitalist exploitation. According to Marxism, it is when the veil of false consciousness is lifted and workers realise where their real interests lie that they can become united by their joint interest in the fight against exploitation. In other words, it is through the development of a common identity as members of the working class that workers can overcome their internal divisions (promoted by the bourgeoisie) and gain the power to overthrow the bourgeoisie.

Nevertheless, although Marx did not claim this would be easy, one could argue that he still underestimated the difficulties in achieving that result, notably by misjudging the hold that "illusory" class-alternative identities can have on social and political actors. Indeed, contrary to Marx's predictions, it has been argued that the development of an overarching class identity uniting all workers within the capitalist system never actually took place, mainly because of the interference of cross-cutting identities at the national level (e.g. Anderson, 1991). Revolutions that, rightly or wrongly, took their cue from Marx framed their fight in national terms: rather than fighting against *the* bourgeoisie, they insisted that the fight was against *their* bourgeoisie (e.g. Inder Singh, 2001; Nimni, 2001). Even more problematic for classic Marxist theory, this hold of national divisions has not been limited to workers; in many historical instances the bourgeoisie also did not act as if moved by a single, transnational common interest, but by what they perceived to be their country's interests. The lessons of history therefore make it difficult to dismiss national identities as mere ideological "illusions" concocted by the bourgeoisie with the sole purpose of dividing the workers. More generally, the role of identity in politics, national or otherwise, has so far proved to be resilient to any reduction to a tool of class warfare.

In one respect, then, Marxism comes close to the Foucaldian approach in that it tends to consider all identities, aside from class, to be little more than the effect of power. As a result, identities lose some of their substance as engines of human action. Their role is restricted to mere intermediaries between power and action. In contrast, the aim of this volume is to examine the bidirectional relationship between power and identity in a way that conceives of them as "equal partners" in that dialogue, i.e. as possessing the same conceptual "thickness" and explanatory power in the shaping of human action. As a matter of fact, one of the key lessons coming out of the contributions in this volume is that the two sides of the dialogue between power and identity are deeply intertwined. Looking at one particular side, be it the ways in which power dynamics shape identity or the ways in which identity dynamics constitute power, merely captures a static picture of what essentially constitutes a feedback loop with no independent starting point.

Outline of the chapters

Aside from this introductory chapter, this volume is comprised of seven chapters that analyse the issues of power and identity in specific empirical contexts, and a concluding chapter that comments on the earlier contributions and teases out some of the common themes and messages. Although both sides of the power–identity relationship can be found in every contribution, the seven chapters in the middle have been organised according to the side on which they place their main emphasis. Thus Chapters 2 and 3 focus mainly on how power shapes the contours and content of identities, whereas Chapters 6, 7 and 8 examine in more detail the role of identity in the constitution of power. In the middle, Chapters 4 and 5 operate as transitions since they address both sides in relatively equal proportions.

Chapter 2, by Xavier, illustrates the ways in which the identities of colonised populations can be shaped by the power of the colonisers. Xavier draws on the case of the colony of Goa under Portuguese rule in the sixteenth century to examine the contradictions in the "policies of identity" put in place to deal with indigenous populations. These contradictions can be traced back to an essential paradox that can also be found at the heart of contemporary debates on acculturation and multiculturalism. They flow from the fact that colonial power sought to assimilate Indians through religious conversion in order to extend the power of the colonial empire, but at the same time aimed to recreate differences to maintain the existing power hierarchy within the empire on which the whole colonial system depended. In that process, the "natives" found themselves in an "identity limbo": irremediably transformed, they could not go back to their original identity, but neither were they truly accepted as members of the colonisers' group.

However, while the role of power in the moulding of identity may be particularly apparent in the case of colonialism, it is by no means limited to that context, nor is it limited to the case of groups using their power to define the identities of those considered to be "others". Power can also be at play in the way groups define the identity of their own members. In Chapter 3, Sobral shows how the implementation of strategies and policies designed to affect identity can be seen as one of the key occupations of the State in its attempt to define and bind the nation. Debates are ongoing as to the modernity or antiquity of nations, but what is clear is that national identities do not "naturally" emerge in a simple bottom-up process. Rather, they need to be actively shaped (as well as continuously maintained), and one of the foremost agents in that process is the State itself. Sobral looks at the means through which this was historically accomplished in the case of Portugal and Portuguese identity. However, the particular means deployed (e.g. the designation of a significant other) are not limited to that specific case, since they can be found in many other instances of nation construction or identity formation in general.

Chapter 4 by Gao looks at the role of tribal identity in the civic life and electoral politics of Jordan, and in doing so provides a good example of how the two sides of the power–identity relationship can be difficult to separate. Gao argues that the persistence of tribal identities in Jordan is related to the persistence of tribal practices in spite of predictions that such practices would slowly disappear with the "modernisation" of Jordanian society. The fact that tribal membership is still the predominant factor in determining who gets elected at both the local and national level is obviously relevant to the ways in which identity impacts on power dynamics. Yet, as Gao stresses, acting in accordance with the wishes of the tribe is not always done out of mere subjective loyalty; it can also be the result of social pressure and of the high practical costs associated with ignoring those wishes. In other words, the pre-eminence of tribes means that they possess the practical power of shaping individuals' behaviour, and ultimately their identity, in tribal terms. What is more, the joint sustenance of tribal practices and identities also results from power strategies deployed by the State. In other words, identity results from power as much as vice versa.

Chapter 5 by Klein, Allen, Bernard and Gervais also deals directly with both sides of the power–identity relationship, since it explicitly contrasts the two vantage points in the context of stereotyping and sexual objectification. Both the ascription of stereotypes to disadvantaged groups and the sexual objectification of women can be seen as particular ways in which the identities of the powerless are defined by the powerful (e.g. by men in the latter case). Much research has been devoted to showing how these phenomena serve to maintain and legitimise the existing social and political hierarchy. However, as Klein et al. argue, this only represents one side of the story. Disadvantaged groups can also use stereotypes (including stereotypes about themselves) to pursue their own agendas, and so can women in relation to the sexualisation of their bodies. The authors illustrate their points through an analysis of the speeches of the leader of the movement for the independence of Congo, as well as the collective actions taken by the Femen movement. In both cases, it is through the reconstruction of the meaning of their (national or sexual) identity that the socially disadvantaged and politically subordinated aim to reclaim the power to shape their own lives.

Chapter 6 by Drury, Evripidou and van Zomeren can be seen as generalising some of the processes illustrated in Chapter 5. Indeed, the chapter provides us with a review of an extensive body of work investigating the empowering consequences of taking part in social movements and collective actions. The power that can ensue from collective as opposed to individual action builds on the development of a shared collective identity, a shared understanding of that identity, and a shared vision about how that identity should be actualised (or objectified) in practice. This creates expectations of mutual support among social actors and allows for the possibility of coordinating social action effectively to achieve the group's goals. Furthermore, through collective action, the identity of the ingroup can be redefined, and with it its specific goals as well as the perceptions of what can be achieved. Thus, it is through the transformation of identity that a more general sense of power (i.e. a sense that it is possible to affect and change the world) can develop.

In Chapter 7, Reicher and Haslam build on their work in the BBC prison study to examine how identity dynamics lead to the actual power or powerlessness to enact the vision of the social world entailed by that identity. As in Chapter 6, the crux of their argument lies with the formation of a shared identity as the medium through which the social coordination of cognitions and actions is made possible. However, where Chapter 6 shows the relevance of those processes in many real social movements and events, Chapter 7 takes advantage of the controlled environment of a week-long naturalistic experiment to examine the evolution of these processes over time, allowing us to appreciate how both identity and power dynamics shift in unison and dramatically affect the overall "system". Both the "revolution" that replaced the initial hierarchical system by a non-hierarchical system, and the reactionary counter-revolution that sought to re-establish it with a vengeance, can be explained by the (in)ability to build a consensual identity, and thereby to achieve the power to actualise the vision of social life it entails. The chilling lesson that powerlessness paves the road to the acceptation of tyranny echoes an idea that, through the fascist experiences of the twentieth century, has become sadly familiar. However, it is also a call to question the modern mistrust of power, for the creation and exercise of collective power may be needed to preserve freedom even in its individual expressions.

Chapter 8, by Sindic, integrates the theoretical resources deployed in Chapters 6 and 7 with work in political philosophy, to offer a reflection on the nature of political power, questioning the adequacy of our existing conceptual tools to capture its specific group-based nature and thereby its intrinsic relationship to identity. Power can be social because of its target (power *over* others) or its means (power *through* others), but also because it depends on the support of others for its very existence (power *with* others). The latter idea would be familiar to the activists in Chapter 6 and is particularly relevant to the case of political power. This argument is subsequently illustrated by examining how the question of political power is addressed in political debates around Scottish separatism and European Union membership. More specifically, Sindic shows that the attribution and meaning of political power in those debates does not only depend on the question of who possesses the "objective" tools of power (i.e. the number of votes in the decision-making process), but is also tied up with the establishment of an identity relationship between political representatives and those they are deemed to represent.

Finally, in Chapter 9, Dovidio proposes an integrative conceptual model of the relationship between power dynamics and identity processes. While this model does not pretend or even seek to subsume every aspect of all the contributions into a single, integrative, overarching theory—an attempt that would threaten to reduce their intended diversity—the chapter nevertheless selectively draws on relevant aspects of every preceding chapter in building that model. By doing so, it therefore makes a significant contribution to the formation of a more coherent and inclusive picture of the issues at stake.

The empirical contexts of power and identity

Despite the disciplinary and methodological diversity exhibited by the various chapters, the above outline shows the strong continuity (and complementarity) that exists between them in terms of their contributions to our conceptual and theoretical understanding of the intersection between power and identity. However, a slightly different (but parallel) story that stresses the connections and commonalities between chapters in terms of their chosen empirical terrains of investigation could also be told. Indeed, several of these terrains appear more than once throughout the volume. This is the case for the issues of colonialism (Chapters 2 and 5), nationalism and national independence movements (Chapters 3, 4, 5 and 8), collective action (Chapters 5, 6 and 7), and electoral politics (Chapters 4 and 8). The relative convergence of the chapters at this level can be taken as an indication that these terrains constitute particularly fertile ground for a joint consideration of power and identity and of their interaction. Of course, there are many other empirical contexts (such as work organisations) that are as important and potentially as fruitful, and to which future work should extend. Nevertheless, the contexts addressed in this volume are particularly suited to move the investigation of power and identity forward, and more generally to promote a due consideration of the interaction between political and psychological processes.

In relation to colonialism, it is no coincidence that we chose to open this prologue with an illustration of its impact on identity and the rest of the volume with a chapter that specifically focuses on this subject. There are good reasons why colonialism provides one of the most striking examples of how power can shape identity on a large scale (Chapter 2). Perhaps nowhere else in the history of mankind can we find a wider gap in power than the one which existed between colonisers and colonised. The effects of this power gap were truly global, since it ended up affecting the great majority of human populations in almost every corner of the world, defining them as colonisers, colonised, or soon-to-be-colonised. One can think of the Portuguese and the Spaniards dividing the world between them at the Treaties of Tordesillas (1494) and Zaragoza (1529), even before their colonising enterprises were fully under way, which for almost any previous government or ruler would have amounted to a delusion of grandeur. Yet the consequences of these treaties are still felt today. To take but one example, Latino identity in America would probably not exist without the particular pattern of colonial expansion the treaties helped create. Perhaps better than any other context, colonialism shows us that power not only moulds the content of existing identities; it can also be responsible for the creation of entirely new groups.

As a worldwide phenomenon, nationalism also shares the same grandeur of scale, but its effects on the constitution of identities can be somewhat harder to spot since we do not enjoy the same historical distance than with colonialism. Whereas colonial empires are from the past, we are still in the era of the nation-state as the primary political entity. We still have to fight against the mechanisms that push us to take for granted and regard as natural the demographic organisation of the world into distinct nations with specific identities, and its concomitant political organisation into nation-states as the mere expression of the right to self-government of those pre-existing national peoples. It takes special effort to reverse the relation and to uncover the ways in which national identities and the very idea of forming a nation can be shaped by the power of the State to justify its existence as a state. Looking into the past of nations and how they were historically constructed may help in this task, since with historical distance practices and patterns of identification that were taken for granted by those living in the past appear less self-evident to us living in the present (Chapter 3).

Another possible point of entry consists in looking at nationally-framed colonial independence movements (Chapter 5) or contemporary national separatist movements (Chapter 8). Indeed, national identities and their relationship with power are brought to the fore by the avowed goal of those movements to establish an alternative political structure based on claims of national identity difference. Since separatist movements strive for a change in the existing political order, their particular versions of identity cannot be taken for granted but have to be openly expounded to legitimise that change. At the same time, the challenge that they mount against those identity versions that help maintain the status quo renders the latter versions less self-evident.

However, this point is not limited to the context of nationalism; it can be generalised to any form of collective action aimed at challenging a status quo that promotes a particular understanding of how the world (or some specific aspect of it) should be organised, as a function of what people are or are deemed to be (Chapters 5, 6 and 7). Any movement seeking to achieve that result cannot afford to take identity for granted since it needs to develop its alternative vision of identities and explicitly link these identities to its version of how the world should be. Furthermore, in mounting such a challenge, collective actors often have no choice but to unpack the opposing identity claims and how they serve to sustain the status quo, in order to boost the credibility of their own claims. Part of the reason why collective action is another pre-eminent empirical theme of this volume, then, is because it allows us to observe the construction of alternative identities and its relationship with alternative political goals, and because it makes taken-for-granted identities and their hidden relationship with power structures (both as their effect and as their legitimising support) more apparent in contrast.

Finally, the interest of electoral politics for an investigation of power and identity should be plain. Electoral politics represent the paradigm of power struggle in democratic societies, and identity plays a key role in that struggle, both because we elect those to whom we can relate and because those seeking to be elected need to establish that relationship. However, looking at the role of identity in electoral politics, particularly in unfamiliar contexts where its operations are made more apparent by cultural distance (Chapter 4) and/or by identity contestations among the actors themselves (Chapter 8), can also serve to demonstrate that this role is larger than what is usually encompassed under the label "identity politics". The latter term assumes the existence of "non-identity politics", when in fact identity is ubiquitous within the political process.

Conclusions

We leave the elaboration of the specific messages as to the ways in which power and identity intersect (and the psychological, political and societal consequences of those intersections) to the individual contributions in this volume. Although many of their conclusions have far-reaching implications well beyond the specific empirical terrain from which they emerged, they are nevertheless more enlightening when considered in the context of the concrete issues that flesh them out. For now, we finish by focusing on the lessons that a study of the interaction between power and identity can teach us at a very broad conceptual level. Indeed, a coordinated analysis of power and identity may not only contribute to illustrate important phenomena in new ways; it may also lead to the mutual enrichment of those concepts.

Thus, on the one hand, the concept of power has often been considered either in individualistic or structural terms. In the first approach, power belongs to individuals (leaders, elites, politicians and other prominent figures, but also "ordinary" people), and/or is the net result of the combination or opposition of the ability of separate individuals to affect the world. Anyone who has ever had to deal with bureaucracy, the power of which can easily overrun even those enacting its rules (making them "victims of the system" every bit as much as anyone else), can see the limits of that view. In the second approach, power is an effect of system organisation and belongs primarily to collective entities (state, administrative and legal apparatus, businesses and other institutions). It is thus irreducible to individuals, but the consequence is precisely that all trace of the human agents exercising that power tends to disappear. One might wonder if power without agency is still power; at the very least, it becomes impoverished as a concept, encompassing too many things to be highly meaningful. What we are perhaps still lacking is a concept of power that is neither reducible to individuals and their agency, nor to structures and their impersonal imperatives—i.e. power as an emergent property of the relations between individuals that may in turn structure them. Since research on group identities had to deal with the same issue and developed fruitful conceptual resources to address it, those resources might be of use in the development of such a concept of power.

On the other hand, the conceptualisation of identity as simultaneously personal and social has often been operated through an emphasis on the ways in which social structures, knowledge and narratives critically shape individuals' self-understandings. In that perspective, identity is essentially a set of socially-saturated cognitions and affects that individuals hold about their selves—it is the social in the mind. Perhaps as a result of this, more emphasis has been put on the psychological function of identity as meaning-making (i.e. how self-understanding relates to understanding of others and the world) and less on its practical function as a guide to action. Yet, if identity matters, it is because it shapes what we do as much as what we think or what we feel. In that context, linking identity to the concept of power, which is essentially bound with action—it is, after all, the capacity to act upon the world—might be a way to restore the balance between cognition and action. It should lead us to consider identity as essentially embedded in practices, and in particular in practices of power. It may also be a way to go beyond the classic opposition between cultural and material factors in the shaping of human social and political behaviour, since identity has typically been associated with (and limited to) the first sphere and power with the second.

Note

1   Here we are glossing over the fact that Marx actually never used the term "false consciousness" in his writings; the term should correctly be attributed to Engels. For the sake of symmetry in the terms we use, we assimilate Marx's parallel criticism of ideology to the notion of false consciousness. Likewise, he rarely used the term "class consciousness" but spoke more readily of the working class becoming a "class for itself". The above

commentary may, if necessary, be seen as directed towards a common version of Marxism that may or may not faithfully reflect Marx's original writings, but it does serve our argumentative purpose.

References

Anderson, B. (1991) *Imagined Communities: A Reflection on the Origin and the Spread of Nationalism* (revised ed.). London: Verso.

Bellofatto, G.A. & Johnson, T.M. (2013) Key findings of Christianity in its global context, 1970–2020. *International Bulletin of Missionary Research*, 37, 157–164.

Foucault, M. (1985) *The History of Sexuality, Volume 2: The Use of Pleasure* (R. Hurley, trans.). New York: Random House. (Original work published 1984.)

——(1986) *The History of Sexuality, Volume 3: The Care of the Self* (R. Hurley, trans.). New York: Random House. (Original work published 1984.)

——(1998) *The History of Sexuality, Volume 1: The Will to Knowledge* (R. Hurley, trans.). London, UK: Penguin. (Original work published 1976.)

——(2002a) The subject and power. In J.D. Faubion (Ed.), *Essential Works of Foucault 1954–1984* (Vol. 3, pp. 326–348). London: Penguin. (Original work published 1982.)

——(2002b) The political technology of individuals. In J.D. Faubion (Ed.), *Essential works of Foucault 1954–1984* (Vol. 3, pp. 403–417). London: Penguin. (Original work published 1988.)

Inder Singh, A. (2001) Communism and nationalism. In A.S. Leoussi (Ed.), *Encyclopaedia of Nationalism* (pp. 31–34). New Brunswick (USA) and London (UK): Transaction Publishers.

Jenkins, P. (2002) The next Christianity. *The Atlantic Monthly*, 290 (3), 53–68.

Marx, K. & Engels, F. (1844) The Holy Family. In *Collected Works* (Vol. 4). London: Lawrence and Wishart.

——(1978) The German Ideology. In R.C. Tucker (Ed.), *The Marx-Engels Reader* (2nd ed.). New York: W.W. Norton. (Original work published 1846.)

Nimni, E. (2001) Class and nation. In A.S. Leoussi (Ed.), *Encyclopaedia of Nationalism* (pp. 25–26). New Brunswick (USA) and London (UK): Transaction Publishers.

Rose, N. (1999) *Governing the Soul: The Shaping of the Private Self* (2nd ed.). London: Free Association Books Ltd.

2

EMPIRE, RELIGION AND IDENTITY

The making of Goan people in the early modern period[1]

Ângela Barreto Xavier[2]

Colonialism is certainly one of the privileged objects of analysis for the multiple ways power can shape identity. In colonialism it is frequent that a powerful minority (the colonisers), often coming from a very different social and cultural background, finds itself in a position to dictate the identity of a majority (the colonised). In fact, the identity labels that colonial power attributed to the colonised usually legitimised the way it could act upon them.

The motivations to dictate identity changes in the world of the colonised could be multiple. The tendency to converge the identity of the colonised towards that of the colonisers usually characterised colonial models based on the principle of assimilation, like the Portuguese in the early modern period and the French (Belmessous, 2013; Crowder, 1962; Diouf, 1998; Lambert, 1993; Silva, 2009; Xavier, 2008), while the tendency to stress the "racial" and cultural differences between the communities of the colonisers and the colonised characterised, in general terms, the British and the Dutch experiences (Bosma & Raben, 2008; McClintock, 1995; Salesa, 2011; Stoler, 2002; Taylor, 1999/1983).

In the context of the assimilationist model, the legitimisation of the process of identity transformation of the colonised could vary. In some cases, it referred to a more or less explicit discourse of a "civilising mission" (either religious, through conversion, or secular, through education). In other cases, it was part of a political culture based on the belief that homogenising society was a condition for building and conserving power. Finally, the adoption of inclusive policies could be a result of strictly pragmatic reasons such as the need for human resources, i.e. the need for more people to become soldiers to defend the colonial institutions.

However, had the equality of colonisers and colonised (theoretically, the ultimate goal of the model) been truly achieved, it would have threatened the dissolution of the imperial relation. Since colonialism is based on hierarchy and difference, how could the colonial relation have been maintained, if hierarchy and difference had been abolished?

In contrast, the model of separation stressed the hierarchy and the difference between the colonisers, mostly represented as superior and with better qualities, and the colonised, whose inferiority was usually emphasised. However, the implementation of this model also frequently entailed many problems such as the risk of conflicts arising from the subaltern community of the colonised (the case of South Africa's *apartheid* being the ultimate example of this). Such conflicts could menace the stability of the political community.

The dangers entailed by the implementation of either model explain why the combination of both—assimilation and emphasis of difference, or emphasis of difference and assimilation—as well as the use of the tools associated with each of these models, were the more frequent situations.

If colonialism is a typical place where power can shape identity, it is also a *locus* that allows us to understand and discuss another (and correlated) dimension of this connection: how identity can be a condition to exert power. In many instances where power openly dictated the labels, those who felt powerless tended to adopt new identities as a way to achieve some measure of power. In that sense, for some of the powerless, colonialism could become, ironically, a "world of possibilities". By transforming themselves, by adapting their identities to the ideal type designed by the coloniser—becoming Christians, becoming like "whites", becoming "civilised"—many of the colonised could enter the world of social mobility. However, colonialism could also be a "world of menace", especially for powerful traditional groups and elites within the colonised population, since it challenged their identities and caused the downgrading of their previous positions. In order to preserve these positions, many traditional elites converged with the interests of the colonial power. Sometimes this convergence (also called "collaborationism") could imply the partial or full transformation of their former identities.

As suggested earlier, the processes that attempted to nullify the differences between the colonisers (the new powerful) and the colonised elites (the old powerful) usually led to new forms of difference, since the former did not accept a complete dissolution of difference. The colonial mimesis that these processes entailed were not supposed to nullify the condition of the colonisers as the ones who dictated the order of society. For this reason, those that tried to converge completely with the world of the coloniser, adopting its identity(ies), were frequently caught in a "liminal condition", that is to say, trapped in an in-between identity (Beech, 2011; Damatta, 2000; Turner, 1969; Van Gennep 1909/1999). In fact, they could never completely possess the same identity as the coloniser and were almost never recognized as equals; on the other hand, they could not "go back" to their previous identity either.

In this chapter I will consider the effects of the transition of a model of separation to a model based on the principle of assimilation on the identities of the inhabitants of Goa (situated in the Konkan region of India) in the early modern period, within the context of the Portuguese imperial experience. I propose that this transition was deeply related to the policies towards "internal others" (Jewish and Moors) developed by the Portuguese crown within the Portuguese homeland. At the same time, this template had to adapt to the Indian conditions, entailing forms of government of difference that were simultaneously familiar and distant from the ones that characterised the situation in the kingdom of Portugal. The result was the invention of "Goans" as a separate—not exactly "Portuguese"—identity. In fact, instead of becoming Portuguese, the Indians who converted to Christianity and to the Portuguese/Western cultures became a "liminal group" (neither Indian nor Portuguese) in ways that were structurally similar to what had happened to the New Christians of Jewish origin in the Iberian world (who were perceived as neither Jewish nor Christians).

Maurice Kriegel (1979) has already demonstrated how the Spanish New Christians (the equivalent of the Portuguese New Christians of Jewish origins) became crystallised as a liminal group with an in-between identity as a result of their conversion (see also Graizbord, 2004). Similarly, Jew converts in the Portuguese kingdom and empire in the early modern period (roughly between the sixteenth and eighteenth centuries) also found themselves in a situation that facilitated neither a full return to their former identity (since reversions could be equally problematic), nor total acceptance by the receiving community (Feitler, 2003, 2005). One can therefore ask in what sense Indian converts in the colonies were subjected to the same conditions.

I will combine different analytical tools in order to discuss these aspects. The works of Arnold Van Gennep and Victor Turner on rites of passage and liminality (Beech, 2011; Damatta, 2000; Turner, 1969; Van Gennep 1909/1999) will be used as template to understand the (ritual) processes of transition from one community (Jewish, Indian) to another community (Christian, Portuguese). In order to assess the social impact of the religious conversion, the initial template will be enriched by the notions of social inclusion and social exclusion, of "established and outsiders", as they were developed by Norbert Elias (Elias & Scotson, 1977/1994). The works on stigma in its formulation by Erving Goffman (1968) and on purity and pollution as they have been discussed by Mary Douglas (1966) provide theoretical tools to understand the stereotypes associated with the Jews, the Indians and, afterwards, with the New Christians and the Indian converts.

The following discussion is divided into four sections. In the first section I address the characteristics of the model of separation between Christian and non-Christian communities both in the Portuguese homeland and in Goa, its most important colony in India. In the second section I consider the transition from this model to a model of assimilation based on religious conversion (and legal equality). In the third section I discuss the mobility of stereotypes that legitimised the extension of the model used in the Portuguese homeland to the imperial territories, and their role in the liminalisation of the converted Indians. Finally, I draw some conclusions from this analysis.

From separated communities to a common society

A snapshot of the general *modus vivendi* of the communities identified as different in medieval Portugal could easily identify legal autonomy and physical separation as two of the principles that structured the political relationship established between the Portuguese crown and the Jewish community in the Portuguese medieval kingdom (Ferro, 1982–1984; Glick, 1979, 1995).[3]

Indeed, until the end of the fifteenth century, the relationship established by the crown of Portugal with its most important "internal other" was based on maintaining separation at several levels: physical separation, which was expressed in the existence of Jewish *ghettos*, as well as the control exercised over the Jews' entrance and exit from such ghettos; legal separation, which manifested itself in the existence of communes and the adoption of Talmudic law; and religious and cultural separation, symbolised by the synagogues where Jews could openly worship, as well as by the libraries and schools and the presence of rabbis that permitted the reproduction of Jewish culture. With respect to economic activities, the urban Jews were mainly engaged in commerce, financial activities (money lending and tax collecting), and "medical" activities. They had in the eyes of outside observers—and I use an anachronistic formulation on purpose—a certain professional specialisation. For this reason they were also easily identified. By living in specific places, bearing different names and practicing activities specific to them, the Jews were considered and treated as "others" (Ferro, 1987; Révah, 1995; Saraiva, 1985).

However, these structuring principles were often violated. Crown decrees in the fifteenth century contained many rules on the "private life" of the Jewish population that were against Talmudic law (Lipiner, 1982, pp. 40–44). This was the case of the regulation of the physical contact between Jewish men and Christian women (Livro das Leis e Posturas, 1971; Ordenações Del-Rei Dom Duarte, 1988). Controlling sexuality was essential to preserve physical separation, but that could mean that legal autonomy had to be sacrificed in order to preserve physical separation (Nirenberg, 1996, 2000).

A similar dilemma emerged in another area central to group identification: religious membership. At the end of the fourteenth century the drive to convert Jews increased, and from 1496 onwards conversion became forceful. Under the threat of losing their assets and their life, all Jews had the choice to be baptised or be expelled from the kingdom (Dominguez Ortiz, 1992). The "hardness of their hearts", their "obstinacy in hate" and their "commission of great evils" against Christ and Christians were some of the reasons invoked in a royal decree of 1521 that ordered conversion or expulsion from the Portuguese kingdom (Ordenaçoens do Senhor Rey D. Manuel, 1797, pp. 212–213).

All children under fourteen from Jewish families in Portugal were to be removed from their families and delivered to Christians. The forced baptism of Jews under the age of twenty-five was decreed in 1497, and an assault on Jewish synagogues, schools and libraries followed soon thereafter. New Christians were not supposed to abandon the kingdom, but rather to take on Christian names and go back to live in their former communities as long as these were Christianised. Old Jewish quarters were now transformed into "new villages" and their lanes and alleyways into "new streets" (Ferro, 1987).

To consolidate this process, in a royal decree of 1514 King Manuel I (1495–1521) gave the New Christians equal legal status to the rest of his Portuguese subjects, subjecting them to the general laws of the kingdom and prohibiting discrimination against them (Ordenaçoens do Senhor Rey D. Manuel, 1797). In fact, given the legal equivalence established between baptism (*regeneratio*) and birth (*generatio*), these conversions also meant the passage from the Jewish to the Christian legal frame. That is to say, it meant the end of legal autonomy for these communities and, at least in theory, the beginning of their inclusion in (or assimilation to) the Portuguese community (Hespanha, 1995).

Ironically, while separation was supposed to be a guarantee of coexistence (Cooperman, 1998), proximity led to the reinforcement of group identification, stimulating what has been called—for the Jewish/New Christian case—the passage from a society of coexistence to a society of conflict (Kamen, 1988). Similar situations can be identified in the context of the Portuguese imperial presence in Goa.

In the first decades of the Portuguese presence in India, which began at the end of the fifteenth century, the relationship between the Portuguese and the Indians was inspired by the regime that had operated in the medieval kingdom of Portugal (Thomaz, 1994). This relationship was also based on the principles of legal autonomy and physical separation. In addition to that, those Indian populations that were not born of Portuguese parentage—the colonised Indians—were not considered as vassals (Hespanha, 1995), which meant they were not under Portuguese rule regarding private matters, although they were for public ones (that is to say, fiscal and military issues).

The consequence of this position was that the daily life of the majority of the population of Goa was regulated by the laws and customs that existed before the establishment of the Portuguese presence in Goa. The legal autonomy of the communities of Indians was complemented by their physical separation, since the Christian (Portuguese) and non-Christian (Indian) populations tended to live in separate neighbourhoods. They existed as parallel spheres that only came into contact with each other when necessary. However, before long divergent dynamics contributed to the destruction of this initial "equilibrium".

Going native and going Portuguese

The first of these dynamics was the promotion of marriages between Portuguese men and Indian women by Afonso de Albuquerque in the second decade of the sixteenth century. Albuquerque, the second Governor of India, conceived an ambitious plan, seeking to establish colonial outposts by conquest to serve as bases to support further territorial advances. In order to overcome the scarcity of human resources—there were few colonisers to conquer and hold vast territories—Albuquerque proposed to the king of Portugal that he would allow his soldiers to marry local women in order to establish a more lasting local presence by transforming the conquered cities in the Indian Ocean—Goa, Kochi, Melaka, Hormuz—into permanent Portuguese colonies.

Despite the more enticing parts of this proposal—the granting of lands and other rewards as compensation for the marriages—the legal terms imposed by the Portuguese crown on these marriages were exacting, both as regards the qualities required of the spouses and the eligibility of the bride. The latter had to convert to Christianity and should have the fairest possible skin for the dowry to be granted by the crown.

The belief that male traits outweighed female ones legitimised the acceptance of the children of these unions as being truly Portuguese. Portuguese men were considered the active force at the moment of procreation which acted, or so they believed, as a shield against Indian contamination. Therefore, the "purity" of the "established" (the Portuguese men) could not be polluted by the "impurity" of the "outsiders" (the Indian women).

A short time after the conquest of the town of Goa, in 1510, the place where these initiatives were most successful, there were hundreds of mixed couples and crossbred children, all considered to be subjects of the Portuguese crown with full rights and obligations in matters of public and private law, as a letter from Diogo Mariz (1960) to the king of Portugal in 1529 indicates. However, compromising its *rationale*, the policy of mixed marriages favoured by Afonso de Albuquerque changed the relation previously established between colonisers and colonised. In fact, these marriages challenged the two pillars of the former system: the principle of physical separation and with it the legal separation between the two "ethnic" communities.

The perception of the Indian territories changed under the government of the next king, João III (1521–1556), and with it the policies towards them and their people. Instead of having Portuguese colonies, colonial officials openly expressed the idea that João III could build a "Greater Portugal" in the Indian territories, a plan that was even more ambitious than the one designed by his predecessor. For the success of this plan, the conquest of territories should be followed by the conversion of Indian people to Christianity, a political imagination that systematically inspired the policies towards the Indians that were imposed in Goa from 1530 onwards.

It was intended that Goa should become as similar as possible to the cities of the kingdom, and its anointing as the capital of the Estado da Índia (State of India) can be understood as a first step in that direction. A political-administrative apparatus very similar to that in Lisbon was established in Goa, with the viceroy, representing the king, occupying the top position (Santos, 1999). Along with this political and administrative dimension the idea of political conformity (that is to say, the conformity of the world of the colonised to the world of the coloniser) also caused changes in perceptions and attitudes towards local society.

In fact, the belief that the homogenisation of society was essential to build and spread the king's power, and that religion was a key instrument in this process, was becoming very strong. In particular, there was the belief that the subjects of the king should share his faith, following the principle of *cuius regius eius religio*, that is to say, "whose realm, his religion" (Hsia, 1989; Paiva, 2011; Palomo, 2004; Prodi & Penuti, 1994; Prosperi, 1996), which would have important practical consequences in the imperial territories (Xavier, 2008). If religion was initially an instrument of distinction, from 1530 onwards this role changed. Religious conversion became the instrument that stimulated political and cultural conformity, and in order to achieve the systematic conversion of local populations and their landscapes, legal and physical violence were combined (Gruzinski & Wachtel, 1997).

Local Hindu temples and objects of worship were destroyed, local priests were expelled and public worship of Indian religions was prohibited in a process of material and symbolic decapitation of the local religious culture. Even temples located within houses were to be destroyed, and the celebration of any local rite, at home or in public, was prohibited. Laws related to family life, land property, labour and political rights persuaded Indian elites to convert to Christianity, while others downgraded the *status* of those that did not convert. Indeed, the First Provincial Council of Goa in 1567 stated that "by depriving them of this honor [that is to say, of their *status*] they shall be more easily converted to our Catholic faith", and that "no office, dignity, honor, preeminence or domain shall be given to a non-believer over a believer" (First Provincial Council of Goa, 1992).

An exponential increase in the number of subjects of the king of Portugal (from only a few thousand in the mid-seventeenth century to over 100,000 by the start of the next century) was the most immediate effect of these policies of conversion. Moreover, at the very moment of baptism, the legal identity of the Indians changed. In practice, that meant that from the moment of conversion onwards, all the converted Indians would be subject to the same tax system, share the same military obligations, and owe the same type of loyalty to the king as the Portuguese colonisers (Hespanha, 1995).

Conversion also meant access to the same legal rights as those enjoyed by the Portuguese. A royal decree of 1542 (confirmed in subsequent decades) defined the landscape of the legal-political effects of the conversion of Indians, by expanding the privileges previously attributed to the couples of Albuquerque to all Portuguese, and to people of "any other nation or generation" that married in Goa and set up house there, provided they were Christian (João III, King of Portugal, 1880).

A special investment was made with women. To interfere in women's local positions was to intervene directly in the process of social and cultural reproduction (or transformation) in Goa. Indian women that converted to Christianity were allowed to have legal independence: they could access their own parents' inheritance and take precedence over their non-converted male brothers—rights they were prevented from having in the local order. Also, widows were allowed to marry again and to receive part of their husband's inheritance, in contrast with the destiny that was reserved for them if they had not converted (João III, King of

Portugal, 1880, 1992). In an explicit way, conversion allowed Indian women to change their social destinies and opened up a world of possibilities.

By contrast, mixed marriages were perceived with growing pessimism, a feeling that was heightened as the role of a Christian upbringing in the establishment of a good society became an increasingly important topic in Portuguese political life. Consequently, the imperial fate of the mixed couples of Albuquerque was fading. Instead of transforming their wives and children into "Portuguese", the husbands were accused of being 'Indianised', and were therefore a threat to the preservation of the new political order.

Once again, the king's inner circle of counsellors did not anticipate the reordering of colonial society that these choices implied. Conversion helped bridge the gap between colonisers and colonised, at the same time challenging the social and political balance of the imperial order. A few converted Indians started to collaborate with and zealously operated within the imperial power system, albeit keeping some traces of their previous identity; others were fully Westernised, wearing Portuguese outfits, speaking proper Portuguese, and living in Portuguese-style houses. By the mid seventeenth century, the Westernised Indian Christian elites started to write treatises trying to demonstrate that they were as noble as the noblest Portuguese. In a few words, to the Portuguese going native (the case of Albuquerque's couples) corresponded effectively the Indian going Portuguese.

But did the Indians who behaved like colonisers—who dressed like the Portuguese, changed their eating habits and the outsides of their houses, spoke and wrote Portuguese—continue to remain truly colonised? How was imperial hierarchy and difference maintained in a situation where the demographic majority of the colonised had been granted "equal" rights to those shared by the demographic minority of the colonisers?

Jewish New Christians and Indian converts: analogies and differences

As described earlier, the Jewish experience was an active part of the template that helped the Portuguese crown and elites to establish new forms of distinction between converted Indians and Portuguese, and the heavy presence of Jewish people and New Christians of Jewish origin in the Portuguese territories in India (Cunha, 1995; Tavares, 1992; Tavim, 1994, 1998, 2003) stressed the connections between them and the Indians. The semantic flows between anti-Jewish and anti-gentile discourses, and the symmetry of the legal solutions applied in the empire and those that had been used in the kingdom in relation to its Jews and New Christians, stimulated these processes (Couto, 1997).

The discourses and the actions of the Archbishop of Goa, Gaspar de Leão, are very telling in this respect. Before leaving for India, Leão was the official chaplain and preacher of the brother of King João III, D. Henrique, a future king of Portugal. That is to say, he was an agent of the Portuguese crown, and a good representative of the strong connections (ideological, but also administrative) between politics and religion. In addition, he had the institutional mission of building the canonical architecture of the Christian Goa.

In my view, the intellectual framework of Leão shows a semantic *continuum* running from the Jews to the Muslims to the Indians. The same *continuum* can also be identified in later treatises, like the ones of João Cardoso (1626) and Joseph Martinez de la Puente (1681). For Leão, Jews, Muslims and Indians all shared many similar aspects (covetousness, avarice, uncontrolled appetites), though they could still aspire to Christian virtues. This *continuum* allowed him (and the Christian clergy) to propose legal decrees that applied norms to the Indians that were similar to those that had already been used in the kingdom.

While in Goa, Leão was the main promoter of the institutionalisation of Christianity in the Estado da Índia. Besides taking energetic action, he also published three doctrinal books, the *Compendio Spiritual da Vida Christãa* (1561), the translation of the treatise of Jerónimo de Santa Fé (1565) and the *Desengano dos Perdidos, feito pera gloria de Deos, e consolação dos novamente convertidos*, published in 1573 (Asensio, 1958). Moreover, he convoked the First Provincial Council, an assembly of the Goan clergy, and wrote the important *Constitutions of the Archbishopric of Goa*, which established the legal template of the diocese of Goa. The similarities between these doctrinal and legal texts are striking, as well as the semantic *continuum* between them and many of the ideas that circulated in the kingdom (and in Europe).

For example, the treatise that he translated had been composed by a New Christian from Saragossa (Spain) who had become a model of religiosity and adherence to Christian identity for other New Christians. Indeed, not only did Santa Fé write this treatise in 1414 seeking to convert his former coreligionists, he also actively participated in their persecution, such as the violent invasion of the Jewish quarter of his home town in 1415, during which his son smote a Jew, in a gesture laden with symbolism (Nirenberg, 1996, 2002). In addressing himself to the Jews and New Christians living in his jurisdiction, the first archbishop of Goa justified the publication of this treatise by stressing "the zeal of the author, compassion for our deluded ones, and also the obligation of the Prelate" (Leão, 1565, Carta do Primeiro Arcebispo de Goa). For Gaspar de Leão it was clear that the Jews of the kingdom had migrated to the imperial territories, and it was his duty as prelate of the empire to see to the conversion of those "lost sheep". In a pastoral letter published in the first pages of the translation, Leão blamed the "error and malice" of the rabbis and the blindness into which the Jews had fallen after the coming of the Messiah.

While the treatise of Santa Fé was directed towards the Jews and New Christians, *Desengano dos Perdidos* sought to encourage conversion of the Muslims, and at the same time it was also particularly intended as a guide for the conduct of the Indian converts. In this treatise Gaspar de Leão established affinities between Islam and the Indian religions, just as he used the treatise of Jerónimo de Santa Fé to establish a parallel between Jews and Indians.

If the desired audiences of these treatises were the different religious communities that inhabited the Estado da Índia, the decrees of the First Provincial Council of

1567 and the Constitutions of the Archbishopric of Goa in the same year expressed in legal canons the ideology behind them. Since this canonical template, as well as the ecclesiastic decrees, supplied in many respects the law of the Crown, it is not hard to imagine the substantial power behind the operations of Leão, one of the political and institutional designers of Christian Goa.

I believe that a similar semantic transfer, if less sophisticated, shaped the attitudes of other travellers who made the long voyage around Africa and arrived in Goa. In that sense, it is not surprising that the Portuguese colonisers resorted to the same methods of dealing with the Jews and New Christians when facing the Indian converts.

It must be remembered that before Gaspar de Leão had arrived in Goa, King João III had given to Indians who had converted to Christianity equal legal status to the rest of the Portuguese, applying to them the general laws of the kingdom (João III, King of Portugal, 1880). Nevertheless, like the decree that King D. Manuel had previously given to the New Christians, this "Indian" decree and its successors were also unsuccessful in achieving their goal.

In fact, almost immediately, other laws, decrees, institutional procedures such as the statutes on purity of blood (Olival, 2004; Rego, 2011), and implicit social norms built a complex architecture of distinctions that would allow an intricate combination between hierarchy and equality (Xavier, 2008). Like the decree of 1542, some of these norms were directly inspired by those in the kingdom whose intention was to prevent New Christians from having the same rights as old Christians. In Goa, they restricted access of the "Christians of the land" (Indian Christians) to the highest local imperial offices, the most important of which were military orders, which were forbidden to people of non-Christian ancestry by a decree of 1602 (Viceroy of India, 1992). A crown officer called the *Pai dos Cristãos* ("Father of the Christians"), whose function was to protect the converts, was given power to decide who among them could exercise functions (and which functions) in the imperial order, channelling them almost systematically to subaltern positions such as doorman, helper and so on. Other rules forbade Portuguese people from being domestic servants of non-Portuguese, or from being treated by local doctors.

As had happened in the kingdom with the New Christians, an effort was made to give Indian converts a transitory *status*, a kind of liminality. They were neither inside nor outside; they were unequal, but not totally different (Fabre, 1999). In short, the equalising power of conversion led to the emergence of other forms of differentiation.

Liminalities

The cases cited above show how the inclusive, assimilating and equalising potential inherent to conversion could be undermined through equally legitimate legal, institutional and social rules, preventing the equalisation of groups that started out at opposite poles on the social *spectrum*. Alongside these legal provisions, of which jurists were well aware since they armed them with more or less contradictory legal statuses and room to conciliate them for specific political purposes, other expedients guaranteed that this legal spirit could be extended by those entrusted with putting them into practice (among which the statutes on pure blood had a symbolic centrality of the greatest importance; see Olival, 2004; Rego, 2011). This permitted social coexistence—albeit tense—as well as the emergence of a social architecture characterised by multiple hierarchies and containing liminal groups; that is to say, groups that were still relegated to the margins of the social order despite being fully part of the legal-political order.

The ways colonisers labelled the different communities that lived in the colonies was a symptom of how identification and differentiation worked. For example, in the letter accompanying a law issued in 1564, reference is made to the city's "residents of Portuguese Christian stock and all other qualities", but in a later passage from the same text, it is stated that the privilege to sell the products of one's farm without paying a tax only extended to "Portuguese and Christian dwellers" of Goa. Some decades previously, along with the decrees that contained more generic designations such as "dwellers", "Portuguese" and "married people", there were many others that listed more precise identities, such as "Portuguese Christians" and "Portuguese Christian dwellers". As early as 1519 King Manuel had made a small concession to the "new Christians of poor lands", already distinguishing the converts from the native Portuguese who lived in Goa (Manuel I, King of Portugal, 1992a). These texts make it clear that the Portuguese and Indians who had converted remained distinct communities.

The descriptive insufficiency of the designation "Christian" became increasingly evident, but there was also the need to abandon the designation "New Christian", in order to distinguish the converted Christians of Jewish origin from those that were of Indian origin. Despite the parallels that had been drawn between these groups, so that they could be treated in similar ways, the "otherness" of the "Jewish community" (who were seen as bearing the ultimate responsibility for Christ's death) was, at the same time, incomparable. Therefore, identifying the community formed by Indian people who had converted to Christianity required an alternative formulation. The labels "Christian of the land", "Christian of India" and "new convert"—all of which began to appear in the rules emanating from the Crown (Manuel I, King of Portugal, 1992b)—became, therefore, a tool of identification and of differentiation. Over time, "new convert" became the preferred label to designate converts of Indian descent, entailing simultaneously their proximity with and distance from the "New Christians" of Jewish origin.

This means that even from the legal standpoint the Christian community that was imagined and constructed in Goa was very complex. The promotion of Indian converts implied more than just a chasm between them and those who had refused to convert. It also implied distinguishing them from the "New Christians" of Jewish origin, and above all from the "old Christians". Similar to what had happened in the kingdom with the "New Christians", the emergence of other distinguishing criteria, other forms of differentiation, prevented the full assimilation of the Indian converts with the colonisers (no matter how much their equality was claimed).

The legal ambiguity of the Indian converts also means that the dissolution of difference intended by some of the decrees did not prevent Christians of Indian origin from being the targets of social discriminatory practices by Christians of Portuguese origin—a pattern that lasted practically until the end of Portuguese imperial domination. It is implied in the royal decree of April 2 1761, which basically repeated in more modern language the state of affairs that had already been defined in the sixteenth century, in order to cope with the new social and political problems that had arisen in the intervening two centuries. In that decree, King José I explained that there were many conflicts between the Indian converted elites and those of Portuguese origin, and ordered that all Christians born in India, in dominions of the Portuguese crown, independently of their nation, be granted the same honours, distinctions, rights and privileges as those born in the kingdom. Beyond this, the king established that the Indian Christians were to be protected from insults, so that anyone who called them "mistiços" (mixed) or "negros" (niggers) was to be strongly punished (Lopes, 1996, p. 39). Yet the very need to legally re-affirm the equal status of Christians of Indian descent shows that the inclusive, assimilationist vision had failed to fully materialise in practice. Instead, the Indian converted to Christianity became "almost the same, but not quite" (Bhaba, 1997, p. 153); they were kept in a liminal state where they still needed special protection against discrimination and hostility from Christians of Portuguese descent.

Unlike in the kingdom—and this is a central aspect that distinguishes the experiences of the "New Christians" and the "new converts"—the conversion of the Indians of Goa to Christianity ended up in a demographic imbalance, and could have had great consequences for the established order. Simply put, in these territories of the Portuguese empire the "new converts" were the majority, far outnumbering the native Portuguese, which meant that the dangers that emerged from potential legal equalisation were exponentially greater, to the point of even jeopardising the very logic of imperial domination. From the third decade of the sixteenth century in both the kingdom and the Estado da Índia, there were few who defended physical miscegenation, but many questioned religious conversion and the dangers it could bring, too. It was the political consciousness of the danger of jeopardising the very logic of imperial domination that led to these political hesitations and to the paradoxical politics of assimilation described above.

Conclusions

I believe that the case discussed above illustrates well how colonialism is a privileged arena to understand the intersections between power and identity. In the case under analysis we have seen how Portuguese colonisers thought and acted from a position that allowed them to dictate the identity of the majority of the Indian population inhabiting those territories, and the mechanics of this process. I have argued that there are many similarities between the processes that were applied in the Portuguese kingdom towards the populations of Jewish origin (who were obliged to convert to Christianity from 1496 onwards, and who became known as New Christians) and those that were put in place in the Estado da Índia to deal with the populations of Indian origins (who were increasingly obliged to convert to Christianity from the 1530s onwards).

These similarities had at least two expressions. The first was discursive and the second legal. The case of Archbishop Gaspar de Leão, a very powerful man in mid-sixteenth century Goa, provides an enlightening example of both. Gaspar de Leão wrote moral treatises where the connections between Jewish and Indians were clearly established, but he was also responsible for legally "inventing" Christian Goa, since it was thanks to him that canonical laws oriented to Christians inhabiting that region were systematically established. This canonical productivity of Leão drew on the legal framework established by the Portuguese crown in order to govern the Jewish population. Thus, the legal architecture established in the Estado da Índia in order to "govern the other" (that is to say, the Indians, "pagans" or "Christians") was a second and extremely powerful expression of the similarities established between the Jewish case and the Indian one.

As in the Jewish case, these laws proposed a cultural conversion of the populations engaged in religious conversion. Jews should not only become Christians, they were supposed to become "Portuguese", since they shared—at least theoretically—the same rights and obligations of Portuguese people. The same was expected from the converted Indians. In Goa, they were also supposed to share the same rights and obligations of the Portuguese colonisers.

However, as we have seen, neither in the kingdom nor in Goa was the "virtual equality" entailed in the legal framework entirely and successfully established. That is to say, neither the Jews nor the Indians became truly "Christian" and truly "Portuguese". Indeed, if it had been fully applied, this legal framework would have dissolved the difference between rulers and the ruled, the colonisers and the colonised, compromising the very foundations of the political community. Furthermore, as previously suggested, in Goa this menace was greater than in the kingdom. Since the majority of the population was of Indian origin, the project of assimilation, if successful, might have inverted the power relations between Indians and Portuguese.

Nevertheless—and for some, tragically—these projects did entail changes in Jewish and Indian identities. In fact, those that had converted to Christianity were trapped inside an in-between identity. They could not easily come back to their previous identity, and they were not fully recognised in the new one either. In the Goan case, in the long-term—that is to say, centuries later—liminality crystallised in a new form of identity, the Goan identity.

Unfortunately, this is not only an early modern closed narrative. Portuguese inclusiveness was still a *topos* frequently enacted in the second half of the twentieth century under Salazar's regime, as being structural to Portuguese identity and proof of their benign colonisation. Known as Luso-Tropicalism, the enactment of this imperial memory contributed to the defence of Portuguese colonialism, and since then it has shaped the ways in which modern Portuguese perceive themselves.

Contemporary Western history with its "civilising" aspirations (frequently considered as new forms of colonialism) under the names of democracy, rationality, and so forth can also be analysed from this angle. Due to temporal distance, these early modern episodes provide a critical perspective on some of the (sometimes unexpected) consequences of these "benevolent" political intentions.

Notes

1 Parts of this text have already been published as Xavier, Â.B. (2011) Conversos and Novamente Convertidos: Law, religion and identity in the Portuguese kingdom and empire (16th and 17th centuries). *Journal of Early-Modern History*, 15, 255–287. This paper is part of the project *The Government of Difference. Political Imagination in the Portuguese Empire (1496–1961)*, financed by FCT, PDTC/HIS-HIS/104640/2008.
2 I would like to thank Denis Sindic, Jorge Vala and Rui Costa-Lopes for their extremely useful comments on this chapter.
3 In this essay I only discuss the relationship with the Jewish community since it ended up being the most relevant source of inspiration for how the Portuguese subsequently dealt with other populations identified as internal "others".

References

Asensio, E. (1958) *Gaspar de Leão, Desengano de Perdidos* [Gaspar de Leão, Disillusionment of the Lost]. Coimbra, Portugal: Universidade de Coimbra.

Beech, N. (2011) Liminality and the practices of identity reconstruction. *Human Relations*, 64, 285–302.

Belmessous, S. (2013) *Assimilation and Empire: Uniformity in French and British Colonies, 1541–1954.* Oxford: Oxford University Press.

Bhaba, H. (1997) On Mimicry and Man. In F. Cooper & A.L. Stoler (Eds), *Tensions of Empire, Colonial Cultures in a Bourgeois World* (pp. 152–160). Berkeley/Los Angeles/London: University of California Press.

Bleich, E. (2005) The legacies of history? Colonization and immigrant integration in Britain and France. *Theory and Society, 34*, 171–195.

Bosma, U. & Raben, R. (2008) *Being "Dutch" in the Indies: A History of Creolisation and Empire, 1500–1920.* University of Michigan, NUS Press.

Cardoso, J. (1626) *Jornada da Alma Libertada* [Journey of a Released Soul]. Lisbon: Geraldo da Vinha. Retrieved from http://purl.pt/14229 [Accessed 5 September 2014].

Cooperman, B.D. (Ed.) (1998) *Iberia and Beyond: Hispanic Jews between Cultures.* Newark: University of Delaware Press.

Couto, J. (1997) Os Judeus de Sinal na Legislação Portuguesa da Idade Moderna [The Jews of "Sinal" in the Early Modern Portuguese Law]. In *Inquisição, Actas do 1º Congresso Luso-Brasileiro* (Vol. 1, pp. 123–134). Lisbon: Universitária Editora.

Crowder, M. (1962) *Senegal: A Study in French Assimilation Policy.* London: Oxford University Press.

Cunha, A.C. (1995) *A Inquisição no Estado da Índia. Origens (1539–1560).* Lisbon: Arquivo Nacional da Torre do Tombo.

Damatta, R. (2000) Individualidade e liminaridade: considerações sobre os ritos de passagem e a modernidade [Individuality and liminality: Considerations on rites of passage and modernity]. *Mana, 6,* 7–29.

Diouf, M. (1998) The French Colonial Policy of Assimilation and the Civility of the Originaires of the Four Communes (Senegal): A nineteenth century globalization project. *Development and Change,* 29, 671–696.

Dominguez Ortiz, A. (1992) *Los judeoconversos en la España moderna* [The converted Jews in Early Modern Spain]. Madrid: Editorial MAPFRE.

Douglas, M. (1966) *Purity and Danger—An Analysis of Concepts of Pollution and Taboo.* London: Routledge and Kegan Paul.

Elias, N. & Scotson, J.L. (1994) *The Established and the Outsiders. A sociological enquiry into Community Problems.* London/Thousand Oaks/New Delhi: Sage. (Original work published 1977.)

Fabre, P.-A. (1999) La conversion infinie des "conversos": enquête sur le statut des nouveaux Chrétiens dans la Compagnie de Jésus au XVIe siècle [The infinite conversion of the "conversos": a study on the status of the new Christians in the Society of Jesus of the 16th Century]. *Annales,* 54, 875–893.

Feitler, B. (2003) *Inquisition, juifs et nouveaux-chrétiens au Brésil: le Nordeste, XVIIe et XVIIIe siècles* [Inquisition, Jews and New Christians in Brazil: the Northeast, 17th and 18th centuries]. Leuven: Leuven University Press.

——(2005) O catolicismo como ideal. Produção antijudaica no mundo português da Idade Moderna [Catholicism as an ideal. Anti-Jewish discourses in the Early Modern Portuguese world]. *Novos Estudos,* 72, 137–158.

Ferro, Mª.J. (1982–1984) *Os Judeus em Portugal no Século XV* (Vols. 1–2) [Portuguese Jews in the 15th century]. Lisbon: Faculdade de Ciências Sociais e Humanas.

——(1987) *Inquisição e Judaísmo* [Inquisition and Jewishness]. Lisbon: Editorial Presença.

First Provincial Council of Goa (1992). In J.H.C. Rivara (Ed.), *Arquivo Portuguez Oriental* (*Vol. 4*) [Portuguese Oriental Archive]. Delhi: Asian Educational Services.

Glick, T.F. (1979) *Islamic and Christian Spain in the Early Medieval Ages.* Princeton: Princeton University Press.

——(1995) *From Muslim Fortress to Christian Castle: Social and Cultural Change in Medieval Spain.* Manchester: Manchester University Press.

Goffman, E. (1968) *Stigma. Notes on the Management of Spoiled Identity.* Harmondsworth: Pelican Books.

Graizbord, D.L. (2004) *Souls in Dispute: Converso Identities and the Jewish Diaspora, 1580–1700.* Philadelphia: University of Pennsylvania Press.

Gruzinski, S. & Wachtel, N. (1997) Cultural Interbreedings: Constituting the Majority as a Minority. *Comparative Studies in Society and History,* 39, 231–250.

Hespanha, A.M. (1995) *Panorama da História do Direito de Macau* [Overview of the History of Law in Macao]. Macau: Fundação Macau.

Hsia, R.P.-C. (1989) *Social Discipline in the Reformation: Central Europe 1550–1750.* London/ New York: Routledge.

João III, King of Portugal (1880). Royal decree. In R.A.B. Pato, *Documentos Remettidos da Índia ou Livro das Monções* (Vol. 2, pp. 66–67) [Documents sent from India or Monsoon Book]. Lisboa: Academia das Ciências de Lisboa.

——(1992) Royal decree. In J.H.C. Rivara (Ed.), *Arquivo Portuguez Oriental* (Vol. 5, I, pp. 175–178) [Portuguese Oriental Archive]. Delhi: Asian Educational Services.

Kamen, H. (1988) Toleration and dissent in sixteenth century Spain: The Alternative Tradition. *Sixteenth Century Journal*, 19, 3–23.

Kriegel, M. (1979) *Les Juifs à lá fin du Moyen Âge dans l'Europe Mediterranéene* [The Jews at the end of the Middle Ages in Mediterranean Europe]. Paris: Hachette.

——(1992) De la "question" des "nouveaux-chrétiens" à l'expulsion des juifs: La double modernité des procès de l'exclusion dans l'Espagne du XVe siécle (From the "question" of the "New Christians" to the expulsion of the Jews: The double modernity of the processes of exclusion in 15th century Spain). In S. Gruzinski & N. Wachtel (Eds), *Le Nouveau Monde, Mondes Nouveaux: L'expérience Américaine* (pp. 469–490) [The New World, New Worlds: The American Experience]. Paris: Éditions de l'École des Hautes Études en Sciences Sociales.

Lambert, M. (1993) From citizenship to négritude: Making a difference in elite ideologies of colonized francophone West Africa. *Comparative Studies in Society and History*, 35, 239–262.

Leão, G. de (1561) *Compendio Spiritual da Vida Christãa* [Compendium of the Christian Spiritual]. Goa: Ioão Quinquencio and Ioão de Endham.

——(1565) *Tratado de Jerónimo de Santa Fé* [Treaty of Jerónimo de Santa Fé]. Goa: Ioão de Endem.

Lipiner, E. (1982) *O Tempo dos Judeus segundo as Ordenações do Reino* [The Time of the Jews according to the Ordinances of the Kingdom]. São Paulo, Brazil: Nobel/Secretaria de Estado da Cultura.

Livro das Leis e Posturas (1971) (N. E. G. da Silva, Ed.) Lisbon: Universidade de Lisboa, Faculdade de Direito.

Lopes, M. de J. dos M. (1996) *Goa Setecentista: Tradição e Modernidade (1750–1800)*. Lisbon: Universidade Católica Portuguesa, Centro de Estudos dos Povos e Culturas de Expressão Portuguesa.

Manuel I, King of Portugal (1992a) Royal Decree. In J.H.C. Rivara (Ed.), *Arquivo Portuguez Oriental* [Portuguese Oriental Archive]. Delhi: Asian Educational Services (Vol. 5, p. 41).

——(1992b) Decrees on the Christians of India. In J.H.C. Rivara (Ed.), *Arquivo Portuguez Oriental* [Portuguese Oriental Archive]. Delhi: Asian Educational Services (Vol. 5, pp. 512–513).

Mariz, D. (1960) Letter to the King of Portugal. In *As Gavetas da Torre do Tombo* (Vol. 20). Lisbon, Centro de Estudos Históricos Ultramarinos.

Martinez de la Puente, J. (1681) *Compendio de las historias de los descubrimientos, conquista y guerras de la India Oriental (…)*. [Compendium of the histories of discoveries, conquests and wars in East India…]. Madrid: Imprenta Imperial.

McClintock, A. (1995) *Imperial Leather: Race, Gender, and Sexuality in the Colonial Contest*. London/New York: Routledge.

Nirenberg, D. (1996) *Communities of Violence: Persecution of Minorities in the Middle Ages*. Princeton: Princeton University Press.

——(2002) Conversion, Sex and Segregation: Jews and Christians in Medieval Spain. *American Historical Review*, 197, 1065–1093.

Olival, F. (2004) Rigor e interesses: os estatutos de limpeza de sangue em Portugal [Rigour and interests: the statutes of purity of blood in Portugal]. *Cadernos de Estudos Sefarditas*, 2, 151–182.

Ordenaçoens do Senhor Rey D. Manuel (1797) [The Ordinances of King D. Manuel]. Coimbra: Real Imprensa da Universidade.

Ordenações Del-Rei Dom Duarte (1988) [The Ordinances of King D. Duarte]. Lisbon: Fundação Calouste Gulbenkian.

Paiva, J.P. (2011) *Baluartes da Fé e da Disciplina: O enlace entre bispos e Inquisição (1536–1750)* [Bulwarks of Faith and Discipline: The alliance between bishops and the Inquisition, 1536–1750]. Coimbra: Universidade de Coimbra.

Palomo, F. (2004) *Fazer dos Campos Escolas Excelentes: Os jesuítas de Évora e as missões do interior em Portugal (1551–1630)* [The making of excellent countryside schools: The Jesuits of Evora and the internal missions in Portugal, 1551–1630). Lisbon: Fundação Calouste Gulbenkian.

Prodi, P. & Penuti, C. (Eds) (1994) *Disciplina dell'anima, disciplina del corpo e disciplina della società tra medioevo ed età moderna* [Discipline of the soul, body discipline and discipline of society between the Middle Ages and the Modern age]. Bologna, Italia: Societè Editrice Il Mulino.

Prosperi, A. (1996) *Tribunali della coscienza. Inquisitori, confessori, missionari* [Courts of consciousness. Inquisitors, confessors, missionaries]. Torino: Einaudi.

Rego, J.F. (2011) «A honra alheia por um fio»: *Os estatutos de limpeza de sangue no espaço de expressão Ibérica (sécs. XVI–XVIII)* ["The honor of others hanging by a thread": Statutes of blood purity in the Iberian world (16th–17th centuries)]. Lisbon: Fundação Calouste Gulbenkian.

Révah, I.S. (1995) *Des Marranes à Spinoza* [From Marranos to Spinoza]. Paris: Librairie Philosophique J. Vrin.

Salesa, D.I. (2011) *Racial Crossings: Race, Intermarriage, and the Victorian British Empire.* Oxford: Oxford University Press.

Santos, C.M. (1999) *Goa é a chave de toda a Índia, Perfil político da capital do Estado da Índia (1505–1570)* [Goa is the key to the whole of India, the political profile of the state capital of India (1505–1570)]. Lisbon: Comissão Nacional para as Comemorações dos Descobrimentos Portugueses.

Saraiva, A.J. (1985) *Inquisição e Cristãos Novos* [Inquisition and New Christians]. Lisbon: Ed. Estampa.

Silva, C.N. da (2009) *Constitucionalismo e Império: A cidadania no Ultramar português* [Constitutionalism and Empire: Citizenship in the Portuguese Overseas]. Coimbra: Almedina.

Stoler, A.L. (2002) *Carnal Knowledge and Imperial Power: Race and the Intimate in Colonial Rule.* University of California Press.

Tavares, Mª.J.F. (1992) Judeus, cristãos-novos e o Oriente [Jews, New Christians and the East]. In *Estudos Orientais: O Ocidente no Oriente através dos Descobrimentos Portugueses* (Vol. 3) [Oriental studies: The West in the East through the Portuguese discoveries]. Lisbon: Instituto Oriental.

Tavim, J.A.R. da S. (1994) Os judeus e a expansão portuguesa na Índia durante o século XVI: O exemplo de Isaac Cairo: espião, 'língua' e 'judeu de Cochim de Cima' [The Jews and the Portuguese expansion in India in the 16th century: The case of Isaac Cairo, spy, interpreter, and "Jew of High Kochi"]. *Arquivos do Centro Cultural Calouste Gulbenkian* (Vol. 33). Lisbon: Fundação Calouste Gulbenkian.

——(1998) Outras gentes em outras rotas: Judeus e cristãos-novos de Cochim—Entre Santa Cruz de Cochim e Mattancherry, entre o Império Português e o Médio Oriente [Other people in other routes: Jews and New Christians of Kochi—Between Santa Cruz of Kochi and Mattancherry, between the Portuguese empire and the Middle East]. In A.T. Matos & L.P. Thomaz (Eds). *Actas do VIII Seminário Internacional de História Indo-*

Portuguesa—A Carreira da Índia e as Rotas dos Estreitos (pp. 309–342). Lisbon: Fundação Oriente.

——(2003) *Judeus e Cristãos-Novos de Cochim: História e Memória (1500–1662)* [Jews and New Christians of Kochi—History and Memory (1500–1662)]. Braga: Appacdm.

Taylor, J.G. (1999) *The Social World of Batavia: Europeans and Eurasians in Colonial Indonesia.* Madison: University of Wisconsin Press. (Original work published 1983.)

Thomaz, L.F. (1994) *De Ceuta a Timor* [From Ceuta to Timor]. Lisbon: Difel.

Turner, V. (1969) *The Ritual Process. Structure and Anti-structure.* New York: Aldine de Gruyer.

Van Gennep, A. (1999) *Les Rites de Passage* [Rites of passage]. Paris: Ed. De la Maison des Sciences de l'Homme. (Original work published 1909.)

Viceroy of India (1992) Decree on military orders. In J.H.C. Rivara (Ed.), *Arquivo Portuguez Oriental* (Vol. 6, p. 739 & p. 776) [Portuguese Oriental Archive]. Delhi: Asian Educational Services.

Xavier, Â.B. (2008) *A Invenção de Goa. Poder Imperial e Conversões Culturais nos séculos XVI e XVII.* Lisbon: Imprensa de Ciências Sociais.

——(2011) Conversos and Novamente Convertidos: Law, religion and identity in the Portuguese kingdom and empire (16th and 17th centuries). *Journal of Early-Modern History*, 15, 255–287.

3

STATE POWER AND THE GENESIS OF PORTUGUESE NATIONAL IDENTITY

José Manuel Sobral[1]

This chapter discusses how state power led to the emergence and reproduction of a Portuguese national identity through the intertwined processes of external differentiation and internal (relative) cultural standardisation. In the view stated here, national identity is mainly a product of the continuous deployment of state agency. While dealing with a specific case, the chapter tries to examine this case within a more general framework, since the connection between state power and national identity is in no way peculiar to Portugal.

Studies of nationalism and national identity have long been divided by different and antagonist paradigms. Some, described as modernists, claim that nations are recent constructions that emerged with modernity, in conjunction with the advent of industrialism (Gellner, 1983), print capitalism (Anderson, 1991) or modern state power (Breuilly, 1993). Others, often referred to as perennialists, conceive of both nationalism and national identities as rooted in a much more ancient past, even in Antiquity (Gat & Yakobson, 2013; Grosby, 2005). Others still, like the self-designated ethno-symbolist Anthony Smith, see both nationalism and the nation as modern phenomena, but view the existence of the latter as depending on older ethnic foundations (Smith, 1991).

This is of course a very simplified view of the debates in the field, and while necessarily taking them into account, this chapter does not deal with these debates per se. However, as it takes the view that national identities should be studied as processes located in the *longue durée* (Armstrong, 1982; Llobera, 1994; Smith, 1991, 1999), it is closer in its approach to the non-modernists than to the others, albeit paying due consideration to the emphasis placed by modernists on the accrued role of nationalism in recent periods and on discontinuities between pre-modern and modern times. It must also be kept in mind that, when referring to nationalism, we have to distinguish between its meaning as a political "theory" and as a "practice". As a theory stating that each "nation" should have its own "state", it is peculiar to modernity (the nineteenth century); as a practice, i.e. as a particularistic feeling about the supreme value of one's ethnic or national tradition, it is far older (Hastings, 1997: 3–4).

Portugal began to exist as a kingdom in the context of Iberia in the twelfth century. This was a dynastic creation by rulers descending from the royal family of Léon and Castile. State power defined a political core, established borders and progressively defined an economic, political, linguistic and cultural space. Considering that with time borders also became cultural boundaries, the interpretation of the genesis of national identity put forward here draws its inspiration from the approach to ethnicity advanced by Frederick Barth (1969) and pursued in the study of nations by others (Armstrong, 1982; Jenkins, 2011). Boundaries, markers of specificity and difference, can be symbolic—like language—but geographical too, although the latter can also acquire intense symbolic meaning (Armstrong, 1982), specifically through the idea of "homeland". This approach also insists on the fact that identities do not develop in isolation but in interaction. Consequently, special attention will be paid to the importance of Castile—the major power in the Iberian Peninsula—in the construction of Portuguese national identity.

Although we will look at the formation of Portuguese national identity as being a process driven by state formation and state power, I will not offer a linear historical reconstruction of that process. Instead, I will consider three moments in history (each of them with different time spans) that were crucial in bringing about Portuguese national identity. The first moment is the medieval period, when state-formation began and when the sign of specific cultural markers attached to the kingdom of Portugal first appeared. This period ended with a dynastic crisis that further separated Portugal from the core power in Iberia (Castile), and the affirmation of the kingdom as an important actor in European overseas expansion. The second period is that of overseas expansion and conquest itself, of the loss and recovery of autonomy, and of the development of the absolutist state, the centralised monarchical regime that began to take shape in the sixteenth century and lasted in Portugal until the beginning of the nineteenth century. The third period, which we can situate between the implementation of political liberalism and the present, is the moment when political and cultural nationalism became hegemonic, due among other things to the conscious building of national sentiment through the activity of state agencies. From an interpretative point of view this latter period is the least problematic, since the relevance of nationalism and national identities at this time is not disputed. Hence, I will concentrate on the first two, whose interpretation is more controversial. I will argue that there were widespread feelings of Portuguese national identity before modernity and that the state was crucial in its formation and maintenance.

The medieval kingdom of Portugal in context

Following the Christian reaction to the Muslim conquest of Iberia in 711, several political entities were formed: Catalonia, Aragon, Navarre, Castile, Léon and Galicia. Their configuration changed due to dynastic disputes and the fortunes of wars both among themselves and against Muslim powers. At the close of the eleventh century the King of Léon, Alfonso VI, managed to get rid of his brothers, the kings of Castile and Galicia, bringing all these kingdoms under his sole command. The king had two surviving daughters, one legitimate and the other a bastard. They were married to two cousins who were members of the ducal house of Bourgogne, which had become an ally in the fight against Islamic power. The legitimate daughter would succeed him as Queen. The other daughter and her spouse would acquire the tenancy of a western earldom, *Condado Portucalense*. This would be aggrandized and converted into a new kingdom, Portugal, under their son Afonso Henriques.

The first thing we must take into consideration is the fact that the new kingdom appeared in the midst of the struggles taking place inside the royal house of Léon and Castile. One branch of this house managed to get hold of a part of the sovereign power, and while initially recognising the superior claims of the main branch, it nevertheless established control over part of the western territory of Iberia that would become Portugal. Second, only a minority (i.e. lords and members of the lower nobility and their retinues) was involved in this matter. Third, although there were strong pre-existing interconnections between the people living within this territory, due to the fact that they were previously part of the same earldom (the *Condado Portucalense*), culturally it was not very different from its northern neighbour, Galicia, with which it shared a common spoken language. Their symbolic and cultural separation would only be achieved during the first centuries of the new kingdom.

When looking at this new medieval state, we must also bear in mind that medieval states should not be confused in any circumstances with their modern incarnations. Although modern states emerged from their medieval roots (Strayer, 1970), it took several centuries before they managed to achieve undisputed political supremacy (Fédou, 1971). Thus, in contrast with the modern Portuguese state, its medieval ancestor could hardly claim full sovereignty over the territory of the kingdom and the monopoly of justice. It had no permanent army and employed few officials. Many areas of social life were under the direct control of the clergy, the nobility and local authorities, the king being a very distant presence. Nevertheless, over time the span for state action grew and its supremacy was established. Furthermore, the king was the symbolic embodiment of the kingdom. These were factors that led to the growing development of feelings of collective self-identification among the inhabitants of the new kingdom. As stressed before, the nation emerged as a product of the state (Disney, 2009, p. 95; Mattoso, 1985a).

The population of the new kingdom was very diverse at the beginning. As already stated, the northerners had close ties, including linguistic ones, with Galicia. They had few contacts with Islam. In the centre, the Mozarabs—Christian populations who previously lived in Muslim polities, adopting their customs and speaking a Latin vernacular influenced by Arabic—were important. In the south, most of the population were Mozarab and Muslim. With the conquest by the Christian northerners of the southernmost part of Portugal, Algarve, from the

Muslims, and the definition of the borders, both achieved in the thirteenth century, the territory of the new kingdom was definitively established. Nowadays Portugal retains the same spatial configuration it had some eight centuries ago, but the ancestors of what would later become the Portuguese were culturally very diverse.

Linguistic historians locate the emergence of a distinctively Portuguese language in the thirteenth century. It evolved mainly from Galician-Portuguese, a language with Latin roots spoken in north-western Iberia, infused with Mozarabic from the centre and south. Most important for linguistic unification was the fact that Portuguese was made mandatory in the king's offices from the thirteenth century onwards (Mattoso, 1985a).

The king's rule and law would be imposed against seigniorial powers through very long and combative processes until the end of the fifteenth century. Suffice to say that the king preserved for himself the privilege of High Justice and imposed control over local lords and authorities, although a written code for the whole kingdom (the *Ordenações Afonsinas*, 1446) was only introduced in the fifteenth century. From the thirteenth century onwards the monarchy imposed control over the clergy, requiring that all decrees and decisions made by church authorities concerning Portuguese religious affairs should have the agreement of the Crown in order to be valid. Nonetheless, in comparison with what would be the absolutist state—from the sixteenth to the early nineteenth century—characterised by the development of bureaucracy on the direct dependence of the Crown, this state still had a limited sphere of action, allowing for the great autonomy of major vassals, some of whom were members of collateral lines of the ruling household.

With the establishment of borders came the circumscribing of an economic space, with its markets and fairs, separated from the outside, where the money of the new kingdom was used. We should bear in mind that besides its economic function, money also played a symbolic role because the name of the king and the arms of the kingdom were represented on it, and hence it operated as a boundary-marker.

Indeed, the first centuries of the Portuguese monarchy saw the appearance of narratives and symbolic devices that became attached to both the kings and the kingdom, such as the first Portuguese flag. Flags are condensed symbols—boundary-markers (Eriksen, 2007). According to legend, the first Portuguese king was accorded the promise of victory over an overwhelming Muslim force by Christ, who appeared to him on the eve of an important battle against the Muslims. The kingdom's flag and arms would later incorporate symbolic elements related to this legend, and the idea of the Portuguese being a chosen people in the pursuit of the triumph of Christianity took hold (Albuquerque, 1974). Additionally, both the names *Portugal*, referring to the kingdom, and *Portuguese*, referring to its inhabitants, made their appearance at this time (Albuquerque, 1974; Mattoso, 1985b).

Besides the direct impact of the state, we should also pay due attention to the role of some specific agents in the symbolic construction of the new kingdom. Historians have signalled how some of the clergy, linked to the Crown and benefiting from its gifts, played a seminal role in the creation of mythical narratives, such as those surrounding the figure of the first king (Cintra, 1989; Mattoso, 1985b). There was a clear attempt to sanctify him. Clergy, but also lay agents, would continue to be active in promoting King and Kingdom. Historical narratives in Portuguese would appear in the fourteenth century, the most important among them being the *Crónica Geral de Espanha* (The General Chronicle of Spain, 1344), which set the history of the Portuguese kingdom in both a universal and a pan-Hispanic framework. At the close of the fifteenth century, with the impact of humanism, intellectuals claimed the Lusitanians—an ancient Iberian people famous for their resistance to Roman conquest—as ancestors of the Portuguese, a mythical claim that would persist until modern times (Albuquerque, 1974). The community of the realm began to be designated by the literate elite, in Latin as in the vernacular, as *patria* (fatherland) and *nation*—with some of their meanings corresponding to contemporary ones (Albuquerque, 1974). Portugal was not exceptional in this: many other European countries came to be represented in the same way at around the same period (Huizinga, 1940/1959).

Both everyday life and exceptional events played their part in the making of Portugal and the Portuguese. The first brought familiarity and naturalness to a social universe initially constructed through war and the conquest of the south. Although we lack documentation on these kinds of processes, we can presuppose that living under the same state provided the moulding of national identity, as suggested by Bourdieu (1994/1998). That is to say, it allowed for the development and largely unconscious reproduction of a specific *habitus* (the sharing of attitudes, values, perceptions) within the area controlled by the State (Bourdieu, 1997/2000). Bourdieu's ideas have broad affinities with the complex of phenomena described as "banal nationalism" (Billig, 1995) or the everyday performance of national identity (Edensor, 2002). These authors insist on the seminal importance of daily life for studying nationalism and national identity—in contrast to "hot nationalism" whose manifestations disrupt routine (Billig, 1995). However, research conducted by these scholars and others (Jenkins, 2011; Skey, 2011) focuses on the present. So, while insisting on the crucial importance of everyday routines for the production and reproduction of national identifications, we have to recognise that we lack testimonies for everyday life in the more distant past. Hence, we turn our attention to exceptional events, like wars.

Wars were rife during the first centuries of Portuguese history. The kingdom would pursue warfare with Muslims in the fifteenth century with conquests in the Maghreb. It was also involved in disputes among the Christian kingdoms in Iberia. The possibility of some kind of pan-Hispanic unification was alive, and the royal households continued to be linked by successive marriage alliances. This would lead to conflict in the centuries ahead.

Conflicts with Castile, the major power in Iberia whose borders met those of Portugal, had a crucial role in the formation of Portuguese identity. Among various conflicts, that which took place in the aftermath of the death of the Portuguese king in 1383 was the most important. According to the dynastic rules of succession, the only daughter of the late Portuguese king, married to the King of Castile, should have inherited the Crown of Portugal, but this aroused fears that Portugal's autonomy would be put at risk, because the Crowns would be reunited and Castile would prevail. There was a strong opposition to that prospect, many insisting that in order to safeguard the autonomy of the kingdom the Portuguese should have someone born and living in Portugal as their king. An illegitimate half-brother of the late king, who fulfilled these criteria, rallied a powerful faction and won the war that followed. This conflict revealed important social cleavages in the networks of supporters of both factions. While the nobility and clergy were split, the popular element seems to have been clearly in favour of an autochthonous Portuguese king and against the possibility of a union of the two Iberian kingdoms that would probably be dominated by the stronger one, Castile.

Eminent Portuguese medieval historians (Mattoso, 1985b) and others (Disney, 2009) agree that some kind of national awareness or consciousness was present among a minority of people, in particular those linked to the Crown, and Albuquerque (1974) documented the presence of feelings of patriotism in medieval and early modern written sources. Since we lack all such testimony for the illiterate masses, we follow the advice that for getting access to their feelings and attitudes "one should look at what they did in lieu of what they said" (Gat & Yakobson, 2013, p. 235).

The conflict with Castile affords a rare glimpse of the behaviour of the masses. It shows us that there was a widespread sense of belonging to the country, and of identification with an autochthonous king, infused with hatred for the foreigner—xenophobia—and for those among the Portuguese who were seen as his allies. There were attacks against anyone seen as an enemy of the Portuguese collective. The Bishop of Lisbon, a Castilian, was the most prominent member of the clergy who was murdered, although he was not the only one (Sobral, 2012). The mobilisation of the people, the violence exacted even against people who were usually highly respected, collective stereotyping such as seeing the Castilians as felons—all this bears witness to a collective behaviour we usually see as linked to nationalism (Albuquerque, 1974). We can say that it is proof of a powerful collective identification, given that the issue of contention was the succession of the King of Portugal and that at this time kings were represented as the "symbolic embodiment of nations" (Hoppenbrouwers, 2007, p. 51).

Hence, the conflict itself revealed and intensified strong and positive self-identification, as well as negative stereotyping of foes, similar to what happened in other parts of medieval Europe. As Schulze stresses, referring to late medieval conflicts and their connection with the expression of national feelings: "Nations do not invariably have their origins in wars, but war often acts as a catalyst" (1996, p. 112). There are reasons for arguing that some kind of "ethnocentric nationalism" (Hoppenbrouwers, 2007) and xenophobia were present at the time, although it was still something very different from the political nationalism that became dominant in the nineteenth and twentieth centuries, which enshrined the nation as "the overriding legitimization of polity formation" (Armstrong, 1982).

Frederick Barth's theory of ethnicity can be useful to explain these points. In his view, ethnicity should be viewed as a form of social organisation, with ethnic groups being "categories of ascription and identification by the actors themselves" and by others that frame their social interactions (Barth, 1969/1998, p. 10). The emergence and maintenance of ethnic groups should be seen as the product of processes of interaction and competition, and not the result of isolation that would account for cultural specificity. The existence of boundaries—social boundaries, which can also be territorial—and boundary maintenance are crucial factors in ethnic group formation and reproduction, and their common culture should be seen as a result, rather than as a prerequisite, of that formation and reproduction (Barth 1969/1998).

However, Barth's theory deals with ethnic groups in general, not with national ones, and as a result it does not focus on the role of the State. In the Portuguese case, the existence of a state that controlled the borders was the crucial factor in the generation and maintenance of boundaries, allowing cultural specificity to develop and thrive and be expressed in language, historical narratives, symbols, separation between the "national" and the "foreign", and stereotyping. In Portugal, as in other places, it was the State that imposed a common language and hence enforced homogenisation, although this was also achieved by other means such as those provided by the law—although we should be aware that no uniform all-embracing common culture ever characterizes a nation. We should bear in mind Jenkins' considerations when he states that "(...) collective identities are imprecise characterizations of many different meanings and points of view, which do not have to harmonize with each other (...) a collectivity—whether it is a nation, an organisation, a sports team, a family or whatever—is more like a large awning than a snugly fitting coat" (2011, pp. 112–113). There is diversity (differences in status or class, gender, region, religion or whatever else) among those who share a collective identification, including in the case of nations. Jenkins (2011) also underlines that, on its own, collective identification does not predict individual behaviour, and hence it should not be treated as an isolated factor, separate from other factors that influence action.

Nevertheless, an awareness of the separation between "us" and "them" is fundamental, since such a separation is at the core of all collective identities (Eisenstadt & Giesen, 1995). In the case of Portugal we have a historical record of its existence, accompanied by xenophobic expressions, at least by the end of the fourteenth century. In the process of production of a distinctive Portuguese identity, which is at the same time a process of "othering", Castilians played the role of the Significant Other, that is to say, of those who offered the (negative) contrast against which the Portuguese self-portrait was constructed (Tryandafyllidou, 1998). Even the patron saint of the kingdom—Saint James the Apostle—would be replaced because of his association with Castile. The new patron would be Saint George, the patron saint of England, an ally in the fight against the pro-Castilian faction (Albuquerque, 1974).

The process of collective identity formation also generally involves enforcing the beliefs of the majority, therefore targeting minorities. Thus, these times saw a rise in attacks towards internal minorities who were seen as different, such as the Jews (Guenée, 1967). In Portugal, both Jews and Moors, who had remained in the country after the Christian conquest, were attributed a subaltern status and discriminated against. After a period of persecution, they would eventually be presented with the alternatives of expulsion or conversion at the end of the fifteenth century (Disney, 2009; Xavier, this volume). Being Portuguese would become synonymous with being a Christian.

Empire, state centralisation and the growing awareness of national identity

It was in the aftermath of the conflict with Castile that the Portuguese crown embarked systematically both on sea voyages and the conquest of places that would mark the first phases of the Portuguese seaborne empire. No one can understand nationalism and national identifications in Portugal without taking the Empire into consideration.

As a minor power in Iberia—the Portuguese population was less than a million in the middle of the fifteenth century (Disney, 2009)—any ambition by the Portuguese crown for conquest over the Muslim polities of Eastern and Southern Iberia was thwarted by Castile. Hence, any further expansion had to be done outside the Peninsula. Ceuta, on the Northern African coast, was conquered in 1415 and other coastal places would follow. The religious motive—the renewal of the Crusade against the "infidel" (the Muslims)—played a part in legitimising the enterprise, in addition to more mundane economic motives (attempts to control traffic in the Gibraltar straight, and trade routes, such as those bringing gold and other produce from black Africa) and socio-political motives (employment and looting for the nobility and the army in general). At the same time, the exploration of the Atlantic and of Africa's west coast began.

Within a century, seafaring and conquests would take the Portuguese from Western to Eastern Africa, India, China, Japan, and to the coastal areas of what is now Brazil. In general, the seaborne empire would not penetrate too far inland, as its purpose was securing the monopoly of trade. The Portuguese only dedicated themselves to agriculture in the Atlantic Islands and in Brazil.

The re-export of exotic commodities to other European countries was a source of enormous profit to the Portuguese and mainly to the Crown, with taxation representing the mainspring of financial revenue at the beginning of the sixteenth century (Disney, 2009, p. 147). Within this period, state centralisation would proceed. The prominence of the King's law and justice were secured both by enshrining the law in a written code (the *Ordenações Afonsinas*, 1446) that would soon be followed by others, and by the division of the kingdom into several administrative and judicial partitions headed by professional magistrates nominated by the Crown. High tribunals were created that were directly dependent on the

Crown (Disney, 2009, p. 138). The State and its head entered the sixteenth century strengthened. They now had an army with important sections, like crossbowmen, who were recruited directly at the local level—equipped by the Crown and therefore not heavily dependent on the nobility and their retainers—, a powerful and modern navy controlled by the Crown, which also controlled firearms and gunpowder, an administration based on bureaucrats, many of them law professionals, and, for the time being, a secure basis of financial revenue (Disney, 2009). At the same time, the king had asserted his prominence, placing himself clearly above both the magnates and the representative assembly constituted by members of the clergy, the nobility and commoners. The building of the Empire also contributed to the magnification of the king's power. Directed by the Crown, the success of that enterprise brought not only economic but also symbolic capital or prestige (in Bourdieu's terms) to the king. There was already an acute awareness of the importance of sea ventures for the kingdom at the time (Sobral, 2012).

In his influential opus on nationalism, Benedict Anderson (1991) draws attention to the importance of the links between capitalism and print in allowing for the possibility of imagining the nation. We can adapt his insights when tackling the subject of national identity in sixteenth century Portugal: works produced and printed at that time were widely influential not only then, but would retain their appeal in the following centuries. When paying due attention to these works, we should also bear in mind that publishing was controlled by the State through censorship. Hence, the published works only reflected views in accordance with state power.

Among those works are historical narratives that offered a genealogy of the Portuguese, inventing mythical prestigious ancestors and celebrating their achievements both in Europe and overseas. However, the most famous work of the time, which would be enshrined as a national epic, is the poem Os Lusíadas (The Lusiads) by Luís de Camões (1578). In it we find topics that would become part of the official vision of Portuguese history. The idea of the Lusitanians as ancestors of the Portuguese and the presentation of sea ventures and explorations— first among them the circumnavigation of Africa and the arrival in India of Vasco da Gama's expedition in 1498—as the most important features of Portuguese history would have a great future in the centuries ahead. They would contribute to the conception of those times as the Golden Age of Portuguese history, a period of unrivalled glory. The State and other ideological agents would regularly invoke this period as a source of inspiration for nationalistic endeavours. Camões would become the national poet, celebrated both as a peerless writer and as a symbol of patriotic attachment to the fatherland. Today the anniversary of his death is still the most important national holiday (Sobral, 2003, 2012). In sum, many of these topics, which were also found in different variants in other parts of Europe (Burke, 2013), would be continuously reproduced and endure for centuries.

There are other manifestations of patriotic feelings towards the nation among the literate elite of that period. For instance, we see the signs of those feelings in the attention paid to the Portuguese language, with the elaboration of the first

Portuguese grammars published in the sixteenth and the beginning of the seventeenth centuries. This fact alone can be seen as a crucial marker of "linguistic pride" (Burke, 2013, p. 30), but the authors of those grammars would go further by developing explicit "patriotic" or "nationalist" apologies of the Portuguese language, in particular vis-à-vis the Castilian (Albuquerque, 1974; Buescu, 1978). Note that in the sixteenth and seventeenth centuries many of the most important Portuguese writers—Camões, for example—also wrote in Castilian, a prestigious language at the time since Spanish power was at its height.

The Lusiads contains an apologetic celebration of the Portuguese compared to other European peoples, showing that the proclamation of Portuguese excellence was indissolubly linked to derogatory representations of others. In the poem, the Portuguese are portrayed as the utmost Christian people—a chosen people, like many other peoples have claimed throughout history (Hoppenbrouwers, 2007)—pursuing the Christianisation of the world through seafaring and conquests, in contrast with the Germans (who rebelled against Rome and invented a new "sect"), the English (who persecuted the Catholics), the French (who saw the emergence of the Huguenots), and the Italian, submerged in vice. Claims of representing true Christianity were of the utmost importance, since together with history and language, religion was one of the domains where "an increasingly sharp national consciousness may be seen in the early modern period" (Burke, 2013, p. 31).

All this self-praise and denigration of others belonged to a context of intensified interaction. Indeed, if the time of humanism was one of cosmopolitanism, it was also one of intensified verbal war facilitated by print. Interaction fed national prejudices, not only keeping alive but probably deepening the divide between peoples. In that respect, it must be underlined that what was happening in Portugal was not by any means an isolated case. On the contrary, and allowing for local variation, this was part of a major Western European trend (Marcu, 1976).

The Portuguese were involved in this verbal war full of hetero-stereotypes and self-stereotypes. A Flemish humanist, Nicolas Cleynaerts, who came to Portugal to teach at the University in Coimbra in the first half of the sixteenth century, portrayed the Portuguese as lazy, possessed by the mania of nobility, and in thrall to vice (Cerejeira, 1949). This contrasted radically with the views of Camões and others who insisted on the "natural endurance" of the Portuguese against adversity as the source of their celebrated feats. Such utterances take for granted the existence of so-called "national characters". We know, of course, that national collectives cannot be thought of as if they were individuals, and we have been warned against any kind of essentialisms, but representations like these were widely believed and have not lost their attraction over the centuries (Leerssen, 2007).

Building the Empire also implied the mobilisation of a great number of Portuguese. People were needed in the armies, in the navy and to conduct trade. Thus, colonisation provided (different) opportunities for diverse segments of Portuguese society. To the nobility went the most important offices or the military commands; to the medium strata, less important offices in the administration; to the bourgeoisie, new territories and opportunities in trade. Every group was involved, from the crown and the clergymen to the commoners. To the more humble artisans and people of peasant or working-class stock, the Empire offered the opportunity to escape poverty at home. As a result, the Empire led to an important diaspora and marked the beginning of an enduring structural feature of Portuguese society—migration. By involving a large proportion of the population in its enterprise, it contributed to a broader awareness among the common people that they were part of a Portuguese collective.

Marriage policies among the Iberian royal households—Spain would be unified by the marriage of the Queen of Castile and the King of Aragon—continued in the fifteenth and sixteenth centuries. At the end of the sixteenth century there was another dynastic crisis in Portugal that was brought about by the defeat and death of the Portuguese King Sebastian in Morocco in 1578. As he died unmarried and without offspring, the crown went to the King of Spain, Philip, a grandchild of a Portuguese king and by far the most powerful of all those who could claim rights to the succession. However, his succession to the Portuguese crown was not without opposition, in spite of having drawn the support of most of the nobility, the high clergy, many of the bourgeoisie and officialdom. His army, under the command of the feared Duke of Alba, and his navy had to invade Portugal and defeat the small forces that supported another claimant, an illegitimate grandson of a former king. Even so, sporadic and localised confrontations kept arising after that defeat. Some in the nobility and probably many commoners resented the fact that Portugal was being ruled by someone who was not Portuguese by birth, since being a native was a source of the king's legitimacy in medieval and modern Europe (Gat & Yakobson, 2013). They also resented the loss of independence, despite the fact that it was agreed that the Kingdom of Portugal, with its Empire, would retain its full autonomy and be in the control of the Portuguese. Philip himself underlined this fact, living in Portugal for two years.

Portugal would be reunited with Spain for sixty years, from 1580 to 1640, until a coup staged by members of the nobility and officialdom placed an autochthonous king (a descendant of the former dynasty) on the throne again, and Portugal became definitively separated from Spain. The backdrop to all this was the decay of Spanish power during the reigns of the successors of Phillip I, and the centralising measures taken by the Spanish Crown (Anderson, 1976/1978). However, history could have been different, in theory at least. A few months before the Portuguese coup, the Catalonians revolted against the centralised state in Madrid—and this began with a popular uprising, not an elite coup. The fact that state authorities had to face this uprising enfeebled their capacities and facilitated the success of the Portuguese coup. Here we should bear in mind that before its attempts at centralisation Spain was not a strongly unified state, being formed by several kingdoms and culturally very diverse. Catalonia had been an earldom and then a principality, attached to the Crown of Aragon by marriage but retaining its own institutions, laws and vernacular. The ascendancy of Castile in the new, more centralised state sparked this uprising, and although it was defeated, the aspiration to independence would resurface in the future.

Portuguese history offers grounds for comparison with Catalonia. Like Catalonia, the Portuguese kingdom was formed during the Middle Ages, and acquired political and cultural distinctiveness in Iberia. Portuguese rebels took the opportunity of the war in Catalonia which further weakened the Spanish, who were already enfeebled by their participation in the Thirty Years War (1618–1648). However, Portugal and Catalonia followed very distinct paths. One of the main factors that explains the difference between the success of the Portuguese rebels and the failure of the Catalonians was the fact that Portugal had an important seaborne Empire—something Catalonia lacked. Under the unification with Spain the Portuguese inhabiting the different parts of the Empire, and particularly Brazil, had to endure the attacks of foreign powers who were hostile to Spain. The Empire suffered enormous losses in Asia. That nourished resentment of a Crown that was suspected of putting Portuguese possessions in danger due to its involvement in European wars. More generally, the Empire would in no small measure provide the resources in men and commodities that would allow for the eventual triumph of the Portuguese in their thirty-year war with Spain as a result of the coup (Schwartz, 2008).

During the Union between Portugal and Spain, a sense of a collective Portuguese identity remained alive. It is true that many families from the higher nobility went to live in the Court in Madrid, the main source of privilege and power, and that some members of the state and literate elites were bilingual, printing important works in Castilian. A few stayed there, loyal to the Spanish Crown of Habsburg lineage. However, neither the fact that members of the elite were servants of the Crown nor that they expressed themselves in another language necessarily meant that their feeling of identification with Portugal weakened. As one Portuguese high official wrote in Castilian, in a work dedicated to King Phillip III of Portugal – (who was also Phillip IV of Spain), "Spain was the better part of the world, and Portugal the better part of Spain" (Sobral, 2012). This is one of several works that illustrates the existence of nationalism among the elites of the time.

What can be said about the more widespread feelings of collective identification among the masses? The role of religious agents in nation-building in pre-modern Europe has already been recognised (Gat & Yakobson, 2013) and we know that the commoners were the targets of patriotic propaganda against Castile-Spain. This was developed by the lower clergy and more powerful agents, like the Jesuits (Marques, 1989). We know this because this propaganda effort left many printed testimonies. However, in themselves such testimonies do not tell us if that effort succeeded in achieving its purpose. To answer that question, we need to look at people's behaviour.

The persistence of the belief that the late King Sebastian had not been killed in the battle of Ksar el Kebir in Morocco in 1578, but was alive and hidden, and that he would return to free Portugal from Spain and restore its greatness, should be read as a protest against what was seen as the subordination of Portugal to Spain. This was a Portuguese version of the messianic myth of the "sleeping king" that had already surrounded many other foreign leaders beforehand (Cohn, 1970). This belief was alive and well, and several people who claimed to be the late king were deemed to represent enough danger that they were executed (Disney, 2009; Serrão, 2006). There were also numerous popular mutinies against taxation that were accompanied by indisputable animosity and xenophobia against Castile-Spain (Oliveira, 1990). Finally, although the initial movement against the Habsburgs was led by some of the nobility and higher bureaucracy, in the end it enjoyed sufficient support from the popular masses (Godinho, 1968), who had to endure a twenty-eight-year war effort ending with the recognition of the full independence of the country. We can postulate that without the spreading of some kind of "popular" nationalism—or "proto-nationalism"—the recovery of independence would not have been achieved.

In studying the historical relation between the State and collective identity, we must also take into account the growth of state apparatus from the late seventeenth century onwards. In general, the State gradually increased its control over several spheres of social life. In Portugal, these were the times of the Absolutist state (Anderson, 1978), which not only assumed a major stake in economic activity, but also secured the *de facto* control of the Church and its feared tribunal, the Inquisition, who lost all autonomy in the second half of the eighteenth century. It established control over information through censorship and made the ruling classes entirely dependent on the Crown as an unrivalled source of distribution of employment and income. Also, it was under the aegis of the Absolutist state that a first effort for basic and generalised public education—through which state nationalism could be disseminated later—began in the second half of the eighteenth century (Sobral, 2012).

National identity from the time of liberalism to the present

So far we have been looking at the question of the formation of national identity in Portugal as a slow process, something that began in the aftermath of the formation of a kingdom in the twelfth century, which first drew the boundaries that allowed for the genesis of the Portuguese. Following other scholars, I have pointed to the role of both exceptional events, such as wars and the collective mobilisations they entailed (Bloom, 1990), and everyday practices in producing and reproducing national identification. The wars that consecrated the separation between Portugal and the core of Iberia (Castile/Spain) belong to the former category, as would the fight against the French Napoleonic invader at the beginning of the nineteenth century (1808). Hatred and xenophobia were mobilised against the enemies of the fatherland, something that also occurred elsewhere from Iberia to Russia (Sobral, 2003, 2012). These are major components of national consciousness. However, operating less notoriously, the workings of daily living, through which, intentionally or not, national identity is performed, are also of the utmost importance. The State and its agencies, as the main frames for collective action and organisation, play a major role in both.

With political liberalism (first introduced by the Constitution of 1822) the nation (understood as the Portuguese people) was defined as the source of sovereignty and legitimisation of power. The nation was understood as being formed by citizens not subjects. All this marks a deep transformation in the nature of the state. The state of the *national monarchy*—a state where sovereigns derived legitimacy not only from the dynastic principle but also from a sense of common identity with the people (Gat & Yakobson, 2013)—gives way explicitly to a *nation-state*, that is to say a state that not only claims to correspond to the nation, but also where the nation is explicitly the only and ultimate source of the ruler's authority (Guibernau, 1996). It is from this time on that we see the development of different nationalist doctrines, from romanticism and liberalism to the racist and authoritarian ideology that would reach their climax in the twentieth century. However, my aim here is not to examine nationalist ideology per se. I only refer to these doctrines insofar as they helped in naturalising national identifications and were reflected in political behaviour, state action and cultural attitudes. Romanticism, for instance, brought a new attention to all things deemed national, be it history, architecture or folk culture (oral literature and ethnography, for example), and interest in those topics would remain alive throughout the nineteenth and twentieth centuries.

However, what is most important to stress here is the fact that it is within this period that the State started to play a decisive role in the "nationalization of the masses" (Hutchinson, 2006; Mosse, 1975). This was done mainly through the army (although universal conscription was only introduced in the twentieth century), the slow enforcement of universal basic schooling (the majority of the population was still illiterate in 1930; Grácio, 2006), the construction of monuments, urban architecture and place-naming, participation in public rituals, and mass media. Public rituals dedicated to national figures and feats attracted massive participation. They began to develop at the end of the nineteenth century, commemorating the third anniversaries of the passing away of the poet Camões (1880) and the circumnavigation of Africa to reach India by Vasco da Gama (1898) (Catroga, 1996). We must bear in mind that the Portuguese and the Portuguese State were not acting in isolation; rather, they were part of contemporary nationalisation dynamics happening everywhere. This context was one of acute international rivalry, for example in relation to the partition of Africa between colonial powers. The Portuguese State, which inaugurated the colonial enterprise in Africa, had to cope with competition in the late nineteenth century from much more powerful European states also intent on building colonial empires, such as the English and the French. It was a time of friction, with the Portuguese State making a strong investment in armies in order to conquer regions of inland Africa and claim them as colonies (for instance in Angola and Mozambique).

After the loss of Brazil in 1822, the Empire still remained at the core of official policies and narratives in Portugal. As previously noted, the Empire already played an immense role in the ethnocentric pride shown both by the state and by the intellectual elite in the sixteenth century. It would continue to be at the fore of nationalist narratives in the nineteenth and twentieth centuries, both under liberal regimes and under the authoritarian fascist-inspired regime of Salazar (the "Estado Novo", 1933–1974), whose insistence on fighting for the preservation of the

Empire led to its own demise by a military coup in 1974. Even today, in post-colonial times, the former Empire still retains its importance in the Portuguese national imagination, conceived as an area connected through the use of Portuguese as an everyday and/or official language, and through the flux of migrants from the former colonies to Portugal and vice versa. Its continuing importance as a central theme in nationalist narratives, promoted by state policy, is shown by the fact that Lisbon's World Exhibition of 1998 was still commemorating the arrival of Vasco da Gama in India (Sobral, 2012).

Mass media has had a central role in "nationalising" the Portuguese by constantly making them aware that they are part of the nation and its history. The modern daily press that appeared in the second half of the nineteenth century would play a central role in this process, a role that was subsequently taken up by the radio and by cinema in the 1930s and television from the late 1950s onwards. Nationalism pervaded most of the media. Although many of the media were in private hands, the State remained the most influential actor, both by indirect and direct means, particularly through censorship, a permanent institution from 1933 up to 1974. The State operated in a direct way through state-controlled broadcasting, cinema and television. Likewise, the State directly shaped the curriculum of schools in order to further a nationalist consciousness, something particularly visible in the teaching of history that magnified Portuguese achievements. An acute sense of national pride was diffused in this way.

Conclusion

In this chapter, I have tried to show how Portuguese national identity is a product of historical processes that began in the twelfth century with the formation of the kingdom of Portugal. State power was the determinant factor in the emergence of the Portuguese collective. The formation of this kind of collective was achieved both by the means of violence and by the slow habit of living together. It was through daily living (e.g. using the same language in conversation, which made its appearance in the thirteenth century) that diverse populations came to believe that they were part of the same people or nation: the Portuguese.

Historical facts like these, which support the claim of a continuity between pre-modern collectives and modern nations, are generally disregarded by modernists but not by all scholars of nationalism. Some have argued, for instance, that the fourteenth century was the turning point in the making of the French nation. It has been claimed that at that time, belief in the nation was present, although probably only among a minority—for in the French case too, the nation as encompassing the masses would undoubtedly be a product of the State (Guenée, 1967). According to Hastings, national awareness first appeared in medieval England (Hastings, 1997), whereas others have argued that in several polities of the Middle Ages "national sentiments" were an incipient fact, though again restricted to minorities (Llobera, 1994). Reynolds, a medievalist historian who examined several kingdoms in Western Europe from 900 to 1300, stressed that "The inhabitants of the kingdoms (…) or at least the politically active among them, seem to have taken for granted that their own kingdoms comprised peoples of some sort of naturally collective character" (1997, p. 301).

The state was the crucible that allowed the formation of the nation. Its physical borders also became the psychological boundaries of self- and hetero-identification. All this did not take place overnight but was the result of a long historical process. People's awareness of a Portuguese national identity, a product of the existence of the kingdom, slowly grew in the following centuries—even though it should be acknowledged that the evidence for such consciousness remains indirect when tackling the beliefs of the majority. The growth of the state apparatus and its involvement in people's lives—as happened through schooling, for example— strengthened its role in the spreading of nationalism and in the naturalisation of national identity.

The Portuguese case is far from being unique as regards the impact of state power on the production and reproduction of national identity. The recognition of the importance of the state in these matters is a point that is shared both by proponents of such diverse approaches to nationalism as the ethno-symbolist (Smith, 1991) or the modernist (Breuilly, 1993; Hobsbawm 1994; Mann, 1993). It should be stressed that the modern state had at its disposal a new array of powers that increased its presence in the day-to-day life of its population, among them the important control it could exert through media and education that allowed for the cultural homogenisation of the population. However, as Guibernau has stated, the effects of state action can be very different, depending on its relation with the nation. In the cases where the state has become coextensive with the nation in the national imagination, as in many European nation-states, (state) nationalism becomes deeply embedded in the daily life of the population and rarely appears at the forefront—and this is what happened in Portugal. In other cases where such correspondence has been less well established—as in the case of multinational or multiethnic states, for example—the enforcement of cultural homogenisation by the State can breed resistance, strengthening alternative nationalisms to that of the state (Guibernau, 1996; Sindic, this volume).

Although this chapter has focused on the particular case of national identities, it may also provide important clues for those interested in the relation between power and identity in other contexts. On the one hand, since it is particularly well documented, the active role of the State in the formation of national identities may provide a useful template for understanding the ways in which the exercise of power in general impacts on the shaping of identity. On the other hand, the historical argument developed here also shows that stressing the formation of identities as the result of human agency is not equivalent to claiming that identities are created without any basis in pre-existing social and historical realities. On the contrary, attempts at forming and mobilising identities, whether or not this takes place at a national level, may be most successful when they can build on and recruit existing realities to their purposes. As such, the present argument should also act as a plea for putting the processes of identity formation back into their historical context.

Note

1 I wish to thank Denis Sindic and Rui Costa-Lopes, who offered critical commentaries on previous versions of this chapter.

References

Albuquerque, M. de (1974) *A Consciência Nacional Portuguesa* [The Portuguese National Consciousness]. Lisbon: Author's edition.

Anderson, B. (1991) *Imagined Communities. Reflections on the Origins and Spread of Nationalism*. London: Verso.

Anderson, P. (1978) *L'État Absolutiste—I—L' Europe de l' Ouest* [The Absolutist State—I—Western Europe]. Paris: François Maspéro. (Original work published 1976.)

Armstrong, J.A. (1982) *Nations before Nationalism*. Chapell Hill: University of North Carolina Press.

Barth, F. (1989 [1969]) Introduction. In F. Barth (Ed.), *Ethnic Groups and Boundaries. The Social Organization of Culture Difference* (pp. 9–38). Long Grove, Il.: Waveland.

Bhabha, H. (Ed.) (1990) *Nation and Narration*. London: Routledge.

Billig, M. (1995) *Banal Nationalism*. London: Sage.

Bloom, W. (1990) *Personal Identity, National Identity and International Relations*. Cambridge: Cambridge University Press.

Bourdieu, P. (1998) *Practical Reason: On the Theory of Action* (R. Johnson, trans.). Cambridge, UK: Polity Press. (Original work published 1994.)

——(2000) *Pascalian Meditations* (R. Nice, trans.). Cambridge, UK: Polity Press. (Original work published 1997.)

Breuilly, J. (1993) *Nationalism and the State*. Manchester: Manchester University Press.

Buescu, M.L.C. (1978) *Gramáticos Portugueses do Século XVI* [Portuguese Grammars of the 16th Century]. Lisbon: Instituto de Cultura e Língua Portuguesa.

Burke, P. (2013) Nationalism and Vernaculars, 1500–1800. In J. Breuilly (Ed.), *The Oxford Handbook of the History of Nationalism* (pp. 21–35). Oxford: Oxford University Press.

Catroga, F. (1996) Ritualizações da história [Ritualizations of History]. In L. Reis Torgal, J. M. Amado Mendes & F. Catroga (Eds), *História da história em Portugal, sécs. XIX-XX* [History of History in Portugal, 19th–20th Centuries], Vol 2 (pp. 547–671). Lisbon: Círculo de Leitores.

Cerejeira, M.G. (1949) *Clenardo e a Sociedade Portuguesa do seu Tempo* [Cleynaerts and the Portuguese Society of his Time]. Coimbra: Coimbra Editora.

Cintra, L.F.L. (1989) A Lenda de Afonso I, Rei de Portugal [The Legend of Alfonso the 1st, King of Portugal]. *Revista ICALP*, 16–17, 64–78.

Cohn, N. (1970) *The Pursuit of the Millennium: Revolutionary Millenarians and Mystical Anarchists of the Middle Ages, Revised and Expanded Edition*. Oxford: Oxford University Press.

Disney, A.R. (2009) *A History of Portugal and the Portuguese Empire, Volume One, Portugal*. Cambridge: Cambridge University Press.

Edensor, T. (2002) *National Identity, Popular Culture and Everyday Life*. Oxford & New York: Berg.

Eisenstadt, S.N. & Giesen, B. (1995) The Construction of Collective Identity. *Archives Européennes de Sociologie*, 36, 72–102.

Eriksen, T. (2007) Some Questions about Flags. In T.H. Eriksen & R. Jenkins (Eds), *Flag, Nation and Symbolism in Europe and America* (pp. 1–13). Abingdon, Oxon: Routledge.

Fédou, R. (1971) *L'État au Moyen Âge* [The State in the Middle Ages]. Paris: PUF.

Gat, A. & Yakobson, A. (2013) *Nations: The Long History and Deep Roots of Political Ethnicity and Nationalism*. Cambridge: Cambridge University Press.

Gellner, E. (1983) *Nations and Nationalism*. New York: Cornell University Press.

Godinho, V.M. (1968) 1580 e a Restauração [1580 and the Restoration]. In *Ensaios II sobre História de Portugal* [Essays II on the History of Portugal] (pp. 257–291). Lisbon: Sá da Costa.

Grácio, R. (2006) Ensino Primário e Analfabetismo [Primary Education and Illiteracy]. In J. Serrão (Ed.), *Dicionário de História de Portugal* [Dictionary of the History of Portugal] (Vol. 2, pp. 392–397). Oporto: Figueirinhas.

Grosby, S. (2005) *Nationalism: A Very Short Introduction*. Oxford: Oxford University Press.

Guenée, B. (1967). État et Nation au Moyen Âge [State and Nation in the Middle Ages]. *Revue Historique, 237*, 17-30.

Guibernau, M. (1996) *Nationalisms: The Nation-State and Nationalism in the Twentieth-Century*. Cambridge: Polity Press.

Hastings, A. (1997) *The Construction of Nationhood: Ethnicity, Religion and Nationalism*. Cambridge: Cambridge University Press.

Hobsbawm, E. (1994 [1990]) *Nations and Nationalism since 1870. Programme, Myth, Reality*. Cambridge: Cambridge University Press.

Hoppenbrouwers, P. (2007). Medieval Peoples Imagined. In M. Beller, & J. Leerssen (Eds), *Imagology: The Cultural Construction and Literary Representation of National Characters* (pp. 45–62). Amsterdam & New York: Rodopi.

Huizinga, J. (1959) *Men and Ideas: History, the Middle Ages, the Renaissance*. Princeton: Princeton University Press. (Original work published 1940.)

Hutchinson, J. (2006) Hot and Banal Nationalism: The Nationalization of the "Masses". In G. D. & K. Kumar (Eds), *The Sage Handbook of Nations and Nationalism* (pp. 295–306). London: Sage.

Jenkins, R. (2011) *Being Danish: Paradoxes of Identity in Everyday Life*. Copenhagen: Museum Tusculanum Press.

Koester, D. (2006) The Power of Insult: Ethnographic Publication and Emergent Nationalism in the Sixteenth Century. In R. Handler (Ed.), *Central Sites and Peripheral Visions: Cultural and Institutional Crossings in the History of Anthropology, History of Anthropology (vol. 11)*. Madison: The University of Wisconsin Press.

Leerssen, J. (2007) The Poetics and Anthropology of National Character. In M. Beller & J. Leerssen (Eds), *Imagology: The Cultural Construction and Literary Representation of National Characters* (pp. 63–76). Amsterdam & New York: Rodopi.

Llobera, J.R. (1994) *The God of Modernity*. Oxford: Berg.

Mann, M. (1993) *The Sources of Social Power, Volume 2: The Rise of Classes and Nation-States*. Cambridge: Cambridge University Press.

——(1994) *A Political Theory of Nationalism and its Excesses*. Madrid: Instituto Juan March de Estudios e Investigaciones.

Marcu, E.D. (1976) *Sixteenth Century Nationalism*. New York: Abaris Books.

Marques, J.F. (1989) *A Parenética Portuguesa e a Restauração 1640–1668* [Portuguese preaching and the Restoration 1640–1668]. Oporto: Instituto Nacional de Investigação Científica.

Mattoso, J. (1985a) *Identificação de um País: Ensaio sobre as Origens de Portugal,* 1096–1325 (Vol. 1: Oposição) [Identification of a country: Essay on the Origins of Portugal, 1096–1325 (Vol. 1: Opposition)]. Lisbon: Editorial Estampa.

——(1985b) *Identificação de um País: Ensaio sobre as Origens de Portugal,* 1096–1325 (Vol. 2: Composição) [Identification of a Country: Essay on the Origins of Portugal, 1096–1325 (Vol. 2: Composition)]. Lisbon, Editorial Estampa.

Mosse, G.L. (1975) *The Nationalization of the Masses: Political Symbolism and Mass Movements in Germany from the Napoleonic Wars through the Third Reich.* Ithaca and London: Cornell University Press.

Oliveira, A. de (1990) *Poder e Oposição Política em Portugal no Período Filipino (1580–1640)* [Power and Political Opposition in Portugal in the Filipino Period (1580–1640)]. Lisbon: Difel.

Reynolds, S. (1997 [1984]) *Kingdoms and Communities in Western Europe, 900–1300.* Oxford: Clarendon Press.

Schulze, H. (1996) *States, Nations and Nationalism.* Oxford: Blackwell.

Schwartz, S. (2008) Prata, Açúcar e Escravos: de como o Império Restaurou Portugal [Silver, Sugar and Slaves: How the Empire Restored Portugal]. *Tempo,* 12, 201–223.

Serrão, J. (2006) Sebastianismo. In J. Serrão (Ed.), *Dicionário de História de Portugal* (vol. 5, pp. 607–615). Oporto: Figueirinhas.

Skey, M. (2011) *National Belonging and Everyday Life: The Significance of Nationhood in an Uncertain World.* Houndmills, Basingstoke: Palgrave Macmillan.

Smith, A.D. (1991) *National Identity.* Harmondsworth: Penguin.

——(1999) *Myths and Memories of the Nation.* Oxford: Oxford University Press.

Sobral, J.M. (2003) A Formação das Nações e o Nacionalismo: os Paradigmas Explicativos e o Caso Português [Nation Formation and Nationalism: Explanatory paradigms and the Portuguese Case]. *Análise Social,* 37, 1093–1126.

Sobral, J.M. (2012) *Portugal, Portugueses: Uma identidade Nacional* [Portugal, Portuguese: A National identity]. Lisbon: Fundação Francisco Manuel dos Santos.

Strayer, J.R. (1970) *On the Medieval Origins of the Modern State.* Princeton, NJ: Princeton University Press.

Thomaz, L.F.R. & Alves, J.S. (1991) Da Cruzada ao Quinto Império [From the Crusade to the Fifth Empire]. In F. Bethencourt & D. Ramada Curto (Eds), *A Memória da Nação* (pp. 81–164) [The Memory of the Nation]. Lisbon: Sá da Costa.

Triandafyllidou, A. (1998) National Identity and the "Other". *Ethnic and Racial Studies,* 21, 593–612.

4

THEY'RE HERE TO STAY

Tribes and power in contemporary Jordan

Eleanor Gao

When the British arrived in what was then TransJordan in 1921, they found a society organised into a number of different tribes. Having been mostly left alone by the Ottomans during their rule of the area, Jordanian tribes governed themselves and had also discovered ways to either co-exist with or dominate other tribes. Members depended on their tribe for protection, marriage arrangements, conflict resolution and social welfare. Without an overarching authority, it made sense that individuals turned to their tribes for assistance. By banding together, members could ensure collective security that they were unable to guarantee on their own— and at the same time, living together led to the development of social arrangements such as deference to sheikhs and the creation of particular mechanisms to settle the disputes that were characteristic of tribes at that time.

Since 1921 much has changed in Jordan, including the establishment of the Hashemite monarchy and a central government, which has managed to stretch administratively to every corner of the country. However, tribes still remain an integral part of Jordanian life despite previous predictions that tribalism would perish. In this chapter, I examine the enduring significance of the tribe in Jordan by highlighting some of the ways in which tribes continue to be relevant and the implications of their presence for power relations in Jordan. While tribes still serve a number of different functions, I focus on the role of tribes with regard to municipal and national elections, patronage, and some aspects of social life such as the formation of civic association and the settlement of disputes between members of different tribes.

The chapter is arranged as follows. In the first section, I define and provide a brief historical background of tribes. I then explain why some scholars predicted the demise of tribalism given the social and political changes taking place in Jordan in the 1950s and 1960s. However, the role of tribes has remained robust, and in the third section I outline some of the ways in which tribalism is still relevant and the implications for political power in Jordan. Finally, I conclude the chapter by exploring the regime's role in ensuring the persistence of tribalism.

Some of the observations that I make in this chapter come from scholars of Jordanian tribes, while others derive from my own fieldwork in the country in 2009–2010. During my time there I travelled to fourteen municipalities, chosen for their tribal composition and ranging from monotribal municipalities (where one tribe is numerically dominant) to those with extremely diverse populations. Throughout this chapter I will also refer to monotribal municipalities as homogeneous and multitribal municipalities as heterogeneous. Five of these municipalities (Showbak, Taybeh, Madaba, Zarqa and Hassa) serve as primary case studies in this chapter. There, I interviewed a number of individuals including mayors, council members, civic leaders, and members of minority and majority tribes. This is complemented by additional interviews in the remaining nine municipalities. All names of interviewees mentioned in this chapter are pseudonyms.

While I argue in this chapter that tribalism is very much present today, I do not wish to imply that it is a phenomenon that is primordial or unchanging. It is not an inherent characteristic of the Jordanian population, but rather a phenomenon that wanes or waxes as a function of social incentives. I also do not wish to imply that tribalism is backwards, primitive or undesirable behaviour. In contemporary Jordan tribalism has a number of different functions, many of which can be deemed socially or politically positive although others are more problematic. For instance, tribes remain an essential source of social and financial support for members, but on the other hand, they can lead to the election of unqualified candidates through automatic support from tribal brethren. What I do wish to underscore in this chapter are the various ways tribalism still matters in contemporary Jordan and its influence on local power relations.

What are tribes?

In *Nationalism and the Genealogical Imagination*, the anthropologist Andrew Shryock (1997) reviews the oral histories of the Bedouin tribes of the Balqa region in Jordan and demonstrates how members of the same tribe negotiate between various versions of their history. What he finds to be evident from these competing histories is that for some members or tribes, their sense of tribal identity comes from their ability to trace their roots back to a single ancestor, even though some of these stories are closer to imagination than to reality. For other members or tribes there is no pretence of sharing a single ancestor, but rather there is emphasis on a long history of collaboration as the basis of their collective identity. Sometimes called confederations, these tribes do not claim to share the same ancestry, including not only those who are supposedly related by blood but also individuals whose descendants either voluntarily or forcibly joined the tribe (such as slaves). Some groups initially allied as a form of protection from enemies, and over time these alliances solidified into a common identity. Another possibility is that over time slaves became incorporated as part of the tribe, even though they shared no familial relationship with the owners (Lancaster, 1981). Whatever the story that binds them together, Jordanian tribes[1] can be defined as groups distinct from each other due to shared heritage and/or notions of common descent, whether real or imagined (Alon, 2007).

The largest tribes are usually those of the confederation type. The Beni Hassan tribe, considered the largest tribe of Jordan, is a confederation that is said to have a membership of 250,000 (bin Muhammad, 1999). Large tribes are divided into several branches, then into clans, and finally into individual nuclear families. Confederational tribes also tended to be nomadic or semi-nomadic in terms of their previous livelihood. Rather than primarily cultivating crops, as in the case of peasant tribes, members of nomadic tribes historically grazed camels or sheep, requiring them to travel to different locations in order to take advantage of feeding grounds. Bedouin tribes specifically grazed camels (Lewis, 1987). Nowadays even members of these semi-nomadic or nomadic tribes are settled for the most part and no longer travel from place to place throughout the year.

In the late nineteenth and up until the first few decades of the twentieth century, members of the tribe often worked together, whether to cultivate crops as in the case of peasant tribes or to graze animals as with nomadic or semi-nomadic tribes (Antoun, 1977; Lancaster, 1981). With the lack of, or only weak, government security forces at that time, tribes relied on themselves or cooperated with others to provide protection. For instance, a nomadic tribe, or a group of nomadic tribes, might police a settled area and in exchange they would ask for *khawa* or protection money from villagers, who contributed to this tax collectively (Lancaster, 1981). As Jordanians prioritise paternal relations, members of the same tribe tended to live next to their patrilineal kin within villages or further out in the desert. Social occasions necessitated not only inviting friends but also prioritising members from the same tribe on the father's side (Antoun, 1977). Visits also tended to occur more frequently between relatives on the paternal side (Antoun, 1979).

Usually no single individual served as the leader of a tribe, but many tribes deemed certain men within the tribe particularly influential, and these individuals were known as sheikhs.[2] Depending on the tribe, the title of sheikh was either inherited or the individual was selected based on his prominence and reputation as a fair and successful arbitrator. Some tribes did not have sheikhs but relied on tribal elites known as *wajaha*.[3] While members handled most of their own affairs on a daily basis, there were certain tasks such as negotiating disputes and proposing marriage for which they had to turn to sheikhs or *wajaha* for assistance. Such issues were never dealt with directly by the main parties but were handled by a group of representatives for each side, which included *wajaha* from one's own tribe but sometimes also from other tribes in the area (Lancaster, 1981). When the settlement of a dispute resulted in the payment of money from one tribe to another, members would be asked to contribute, with those closer in relation asked to contribute more than more distant others. If the punishment resulted in banishment from the tribe, the perpetrator and five generations of relatives, either previous or future, were asked to leave the area (Gubser, 1973). In farming areas where land was shared and rotated among a number of tribes, elders from each of the tribes sometimes also gathered together to distribute land (Antoun, 1977).

Modernisation and the waning of tribalism

Historically, tribes were critical in the lives of Jordanians. They provided protection and served as the basis of order and justice within the community. Disputes were solved by tribal elites, and punishment, if applied, was borne collectively by the entire tribal community. Tribes were also at the heart of social activity with members frequently visiting and inviting one another to mark momentous occasions. Preference for social relations with one's tribe also extended to marriage, since unions between first paternal cousins were favoured. Some tribal scholars describe incidences where male cousins had "claims" on their female cousins or where sheikhs declared upon the delivery of a baby girl that she was to be the bride of a particular individual (Antoun, 1977). Furthermore, there was little or no central governance, and with nomadic tribes moving to different locations throughout the year it was also difficult to reach them with public services.

With time, this began to change as the Hashemite monarchy became more firmly established in Jordan after being invited to rule by the British in 1921. During the process of consolidating their rule, the Hashemites enlisted the support of various tribes, particularly specific Bedouin tribes, whom the monarchy rewarded by placing members of these tribes in prominent government positions. The government also began encouraging nomadic tribes to settle, and by the 1970s less than 3 percent of the population was still travelling between locations (Jureidini & McLaurin, 1984). With the increasing settlement of nomadic tribes and the extension of the central government's authority and public services even to locations far out of the capital, it was believed that tribalism would erode away.

For instance, sedentarisation of the tribes facilitated government control and reduced local tribal independence because settled tribes could no longer simply relocate when they experienced hardship or objected to government policy. More importantly, however, the settling of tribes made it easier for members to receive education and other services from the central government (Jureidini & McLaurin, 1984). The improvement of road networks and transportation facilities also enabled the government to erect schools and health facilities, and to send civil servants to these areas. Education in particular was seen as critical in facilitating movement from a tribal to a national identity. Previously, because nomadic tribes moved according to the seasons, it was difficult for children to attend school. Now Jordanian schoolchildren were encouraged to develop national rather than tribal identities through education. Education also promoted notions of meritocracy where individuals were rewarded not according to the tribal hierarchy but as a function of their achievements (Fathi, 1994). Low status tribes—such as those whose members are former slaves, tribes that had not been politically favoured by the monarchy, or those with small membership sizes—readily adopted this meritocratic attitude, while high status tribes were more resistant to the idea (Layne, 1986). Finally, education resulted in new opportunities which sometimes required individuals to move away from their tribe, which was also believed to have the effect of decreasing the social power of the tribe over its members.

It was also posited that as the government began to assume many of the duties previously performed by tribes, the latter would become less relevant. The state now provided education, ministries organised the construction of roads, and rather than relying on the tribe for protection, both internal and external security forces had now been established. In place of working alongside members of the tribe in the herding of animals or in agriculture, Jordanians also increasingly found employment in the public and the private sectors. Finally, in 1975, tribal law was abolished (IRB, 2013). While the tribe had historically been the intermediary between the individual and the State, according to Dr. Muhafiza, former president of Yarmouk University in Jordan:

> [But now] the state has direct impact on an individual by offering him more services, by issuing laws, providing education, etc. In three decades the whole society has changed and the relationship between individuals and the state became stronger. Nobody is in need of his tribe or clan anymore to get rights.
>
> *(quoted in* Fathi, *1994, p. 179)*

As Jordan moved from being a "traditional" to a "modern" society, the role of the tribe was expected to ebb away as well. According to modernisation theorists writing in the 1960s and 1970s, migration, industrialisation, mass communication and the proliferation of education transformed societies from agrarian, inward-looking and politically apathetic to urban, more worldly and participatory counterparts (Deutsch, 1971; Inkeles, 1966; Lerner, 1958; Lipset, 1960). These processes were also predicted to reduce the level of tribalism in Jordan. Paul A. Jureidini and R.D. McLaurin wrote in 1984 that, while they could not proclaim the death of tribalism, its influence was diminishing:

> This is not to say that tribal loyalties are a thing of the past, but that tribal linkages can no longer lay exclusive claim on tribe members' allegiance. All Jordanians (East Bankers) are tribal in the sense that they can trace their descent from one or another of the hundreds of Jordanian or nearby (Syrian, Iraqi, or Arabian) tribes. Yet, for a steadily increasing number, tribal allegiance is either meaningless or peripheral to their lives and feelings.
>
> *(p. 40)*

Indeed, these changes were accompanied by indicators of waning tribalism such as the weakening of the authority of tribal leaders and the disintegration of previous tribal alliances. The anthropologist Linda Layne (1994) noticed in her fieldwork during the 1980s that tribal members no longer systematically followed the directives of sheikhs with regard to which candidate to support in elections. Candidates were also no longer limited to paramount sheikhs; instead, sheikhs of smaller tribal units also ran.

Migration toward urban centres also decreased the ubiquity of tribalism in the life of many Jordanians. In 1980 the percentage of Jordanians living in urban areas was 60 percent, but by 2010 this had grown to over 80 percent as individuals left rural areas to search for employment in cities (UN ESCWA, n.d.). In rural areas, where levels of migration are low, residents are more likely to live among other members of their tribes due to historical patterns of land ownership. In contrast, the increasing numbers of migrants in urban areas has led to a more chequered pattern of settlement as tribal land is sold to migrants or migrants rent properties constructed on these lands. Because members of the same tribe in urban areas may be distributed across several neighbourhoods, interactions occur less frequently and there is less ability to monitor the fulfilment of social obligations such as voting for a tribal candidate in elections. Furthermore, the large concentration of ethnic Palestinians in urban areas also dilutes tribalism since Palestinians are known for being less motivated by tribal considerations and are strong supporters of political parties, which are non-tribal in nature.

Compared to their counterparts in rural areas, members of tribes in urban settings may also be less able to exploit clientelistic relationships because of the greater difficulty in clearly identifying an appropriate individual to help, or from whom to solicit help. In rural locations, smaller numbers of people and closer social relations imply that tribal members are more likely to know each other and to be able to locate someone relevant to assist them. This is difficult in municipalities with large populations where the resident is less likely to have a connection to the individual they wish to persuade. Finally, urban areas tend to have a higher number of educated individuals and education is correlated to the weakening of tribal ties. This does not mean that tribalism is absent in urban areas, merely that its influence is attenuated as meritocratic hiring is more acceptable and there is less pressure to behave "tribally" in these places. In other words, the number of demands to provide patronage may not decrease in urban areas, but the obligation to fulfil them is often diminished.

But tribalism didn't go away

According to the predictions of yesteryear, one would expect to have few indications of tribalism in contemporary Jordan. Hiring policies ought to be meritocratic, social interactions and marriages ought to occur with as much frequency between friends as between family members, and the powers of tribal leadership ought to have continued to crumble to near extinction. While it is true that tribes no longer provide many of the services that they used to and that tribal hierarchies are no longer respected to the same degree, "tribal mentalities" have not disappeared (Masri, cited in Fathi, 1994, p. 208).

Hani Hourani, director of the former New Jordan Research Center, argues that there are two aspects to tribalism. On the one hand, there is the tangible relationship between tribes and the regime, which has weakened as the central government has adopted many of the previous obligations of tribal authority. The second important aspect of tribalism is tribalism as a mentality, which can assume a number of different contours and seems very much an ingrained part of Jordanian society. Whereas change has been observed in the first aspect, the second seems to have been less affected. When voting in elections, helping someone find a job, adjudicating a dispute or participating in charitable organisations, Jordanians continue to take account of tribal considerations, although the extent to which this is the case varies across socioeconomic, ethnic and geographic groups.

Therefore, despite portents of the death of tribalism thirty years ago, it seems that tribes are still very much present in Jordanian society today, particularly in the context of elections or situations where patronage can be provided, as well as many other aspects of social life. While Jordan holds both parliamentary and municipal level elections, here I focus on the latter since they have received less scholarly attention, but I will also consider parliamentary elections in a later section.

Elections

In recent years, municipal councils as well as parliaments have been dominated not by members of political parties but by members of tribes. In the 2007 municipal elections, the majority of candidates for the mayor and the municipal council were not members of parties. In the 2013 parliamentary elections, despite an increase in the number of seats allocated to parties from 17 to 27 as a result of the Arab Spring protests, the number of MPs representing parties has remained low (BBC News, 2012). The remaining 123 seats in parliament can be won either by members of political parties or by those running as independents, but the number of seats won by members of political parties has not exceeded the 27 allocated specifically to parties.

At the municipal level, the type of electoral system used in Jordan is the single non-transferable vote (SNTV) system, where the top n vote-getters become members of the municipal council, n being the number of council seats. Mayors are elected using the majoritarian system, however, and under this system the candidate receiving the greatest number of votes is elected. There is also a women's quota whereby 20 percent of the seats on the council must be allocated to women. Prior to 1993 Jordan used the block system where a voter could vote for as many candidates as there were seats on the council, but in 1993, the government changed this to the "one man, one vote" system whereby a voter could only support a single candidate (El-Shamayleh, 2013).

The influence of the tribe begins with the nomination process, as it is often tribes rather than political parties that bring candidates forward. Some tribes discuss collectively how many candidates to nominate and who they wish to select through the holding of a tribal primary or meetings between the *wajaha* or tribal elites (Layne, 1986). They can also devolve the decision to a particular branch of the tribe, in which case the right to make nomination decisions would normally rotate among branches of the tribe. These decisions can greatly influence how many candidates are offered in each electoral district, and hence the level of electoral competition, especially in monotribal municipalities. In such municipalities it is the dominant tribe that offers the majority of candidates since members of other tribes are aware that they often do not have enough supporters to win. Hence, if the dominant tribe offers a large number of candidates then the level of competition is high, and vice versa if the number of candidates is low.

For instance, in the municipality of Hassa in southern Jordan, where a large percentage of the population is from the tribe of Hajaya, this dominant tribe decided in the 2007 municipal elections to nominate Rana Hajaya, one individual from the tribe, for mayor. As some of my respondents indicated, prior to the elections discussions between various branches of the tribe had led to agreement on Rana's candidacy. One other candidate from the same tribe ran against Rana, but this individual was not endorsed by the tribe and received only half of the votes accorded to Rana. In effect this meant that there was very little competition for the mayoral position.

However, while the Hajaya tribe was organised and cohesive enough to control the number of candidates, not all dominant tribes have the capacity or desire to exert such control. For example, in the electoral district of Ghernata in the municipality of Madaba, located in central Jordan where the Shawabkeh tribe is dominant, five candidates vied for one council seat as the Shawabkeh tribe was not able to come to a consensus on a candidate prior to the elections. Therefore the level of electoral competition was high in that municipality, but the role of the dominant tribe in shaping elections was no less important.

Once candidates have been selected (either by the tribe or through self-nomination), the next step is to mobilise members of the tribe to support these candidates. Members may receive visits (Langston, 2005) and/or phone calls to encourage them to vote for the candidate. Those who are living far away are also encouraged to return to vote for that individual. As expressed by Qasim, a resident of Amman municipality who participated in my field study, there is a great deal of social pressure to support the candidate(s) from one's tribe, and members who do not vote for their tribal candidate often refrain from saying so in order to avoid causing any problems for themselves (5/7/2010). In the 2007 municipal elections, exit polls showed that a minimum of 25 percent and a maximum of 55 percent of voters supported their tribal candidate for the municipal council across the municipalities of Oyoun, Hassa, Madaba, Karak, Rashid and Barha[4] (JCSR, 2007).

These electoral processes demonstrate that in contemporary Jordan, the ability to achieve political power is related to the size of the tribe as well as to the cohesiveness of the tribe. Because winning elections depends on the number of votes the candidate is able to garner, large tribes have an advantage. An example of the power of large and cohesive tribes is their ability to nominate weak candidates and still win elections. The same possibility is not available to small tribes. Karim, a previous member of the municipal council in Hassa, informed me that even illiterate members from his tribe can win elections simply because they can depend on the support of their own tribe (21/4/2010). Describing his own case, Karim also noted that he was guaranteed to win a position on the municipal council because he could depend on the votes from his branch, which were large enough in number to secure a seat. Because Karim is from a monotribal municipality where candidates from various branches of the tribe compete against one another, his focus was on gaining the necessary votes from the branch rather than from the overall tribe. However, the logic that he describes is also applicable to situations where tribes compete against one another.

On the other hand, it is difficult for strong candidates from small tribes to win, even if the tribes from which the strong candidates originate are extremely cohesive, simply because they cannot generate enough votes from their members. To overcome this obstacle, small tribes campaign vigorously amongst members of other tribes, including their tribal in-laws. Small tribes can also form coalitions with one another, but the coordination of who to nominate can be difficult, and as members are from different tribes, there is less social pressure to support the coalition candidate (Hesham, resident of Madaba municipality, personal interview, 9/5/2010).

With the exception of municipalities with high numbers of migrants, political power is also circumscribed to individuals from the "original" tribes of the area. Members of these tribes see themselves as being the rightful holders of power and entitled to the political positions. This phenomenon is perpetuated by the fact that it is difficult for members of migrant tribes to win enough votes to hold office because their tribes are not with them in sufficient numbers. In locations with many migrants, these candidates are able to obtain support from other migrants from their region of Jordan, but because these voters are not from the same tribe as the candidate, the social pressure to support such candidates is not sufficient to guarantee their votes (Yazid, resident of Zarqa municipality, personal interviews, 4/4/2010 and 7/7/2010).

What about the reputation of the tribe? Historically, the relations between Jordanian tribes have been hierarchical with some tribes serving as the patron tribes and others as their clients. Some tribes were also the former slaves of other tribes, and in previous elections members of client or slave tribes have generally supported the candidate(s) from their former patron tribes (Gubser, 1973). Given that this has not been the focus of much research, I can only offer a few speculative thoughts on this subject. As traditional leadership has waned and now that being a sheikh is no longer a requirement for nomination, I suspect that such hierarchical relations are also declining as elections become a game in which tribes win based simply on the number of votes they are able to gather. The deterioration of former political alliances noted earlier is further evidence that each tribe that can win seats due to its numbers is eager to go it alone.

Patronage

Given that electoral support and tribalism are intertwined, it should not be surprising that the same relationship exists between patronage and tribalism. It is acceptable and typical to use *wasta* to facilitate the achievement of a number of goals, whether it be employment, the waiving of a local fee, obtaining a passing grade for a student, or a host of other activities. In written and formal Arabic, *wasta* literally means "the middle", but colloquially it has come to mean an intercessor who "achieve(s) that which is assumed to be otherwise unattainable by the supplicant" (Cunningham & Sarayrah, 1993, p. 1). To use *wasta* is to turn to a patron to achieve some sort of goal, whether it is mediation in disputes, the introduction of "flexibility" to laws or regulations, or facilitation in gaining employment. In this section, I discuss how tribalism leads to the prioritisation of kinfolk in patronage relationships and with regard to social support. I also discuss briefly the consequences for those who prefer not to abide by these obligations.

In general, where there is discretion in decision-making and where patronage will not create harm for the patron, there is potential for clientelism to arise. The problem of patronage is so pervasive in some areas of Jordanian life that the government has taken explicit measures to prevent its usage. Because elected officials like mayors and council members hired so many additional but unnecessary municipal employees, the Ministry of Municipal Affairs has turned the hiring process into a central rather than a local decision. In order to acquire additional employees, the municipality must ask the Ministry for permission, which must also approve of the individual who is offered the job. A job in the public sector, even at the municipality where salaries are low, is desirable as it is guaranteed for life, not demanding, and with short work hours. This popularity of jobs at the municipality grants power to mayors and council members who are therefore in a position to offer attractive employment (Gao, 2012).

Wasta can be provided by members of one's tribe, a friend, or even a stranger. However, there are differences in clientelistic relationships between those who are related and those who are not. First of all, the obligation to help a member of the tribe may be greater than the obligation to assist a friend from another tribe because Jordanian social customs dictate the prioritisation of kin. Mayors who do not make an effort to hire relatives, or assist them in other ways once in office, are criticised and may lose the support of their tribe. It is possible that a refusal to help a member of another tribe may also lead to poor relations with members of that tribe, but this consequence is less certain and may also be less problematic for the patron as he does not interact with members of other tribes as frequently as with his own. Furthermore, when patronage is offered within a tribal relationship, it is not obligatory for the client to repay the patron—support for the official in the next round of elections may be all that is expected. Robert B. Cunningham and Yasin K. Sarayrah (1993), scholars of the usage of patronage in Jordan, note that "family members seeking *wasta* assistance are not expected to reciprocate for services rendered beyond effusive thanks to the *wasta* and spreading his reputation, although some family members may bring gifts" (p. 14).

Conducted in 1993, the Jordanian Living Conditions Survey, which includes a number of questions regarding living and social arrangements, confirms many of Cunningham and Sarayrah's findings. Hiam Omar Kalimat and Jon Hanssen-Bauer (1998), in their analysis of the survey, find that those who benefit from patronage are more likely to return the favour to benefactors within a specified period of time when they are unrelated. Family networks also served as an important source of social security, with wealthy relatives providing financial transfers to poorer households. For example, 14 percent of households stated that remittances from relatives were one of their most important sources of income (p. 290). This figure was as high as the percentage of respondents who noted that receiving government assistance through retirement pensions or social security was one of their three most important sources of income. In short, compared to many countries where the State is seen as the main provider of social welfare, kinship networks in Jordan are as critical as government contributions.

The use of patronage in Jordan, and its intersection with tribalism, tends to reinforce power relations between tribes. Because of family obligations to assist one another, members of tribes in prominent positions tend to help their own, perpetuating the existing hierarchy of relations between tribes. Furthermore, it is difficult to escape from the practice of patronage and to adopt a more meritocratic system, even if some disagree with the principles of clientelism. In their book on *wasta*, Cunningham and Sarayrah (1993) present the case of an idealistic employee in the customs department, Shtayan, who approached his superior, also his uncle, with a staffing plan that detailed the positions needed and the technical requirements that applicants had to meet. Looking to hire typists, Shtayan gave all candidates typing tests and suggested that his uncle employ the fastest one. Such suggestions were met with laughter by the uncle, who proceeded to appoint three individuals who did not even take the typing test, asserting to his nephew: "You want me to appoint on the basis of gimmicks while I have to find jobs for all these family members who graduate in ever increasing numbers every year?" (p. 54). Taking a meritocratic route would mean having to face the displeasure of the tribe.

The ability of an employer to have discretion over who to hire, irrespective of candidates' merit, is a form of power, and this is a decision that, depending on who the patron chooses, obliges the chosen one to return the favour, which further grants power to the patron. For instance, mayors who do not hire family members and who wish to be re-elected or have other political ambitions must develop ties with members of other tribes to compensate for the disaffection of members of their own tribes. One mayor in a southern Jordanian municipality stated that many members of his tribe would no longer support him in future elections, even though he is widely considered one of the best mayors in Jordan, because he had initiated a number of successful development opportunities in his municipality (personal interview, 14/4/2010). Another mayor in a nearby municipality, also known as exemplary, added that his transparent and meritocratic hiring practices has led him to be ostracised by members of his tribe, who expected to benefit directly from a relative in power (personal interview, 4/4/2010).

Nevertheless, there are limits to the use of *wasta*. In terms of employment *wasta* is not always necessary, and even when it is utilised it does not always work. In a system where many employ *wasta*, the result is often down to who has the most influential connections. Its over-use to hire members of one's tribe may also elicit disapproval from other Jordanians (Cunningham & Sarayrah, 1993). Still, despite its potential limits, there is no current indication that the desire to seek a powerful patron to influence outcomes in one's favour will cease any time soon.

Social and Civic Life

Whether with regard to gatherings, civic associations, or legal disputes, tribes continue to influence the conducting of Jordanian social affairs. Many tribes have a *diwan* or space in which to gather together as a tribe (Fathi, 1994). Usually this is a specific building, or a room in a building, that the tribe either owns or rents where members can meet to discuss who to nominate for elections or to collect financial contributions from all members to aid in the payment of a fine (which is a possible penalty for violation of the Jordanian law, or which may be required in the resolution of tribal disputes). The *diwan* also provides a social space for weddings and funerals of members of the tribe, although it can be rented to members of other tribes.

Civic associations can also be tribal in character with most of the members, especially those on the executive board, stemming from one particular tribe. In such cases services are targeted toward members, and fees for renting items belonging to the club (e.g. a bus) are reduced for members. It is impossible for visitors to use the names of these associations to identify which are tribal in character, but residents of the local community are able to discern.

Tribal law was banned in 1975 but continues to be used to settle disputes such as blood crimes (i.e. murder, rape), honour crimes,[5] land claims, and disagreements between tribes. Preference for tribal methods for settling problems between tribes seems to be particularly high in rural areas and in urban areas with large tribes (IRB, 2013). The use of such tribal methods generally involves a group of *wajaha* or elites visiting the *wajaha* of the second tribe in order to negotiate a settlement.

As in the case of elections and patronage, power relations play a part in the degree to which residents can be fully integrated into communities and whether they are accorded justice in tribal disputes. With regard to most aspects of municipal life and daily social interactions, residents from minority tribes may feel welcome and integrated into the community. Members of minority and majority tribes do not segregate, but instead mix freely. They develop close friendships, participate in social functions, worship in the same mosques, and send their children to the same schools. However, when an element of power is involved the boundaries separating minorities from the majority are clarified and reinforced. For instance, while most civic associations welcome members in general, they are selective with regard to who is permitted to serve on executive boards. This means that in monotribal communities, where most associations are dominated by members of a particular tribe, it can be difficult for members of minority tribes to fully participate in civic life. Even the establishment of a civic organisation by a member of a minority tribe in such areas might be viewed with hostility by members of the dominant tribe, who may feel that only they ought to have the right to do so (Taysir, resident of Madaba municipality, personal interview, 4/5/2010).

Problems can also arise in homogenous municipalities when there is a dispute between a member of a dominant tribe and a member of a minority tribe. If the problem is solved through tribal methods, which involve the elites of each tribe visiting one another to reach a negotiated settlement, then the member of the minority tribe is likely to be at a disadvantage simply because most of the members of his tribe do not reside there. Qasim, who lives in a southern Jordanian municipality, became involved in a dispute where he was physically struck by a member of the dominant tribe. Members of Qasim's family live mainly in another municipality but many of them came down to help negotiate the settlement. While their physical presence helped, he felt that it was no match for the large membership size of the dominant tribe present within the municipality (personal interviews, 25/4/2010 and 1/5/2010). As a result, Qasim was dissatisfied with the settlement and with his subsequent work transfer to a different municipality, but as a member of a minority tribe he felt pressured to accept what was offered and to end the case.

But why is tribalism still prevalent?

Despite the growing importance of the central government and the wide reach of its services, tribalism continues to influence Jordanian life for a number of different reasons. Except for a few municipalities, levels of internal migration are still relatively low in Jordan. Migration reduces tribalism because the tribe is less able to act as a unit when members are distributed across the country; it also diminishes the ability to monitor the behaviour of individual members and whether they comply with tribal directives such as voting for the appropriate candidate. As noted earlier, internal migration has substantially increased as a result of Jordanians leaving behind farming or the grazing of animals to migrate to some of the larger and economically vibrant municipalities in search of employment. Indeed Jordanians do travel in the search for jobs, but there is also a reluctance to leave families behind, or to relocate to areas where they feel that they are regarded as "outsiders". Many prefer to work far away during the week and return to their homes at the weekends. Although current statistics are unavailable, the 1993 Jordanian Living Conditions Survey provides some indication of the importance of family. At the time of the survey, 74 percent of Jordanian households lived in an area close to relatives, i.e. with relatives residing in "one's *hara* (neighbourhood) or so near to it that one is able to walk and visit them" (p. 264). Only 15 percent of respondents had not had a visit from a relative in the two weeks prior to the interview, and only 1 percent of households claimed that "distance to friends and family is not important" to them (p. 271).

The integration of migrants into local communities is also further impeded by the construction of housing units specifically for them. When Al Hussein bin Talal University was established in 1999 in the municipality of Ma'an, faculty housing was constructed for university staff (a significant number of whom were not from Ma'an itself) so that they did not need to rent places in the town. Certainly the lack of housing available for occupation at the time makes the construction of new units logical, but at the same time their presence discourages the integration of migrants into local society. Relatively low levels of migration and few incentives to interact with migrants have meant that migrants can still be referred to as "strangers", reinforcing the idea that local tribes ought to dominate both socially and politically.

While the awareness of health risks from consanguinity has decreased marriage between members of the same tribe, it still occurs. Jordan is a patrilineal society where consanguineous marriages have been traditionally preferred. The ideal suitor for a daughter, according to such customs, was her paternal cousin (Hamamy, Al Hait, Alwan & Ajlouni, 2007). At the time of the Jordanian Living Conditions Survey in 1993, almost one half of all marriages were contracted with someone within the tribe (p. 273). It is likely that fewer marriages today involve the union of cousins, but it is still a regular occurrence.

It is difficult to ascertain whether there is little migration and many consanguineous marriages *because* of the enduring strength of tribalism, or whether the paucity of migration and marriages outside of the tribe simply *reinforce* the existence of tribalism. In reality it is probably a combination of both factors, with strong tribal ties decreasing the desire to migrate and to marry outside of the tribe but also the preservation of traditional communities and customs strengthening tribal ties between members. Certainly, there are indications that where levels of migration are high, tribalism seems to be less important. Results from the Jordan Living Conditions Survey showed that the proximity to family members, the frequency of visits and the degree of in-marriages varied across governorates, with urban governorates like Amman scoring lowest on these measures.

The manufacturing of tribalism?

The persistence of tribalism may also be one consequence of regime policies that reinforce tribal ties. While political parties are permitted by the Jordanian monarchy, the opposition claims that the regime purposely manipulates electoral laws so that it is difficult to establish parties and for parties to gain votes (Wakeman, 2009). The Islamic Action Front, the main opposition party since its formation in 1992, accuses the regime of purposely encouraging tribalism in order to reduce the power of political parties. They allege that the regime introduced the single non-transferable vote (SNTV) electoral system (permitting citizens only one vote) to urge citizens to support tribal candidates. The basis for their claim is that this introduction occurred after the IAF won 30 percent of the seats in the 1989 parliamentary election, with independent Islamists also increasing their number of seats in that election. Prior to 1993, all Jordanians had multiple votes and as a result parties and tribes often formed coalitions and voters were encouraged to support all members of the coalition. However, the use of the single vote has motivated Jordanians to vote primarily for tribal members. With only one vote, Jordanians prefer to support a tribal as opposed to a party candidate, and indeed, in subsequent elections with the abolition of the block vote Islamists have won fewer seats, demonstrating that the new electoral system favours tribal representatives at the expense of political parties (Kao, 2012). The choice of the SNTV electoral system is also to the advantage of the regime because it encourages members of large tribes to run against one another (Cox & Niou, 1994). Scholars have found that where the SNTV has been used, large parties in multi-member districts ran the risk of fielding more candidates than they could possibly place into seats. While large parties did try to coordinate appropriately, it can be difficult to predict how many candidates will win and also to encourage voters to distribute their support among the candidates equally so that all candidates are elected (Cox & Niou, 1994). Therefore, the use of the SNTV system brings two advantages to the regime: it encourages tribal organisations over political parties, and it divides large parties.

Since the establishment of Jordan the monarchy has attempted to centralise the country and to consolidate power, and while past monarchs have worked with the tribes in order to gain their support, this has also decreased their influence by usurping many of the previous functions of the tribes. Nowadays one could say that, to some extent, the opposite is happening since tribalism is encouraged to flourish at the expense of political parties. Indeed, as a result of the policies of the current monarchy, parliaments have been dominated by independent candidates who win primarily through their appeal to their tribes. It is said that even ethnic Palestinians who are known to be less "tribal" have also become more so in response to this phenomenon among ethnic Jordanians.

Nevertheless, this has also led to friction between the regime and tribes. By empowering tribes, the regime has also increased their sense of entitlement. Indeed, recent news stories in Jordan have emphasised increasing tensions between Jordanian tribes (Khalidi, 2011; Ma'ayeh, 2013; Majdoubeh, 2013). For instance, incidents of tribal violence at Jordanian universities have increased dramatically in recent years. According to Thabahtoona, a national campaign for student's rights, there were over fifty clashes at universities between January and April 2013 (Al Monitor, 2013). In 2011 there were sixty-one such incidents and in 2010 there were only twenty-nine clashes (Sweis, 2013). Some of these incidents have led to deaths, riots in nearby towns, and the suspension of classes for weeks (Al Monitor, 2013; Ammon News, 2012; Melkawi, 2013). Because of tribalism, arguments between students have the potential to escalate into inter-group brawls, as members of each tribe pledge to defend the honour of a fellow tribesman regardless of whether they agree with their behaviour (Sweis, 2013).

Tensions between the regime and tribes are also present with regard to the creation of new municipalities in Jordan. In 2011, the Ministry of Municipal Affairs permitted areas to petition for the creation of additional municipalities if they fulfilled particular criteria. The Ministry was flooded with applications, and had they not amended the criteria so that they became more stringent, the number of municipalities in Jordan would have more than doubled (Ammon News, 2011; *Jordan Times*, 2011; Neimat, 2011a; Neimat, 2011b). According to Janine Clark (2012), a scholar of Jordanian municipalities, the large number of applications reflects the aspiration of smaller tribes to gain control over particular municipalities, thereby overcoming neglect, or even bias, experienced at the hands of dominant tribes. Clark also claims that the government's push for municipalities to adopt private–public partnerships has only served to reinforce the dominance of large tribes even within diverse municipalities, as larger tribes are more able than smaller tribes to manoeuvre projects to specific locations or partner with business associates beneficial to them. Overall, these increased clashes between tribes can be viewed as another sign of the "revival" of tribalism, a revival that may be due partly to the regime's policies, as the last example demonstrates.

Tribalism and power

Despite earlier predictions that tribalism would become irrelevant in Jordan, it has continued to remain prominent and prevalent in social and political life. During elections, there is strong pressure to support the tribal candidate. It is frequently tribes rather than political parties that nominate candidates, and depending upon whether they are cohesive they can significantly reduce the degree of electoral competition between all candidates. Requests for patronage may not have tribal boundaries but the obligation to carry out demands is particularly strong when the individual requesting help is a member of the same tribe. Tribalism can also affect which civic associations residents participate in and how disputes are resolved.

Tribalism also has obvious repercussions with regard to power relations between groups. It seems evident that the power and the size of the tribe are intertwined, with large tribes able to dominate in their municipalities. Large tribes are able to monopolise the most powerful elected political positions for themselves simply because they have enough votes to win these positions. Knowing this, smaller tribes often do not even bother to challenge large tribes by contesting these positions (Gao, 2012). In municipal elections, candidates for the mayor are almost always from the largest tribes while smaller tribes will offer candidates for the council positions, which require fewer votes to win. In monotribal municipalities, dominant tribes also feel that the most influential political and social positions *ought* to be held by members of their tribe as they comprise the greatest percentage of the population.

The significant role of tribes in contemporary Jordan demonstrates that identity is indeed still related to power; belonging to a large and socially prominent tribe relative to other tribes within one's place of residence does not guarantee the acquisition of social and political positions, but it does facilitate it. Hard work and a good education does matter and members of small tribes also have connections that they can use to their advantage. Nevertheless, one's tribal background can simplify, ease and accelerate this process.

Dominance by large tribes signals that in Jordan, particularly in locations where tribalism is strong, it is easy for majority rule to trump minority rights. While this may be seen as democratic with large tribes winning elections through their larger membership size, the effect of such control can be stifling to other segments of society and result in political apathy on their part. But do Jordanians act for the benefit of their tribes out of an internalised sense of loyalty, or can it also be the result of social pressure from the tribe? In the areas where residents demanded new municipalities, for example, did local officials actually *want* to prioritise their tribe over others, or did they feel that they *had* to act in this way for practical reasons? The examples in this chapter suggest that tribalism is not only based on subjective feelings of identity or solidarity with the tribe. That is, even individual members who do not wish to provide preferential treatment to members of their tribe, or who believe that employment should be meritocratic rather than an exercise in tribal loyalty, are often expected to behave according to these social customs. Of course, there are those who defy such conventions, but this is not without repercussions from their tribe. Indeed, in part, the power of tribal identity lies in the power it has over its individual members and the repercussions they may face if they do not act accordingly. The more cohesive the tribe, the greater this power and the less its members are likely to perceive opting out as a possibility.

In the same spirit, one may also argue that the persistence of tribalism is partly the consequence of political machinations on the part of the regime. When the Hashemite monarchy was first established in Jordan, the regime wished to centralise power and to decrease the influence of tribes. Now that the legitimacy of the monarchy is no longer threatened and it is firmly entrenched within society, elites seem to have decided to re-emphasise the role of tribes in the hope of curtailing the influence of opposition movements. The strengthening of tribal identities is not limited to Jordan but occurs in other authoritarian regimes as well. In Iraq Saddam Hussein also revived tribalism, even though his Ba'athist party regarded tribalism "as a major obstacle on the road to 'social transformation'" and "equated tribalism with feudalism" (Baram, 1997, p. 2). For many political leaders, manipulating tribalism has proven an effective method to factionalise and to control their populations.

The examples in this chapter demonstrate that tribalism is still very much a part of the fabric of Jordanian contemporary life. It is clearly a complex phenomenon, with costs and benefits both within and outside tribes. On the one hand tribal solidarity can provide the much-needed social security to persist through a difficult situation as relatives lend a helping hand or provide financial assistance. It means that members never need to endure hardship alone but are always helped, whether it is planning for a wedding, adjusting after the birth of a child, or defending oneself during a dispute. On the other hand, tribalism can lead to tension and violence that is merely based on membership of different tribes. It can result in the election of leaders, who are supported not so much for their ideology or popular appeal but because of the size of their kinship network, and who may be predisposed to reward their supporters with employment or better services.

However, one thing seems definite: it will be a long time before tribalism fades from its prominent role in Jordanian society. As such, it will continue to be a critical factor affecting how Jordanians' identities, social lives and power relations are jointly shaped. Further research in this area, especially regarding the role of tribal identities in both local and national electoral politics, should therefore be of prime interest to anyone interested in the ways in which dynamics of power and identity intersect.

Notes

1 Throughout this chapter, I use the term "tribe" to refer to kinship or heritage networks for both ethnic Jordanian and ethnic Palestinians living in Jordan. After the 1948 Arab-Israeli War, a large number of Palestinian refugees left their homes and resettled in Jordan. Today they and their descendants are Jordanian citizens and now comprise approximately 60 percent of the Jordanian population. Ethnic Jordanians are often referred to as "East Bankers" because they originated from the east of the River Jordan, while ethnic Palestinians are known as "West Bankers" as they came from west of the same river. Some scholars argue that the term "tribe" should only be used with reference to ethnic Jordanians because they act "tribally" while ethnic Palestinians do not, or to a much lesser extent. While this may be true with regard to the degree of tribalism that ethnic Jordanian tribes exhibit compared to ethnic Palestinian tribes, I still consider the latter to be organised according to tribes because, like ethnic Jordanians, they have families and therefore kinship networks.

2 Sheikhs are not religious leaders but prominent members within their own clans, branches, or tribes. Within large tribes, each individual clan or branch might have its own sheikh. The leader of the entire tribe, or the sheikh of all of the individual sheikhs, is the paramount sheikh.

3 There is usually only one sheikh per clan, branch, or tribe, but each of these entities may have several *wajaha,* or tribal elites, who undertake the same mediation role of sheikhs but collectively.

4 The figures for each of the municipalities were Barha (51 percent), Rashid (28 percent), Karak (37 percent), Madaba (25 percent), Hassa (55 percent) and Oyoun (38 percent).

5 An honour crime occurs when a woman is killed to protect her honour or the honour of her family. If a woman was deemed to have had inappropriate relations with a man prior to marriage, she might be killed by a family member in order to protect the honour of the family.

References

AlJazeera Center for Studies (2012, November 18) Jordan's struggle over the rules of the game. Retrieved from http://studies.aljazeera.net/en/positionpapers/2012/11/2012111810 3353939827.htm [Accessed 3 September 2014].

Al Monitor News (2013, June 4) Jordan universities become 'battlefields'. Retrieved from www.al-monitor.com/pulse/security/2013/06/jordanian-universities-battlefields-tribes.html [Accessed 3 September 2014].

Alon, Y. (2007) *The making of Jordan: Tribes, colonialism, and the modern state.* New York, NY: I.B. Tauris and Company, Ltd.

Alrababa'h, A. (2011, July 10) Jordan's transition to democracy. *Ammon News.* Retrieved from http://en.ammonnews.net/article.aspx?articleNO=12788 [Accessed 3 September 2014].

Ammon News (2011, October 2) Irbid, Ajloun residents protest against municipalities merger. Retrieved from http://en.ammonnews.net/article.aspx?articleNO=13960#. UuH_f_04kd [Accessed 22 August 2014].

——(2012, March 11) Violence breaks out at University of Jordan. Retrieved from http://en.ammonnews.net/article.aspx?articleNO=15942#.UoonYqVgwdA [Accessed 22 August 2014].

Antoun, R.T. (1977) *Arab village: A social structural study of a Transjordanian peasant community.* Bloomington, IN: University of Indiana Press.

——(1979) *Low-key politics: Local-level leadership and change in the Middle East.* Albany, NY: State University of New York Press.

Baram, A. (1997) Neo-tribalism in Iraq: Saddam Hussein's tribal policies 1991–1996. *International Journal of Middle East Studies,* 29 (1), 1–31.

BBC News (2012, July 13) *Jordan's Muslim Brotherhood to boycott early elections.* Retrieved from http://www.bbc.co.uk/news/world-middle-east-18825221 [Accessed 11 August 2014].

bin Muhammad, G. (1999) *The tribes of Jordan at the beginning of the twenty-first century.* Jamiyat: Turath Al Urdun Al Baqi.

Clark, J. (2012) Municipalities go to market: Economic reform and political contestation in Jordan. *Mediterranean Politics,* 17 (3), 358–375.

Cox, G.W. & Niou, E. (1994) Seat bonuses under the single nontransferable vote system: Evidence from Japan and Taiwan. *Comparative Politics,* 26 (2), 221–236.

Cunningham, R.B. & Sarayrah, Y.K. (1993) *Wasta: The hidden force in Middle Eastern society.* New York, NY: Praeger Publishers.

Deutsch, K. (1971) Social mobilization and political development. In J. Finkle & R. Gable (Eds.), *Political development and social change* (pp. 384–401). New York, NY: Wiley.

El-Shamayleh, N. (2013, January 22) Understanding Jordan's parliamentary election. *Al Jazeera,* available from http://blogs.aljazeera.com/blog/middle-east/understanding-jordan%E2%80%99s-parliamentary-election [Accessed 4 September 2014].

Fathi, S.H. (1994) *Jordan: An invented nation? Tribe-state dynamics and the formation of national identity.* Hamburg, Germany: Deutsches Orient-Institut.

Gao, E. (2012) *Diverse but not divisive: Tribal diversity and public goods provision in Jordan* (Doctoral dissertation). Retrieved from ProQuest Dissertations and Theses Database (UMI 3531235).

Gubser, P. (1973) *Politics and change in Al-Karak, Jordan: A study of a small Arab town and its district.* New York: Oxford University Press.

Hamamy, H., Al Hait, S., Alwan, A. & Ajlouni, K. (2007) Jordan: Communities and community genetics. *Community Genetics,* 10 (1), 52–60.

Immigration and Refugee Board of Canada (IRB) (2013, May 31) *Jordan: Tribal law, including whether it allows murder as revenge; whether tribal law overrides the legal justice system, as well as areas it is applied; government protection.* Retrieved from www.ecoi.net/local_link/256891/368860_en.html [Accessed 22 August 2014].

Inkeles, A. (1966) The modernization of man. In M. Weiner (Ed.), *Modernization* (pp. 138–150). New York: Basic Books.

Jordan Center for Social Research (JCSR) (2007, August 23) *The 2007 municipal elections in Jordan: An exit poll conducted in six electoral districts located in six municipalities* (Report). Amman, Jordan: Jordan Center for Social Research.

Jordan Times (2011, October 15) Jordan: New municipalities emerge as violent protests continue. Retrieved from http://thevotingnews.com//new-municipalities-emerge-as-violent-protests-continue-jordan-times/ [Accessed 22 August 2014].

Jureidini, P. & McLaurin, R.D. (1984) *Jordan: The impact of social change and the role of tribes.* New York, NY: Praeger Publishers.

Kalimat, H.O. & Hanssen-Bauer, J. (1998) Social network. In J. Hanssen-Bauer, J. Pederson & A.A. Tiltnes (Eds), *Jordanian society: Living conditions in the Hashemite Kingdom of Jordan* (pp. 259–292). Oslo, Norway: Fafo Institute for Applied Social Science.

Kao, K. (2012) *Jordan's ongoing election law battle*. Retrieved from http://carnegieendowment. org/sada/2012/07/05/jordan-s-ongoing-election-law-battle/fbdu [Accessed 11 August 2014].

Khalidi, S. (2011, January 13) Tribal feuds threaten Jordan's stability. *Reuters*. Retrieved from www.reuters.com/article/2011/01/13/jordan-tribes-idUSLDE7051QR20110113 [Accessed 22 August 2014].

Lancaster, W. (1981) *The Rwala Bedouin today*. Cambridge, UK: Cambridge University Press.

Langston, E.M. (2005) *The Islamist movement and tribal networks: Islamist party mobilization amongst the tribes of Jordan and Yemen* (Doctoral dissertation). Retrieved from ProQuest Dissertations and Theses Database (UMI 3200329).

Layne, L. (1986) *The production and reproduction of tribal identity in Jordan* (unpublished doctoral dissertation). Princeton University, New Jersey.

——(1994) *Home and homeland: The dialogics of tribal and national identities in Jordan*. Princeton, NJ: Princeton University Press.

Lerner, D. (1958) *The passing of traditional society*. Glencoe, IL: Free Press.

Lewis, N. (1987) *Settlers and nomads in Syria and Jordan 1800–1980*. New York: Cambridge University Press.

Lipset, S.M. (1960) *Political man: The social bases of politics*. Garden City, N.Y.: Doubleday.

Ma'ayeh, S.P. (2013, July 29) New violence raises concerns about Jordan. *The Wall Street Journal*. Retrieved from http://blogs.wsj.com/middleeast/2013/07/29/new-violence-raises-concerns-about-jordan/ [Accessed 22 August 2014].

Majdoubeh, A.Y. (2013, April 4) University violence, again. *The Jordan Times*. Retrieved from http://jordantimes.com/university-violence-again [Accessed 22 August 2014].

Melkawi, K. (2013, August 4) Mutah University, UJ expel students over campus violence. *The Jordan Times*. Retrieved from http://jordantimes.com/mutah-university-uj-expel-students-over-campus-violence [Accessed 22 August 2014].

National Democratic Institute (NDI) (2010, November 10) *Preliminary statement of the NDI election observer delegation to Jordan's 2010 parliamentary elections*. Retrieved from www.ndi. org/files/Jordan_2010_Election_Delegation_Statement.pdf [Accessed 11 August 2014].

Neimat, K. (2011a, October 5) Protesters demanding new municipalities temporarily block Amman-Aqaba highway. *The Jordan Times*. Retrieved from www.mobilitytechzone. com/news/2011/10/13/5852385.htm [Accessed 22 August 2014].

——(2011b, November 27) Jordan: Over 40 applications for independent municipalities received. *The Jordan Times*. Retrieved from www.themuslimtimes.org/ 2011/11/ countries/jordan/jordan-'over-40-applications-for-independent-municipalities-received' [Accessed 11 August 2014].

Shryock, A. (1997) *Nationalism and the genealogical imagination*. Berkeley, CA: University of California Press.

Sweis, R.F. (2013, April 24) Tribal clashes at universities add to tensions in Jordan. *The New York Times*. Retrieved from www.nytimes.com/2013/04/25/world/middleeast/tribal-clashes-at-universities-add-to-tensions-in-jordan.html?_r=0 [Accessed 22 August 2014].

United Nations Economic and Social Commission for Western Asia (UN ESCWA). (n.d.) *The demographic profile of Jordan* (report). Retrieved from www.escwa.un.org/popin/members/Jordan.pdf [Accessed 11 August 2014].

Wakeman, R.L. (2009) *Containing the opposition: Selective representation in Jordan and Turkey* (Master's dissertation). Retrieved from http://dspace.mit.edu/handle/1721.1/53083 [Accessed 22 August 2014].

5

ANGRY NAKED LADIES

Can stereotyping and sexual objectification be used to transform social systems?

*Olivier Klein, Jill Allen, Philippe Bernard and
Sarah J. Gervais*[1]

In March 2013 Amina Tyler, a young Tunisian woman, posted a topless photo on Facebook. Alluding to the rise of Muslim fundamentalism in Tunisia, she exhibited the following words (in Arabic) on her bare chest: "My body belongs to me and is not the Source of anyone's Honour". She was subsequently kidnapped by members of her family, stoned and drugged, among other niceties (Tayler, 2013). This example illustrates how an isolated woman purposefully displayed her naked body to highlight a political message aimed at contesting the social status of women in her society. However, from a (Western) feminist perspective, such a display of nudity could be viewed as a manifestation of sexual objectification, thereby reinforcing the notion that women can be reduced to their bodies. Further, although baring her chest revealed some power inasmuch as Tyler controlled the display of her body, the subsequent response from her family showed that Tyler was still not in complete control; her family exerted significant power over her body through physical violence.

In this chapter, we consider two interrelated phenomena: stereotypes and sexual objectification. These two phenomena, as they have been appraised in the social psychological and also the feminist literatures (Code, 1995), tend to be viewed as ideological tools favouring the oppression of women. We propose that, in addition to functioning as tools of oppression, stereotypes and objectification can be used by the oppressed to question existing power relations. Turning first to stereotyping, we consider how social psychological research may have neglected the role stereotypes can play in challenging social systems. We suggest that stereotypes can play a crucial role in mobilising ingroup members in support of collective projects aimed at transforming social systems. We then examine the parallels between stereotypes and sexual objectification and consider whether self-objectification can also serve this function, as seems to be the case in our opening example. Indeed, feminist scholars have suggested that self-objectification is a means for women to reestablish some control and power in contexts where they are objectified (Fredrickson & Roberts, 1997). Nevertheless, they argue that the outcomes of this self-objectification are primarily negative. We provide a more nuanced picture, suggesting that stereotypes and sexual objectification may sometimes be used to effectively transform power relations. To embark on this journey, let us turn first to stereotypes.

Stereotypes and domination

Stereotypes are traditionally considered as mental representations of the psychological traits possessed by members of social groups. What is the relation between social stereotypes and the social structure? We shall consider two perspectives here: one that portrays stereotypes as consequences of the social structure, and another that envisions how they may contribute to modifying the social structure.

Stereotypes as ideological tools

There is a clear relationship between the content of social stereotypes and objective indices of power or status. Among many other examples (see e.g. Fiske, Cuddy, Glick & Xu, 2002; Oakes, Haslam & Turner, 1994), Poppe (2001) showed a correlation between the evolution of the Gross Domestic Product of various Eastern European countries and the ascription of competence to their citizens by neighbouring nations. However, this does not tell us what the psychological relationship between the social structure and the content of shared social stereotypes may be. Three forms of such relationships can be envisioned.

In the first, stereotypes *derive* from the social structure because they describe actual psychological differences that emerge between groups due to their social position (e.g. Jussim, 2012). For example, in the context of social role theory (Eagly, 1987), the distribution of social roles between men and women leads each gender group to adopt behaviours that are required to perform these roles. Sexist stereotypes incorporate these traits because they partially reflect the gender group's "real" characteristics. Thus, women may be construed as less assertive than men because their social roles (e.g. as a mother) require them to be so.

In another perspective (e.g. Oakes *et al.*, 1994; Yzerbyt, Rocher & Schadron, 1997), stereotypes serve to *explain* the social position of groups. For example, Hoffman and Hurst (1990) found that stereotypes could emerge in the absence of actual psychological differences between the groups because they account for existing divisions of labour (a socio-structural difference) between the groups involved (e.g. women are at home *because* they are more capable of taking care of children).

In a third perspective (e.g. Jost & Banaji, 1994; Sidanius & Pratto, 2001), stereotypes not only explain but legitimise the positions of social groups. For example, by describing southern Italians as "lazy", the lesser prosperity of southern

Italy is justified as originating in their lack of hard work. This function may play out not only for the members of privileged groups, who find solace in the belief that those who are below them deserve their social position, but also among members of disadvantaged groups. For instance, women may endorse benevolent sexist stereotypes suggesting that they are more relational and warm, but less assertive and autonomous, than men. Such an approach is also present in the Stereotype Content Model (SCM; Fiske *et al.*, 2002). Proponents of this model argue that mixed or ambiguous stereotypes of high status groups (i.e. competent yet cold) and low status groups (i.e. incompetent but warm) justify the social system (Jost & Kay, 2005). By suggesting that all groups' negative characteristics are offset by positive ones, they indeed convey a perception that no single group is blatantly advantaged or disadvantaged. This idea is at the core of system justification theory (Jost & Banaji, 1994), which argues that people have an inherent motive to preserve the social system and view it as fair, even if they are objectively disadvantaged. Stereotypes are a very convenient tool in this respect.

These three perspectives envision stereotypes as consequences of the social structure. The legitimisation approach has an additional twist: it suggests that there may be a positive feedback loop between the social structure and the content of social stereotypes. Indeed, when group members endorse social stereotypes that justify their stigmatisation, they fail to contest the existing hierarchy. Social stereotypes work effectively as a social glue maintaining the inertia of the social system. This is one of the many reasons why they have earned a bad reputation. Given that social systems are generally viewed as inherently unjust by the (often liberal) social scientists who describe them, the mental entities (i.e. stereotypes) assumed to hold these systems together are understandably vilified.

Marxian approach

It is possible to frame these perspectives in Marxian terminology. To a large extent, social psychological perspectives on the role of stereotyping in the maintenance of social systems, including social identity theory (Tajfel & Turner, 1986), system justification theory, and social dominance theory (Sidanius & Pratto, 2001), have been influenced by Marx. The position of groups in the social system roughly corresponds to what Marx (1859/1979) called "the base": the latter term referred precisely to relations of production. In contrast, people's shared beliefs about social groups emanate from these positions and are part of the "superstructure" (i.e. the "ideology" and social relationships other than those based on production). For example, paternalism, which involves both an ideology and specific forms of relationships, emanates from the division of labour between coloniser and colonised, or between master and slave. In this view, the group who controls productive forces controls ideas as well. Hence, ideology distorts or hides reality, making differences in social status justified or invisible and leading to "false consciousness" (Jost, 1995) when an oppressed group endorses ideas and beliefs, such as social stereotypes, that are in contradiction with its interests.

When stereotypes serve utopias

Although the above description is the widely accepted narrative on stereotypes, it is not the only possible story. Let us take another angle: stereotypes help groups understand the world that surrounds them. However, rather than assuming an inherent motive to maintain the *status quo*, one can presume that these understandings may also justify social systems that have yet to be. Collective action on the part of low status groups, arguably the most important ingredient in any successful attempt at changing the social system, is predicated on a minimally shared understanding of the positions of groups in this system. In social dominance parlance (Sidanius & Pratto, 2001), stereotypes can be an important ingredient of hierarchy-attenuating ideologies, as well as of hierarchy-enhancing ideologies.

Second, when shared, hierarchy-attenuating stereotypes can be empowering as much as hierarchy-enhancing stereotypes can be disempowering. Coordination between group members, which is the basis of collective action, demands some common ground (Reicher, Hopkins, Levine & Rath, 2005). Thus, knowing that group members share the same view of the outgroup can induce a sense of empowerment and solidarity as well as form a precondition for actual power, given that a group's power is predicated on its capacity to coordinate its members' actions (see Reicher, 2008; Reicher & Haslam, this volume).

Appraised in this light, the relation between social stereotypes and social change involves a transition from hierarchy-enhancing to hierarchy-attenuating stereotypes. Mobilising ingroup members—that is, convincing them that this political project is worth fighting for—may often involve disseminating the stereotypes that justify this project. Rather than fulfilling an intrapsychological justification function (by reinforcing the belief that the social order is legitimate), these stereotypes may serve an intragroup or intergroup rhetorical function.

From ideology to utopia

In the Marxian view of ideology, ideology completely encloses the mind (Marx & Engels, 1932/1998). Ideologies are taken for granted and cannot be contested. Thus, in early medieval Europe, people took for granted that God created men and that, through the Catholic Church and its head, the Pope, He ruled their existence in a just way (Bagliano, 2006). Such a set of assumptions may have prevented social change. Given that an ideological belief is necessarily experienced as self-evident, perceiving an ideology as such demands an alternative worldview (e.g. in which God does not exist), or "utopia" (Mannheim, 1954; Ricoeur & Taylor, 1986).

According to Mannheim (1954), such a utopia, like ideology, is divorced from reality, but rather than being oriented toward the past and present (as ideology is viewed in the Marxian perspective), it is oriented toward the future. Nothing in the substance of stereotypes makes them more apt at justifying ideologies than at justifying utopias. The question then naturally arises: why has research on stereotypes focused on their ideological dimension and neglected their utopian function?

Automaticity and bias

Research on stereotyping has focused on the following issue: given that stereotypes are mental representations, how and when do they colour the impression of members of the target group (see e.g. Fiske, Lin & Neuberg, 1999)? When, meeting a (female) secretary, is a (male) executive likely to categorise her as a "woman" and to activate a specific gender stereotype that will inevitably fail to capture her "true", idiosyncratic, qualities? And if the stereotype is activated, will the executive apply the stereotype to this specific secretary and actually perceive her in line with the stereotype? Ample research (Fiske, 1998) suggests that the activation of stereotypes is largely automatic: it is unconscious, unintentional and/ or cannot be monitored. Cultural stereotypes (Devine, 1989) are an inescapable consequence of our socialisation (Bargh, 1999). They remain in the back of our mind, but they may "pop out" each time we are in the presence of a person we categorise in the relevant social group. In this view, stereotypes appear to be the ultimate weapon of false consciousness: not only does their content justify the position of the dominant, but all members of a society may use them unintentionally even when they do not endorse them, and even when they hurt their own interests. Thus, viewing stereotypes as automatically activated and as biased mental representations contributes to emphasising their ideological function in the reproduction of social systems (for a review, see Macrae & Bodenhausen, 2000).

When stereotypes serve social change

How have researchers within these perspectives examined the relationship between stereotypes and social change? Social change can be said to occur when the positions of salient social groups within a society change. Thus, women's acquisition of the right to vote, or their massive entry into the workforce in industrialised countries after World War II, can be considered as forms of social change as they helped reduce gender inequality.

We have suggested that stereotypes could—theoretically—serve a "utopian" function (i.e. justifying ideal social systems), but let us now consider some empirical evidence for this function. In our work (Klein & Licata, 2003), we examined the role of stereotypes in a situation of rapid social change: the decolonisation of the former Belgian colony of Congo,[2] a process that occurred in less than two years (1958–1960). Specifically, we addressed the use of stereotypes in the speeches of the Congolese nationalist leader Patrice Lumumba, who sought to represent the oppressed Congolese people. Importantly, Lumumba nurtured a single political project during the whole period: that of an independent and unitary Congo. Using content analysis, we found that stereotypes were not solely the tools of the dominant insofar as Lumumba relied heavily on stereotypes during this period. However, the content of the stereotypes varied depending on the specific point in time and on the audience of Lumumba's speeches. Thus, when talking to a Congolese audience (especially at the beginning of the decolonisation process), he tended to rely on classic anticolonialist rhetoric by depicting the Belgians as ruthless oppressors and the Congolese as innocent victims. During the same period, Lumumba also visited Belgium and addressed Belgian audiences (directly and via the media). In this context, his speeches were much more moderate and emphasised the interdependence between Belgians and Congolese, sometimes depicting Congolese as infants in need of the help of the more experienced Belgians. A surface analysis of such discourse could mistake it for an endorsement of colonial paternalistic stereotypes. In our view, however, these stereotypes were used here to advance a revolutionary agenda. Lumumba knew that his project required collaboration from the Belgians, who controlled most of the colonial state and had the necessary technical skills to make the project work.

In this context, the use of such stereotypes cannot be considered as merely reflecting the automatic activation of cognitive representations. Rather, such stereotypes should be understood as rhetorical tools helping Lumumba achieve his political goals, here the "utopia" of an independent Congo. Specifically, Lumumba used stereotypes to mobilise his audiences into supporting specific forms of actions to serve his political project. When addressing the Congolese people, especially in the beginning of the period considered here, the success of his project depended on his capacity to raise an anticolonial consciousness among the Congolese who, until then, had not manifested much enthusiasm for independence. When addressing Belgians, the success of his project depended on alleviating their fears about his capacity to govern his country in ways that would preserve the interests of the Belgians.[3]

When considering the stereotypes expressed by Lumumba, whether they are accurate or biased is less important than their function within this particular project. They should be considered in the context of his utopia: thus, his anticolonialist stereotypes (Africans of the past as victims of European oppression) are a prelude to a desired brighter future that will see the liberation of Africans.[4]

Stereotype expression as identity performance

In this context, stereotypes are tales of social identity, with social identity conceived in a dynamic way leading to the achievement of the utopia. Thus stereotypes, like social identity itself, appear to be guides for actions (Reicher, 1996).

When group leaders express their view of the group to which they belong in front of an audience, they manifest what they believe the group identity to be. In doing so, they will often develop nuanced views of the traits composing these stereotypes. Some of these traits will be construed as stable and inherent to the ingroup, whereas others will be construed as the result of social pressures from a relevant outgroup. Thus, as in Lumumba's example, ingroup stereotypes may incorporate a historical dimension: past, present, and future.

However, stereotypical expressions of the outgroup can also be viewed as a way to express the identity of one's ingroup. When emphasising the moral depravity of the colonialists, Lumumba indirectly affirms the virtues of the Congolese. Here we follow self-categorisation theory's assumption that stereotypes are inherently comparative: stereotypes of a target group maximise distinctiveness from relevant comparison groups. Hence, stereotypical expressions of the outgroup can be viewed as a way to express the identity of one's group, albeit indirectly.

Stereotypes can be expressed strategically without necessarily implying adhesion to the relevant representations. When moving to the laboratory, such a strategic use of stereotypes can be best evidenced when observing how people use stereotypes as a function of the communicative context, and especially the audience they address (Klein, 2004).

To capture the strategic or rhetorical aspect of such behaviour, we (Klein, Spears & Reicher, 2007) have coined the term "social identity performance". The concept refers to "the purposeful expression (or suppression) of behaviors relevant to those norms conventionally associated with a salient social identity" (Klein et al., 2007, p. 30). The concept of social identity performance is rooted in the proposition that, depending on the social context, different identities can be cognitively salient (a central tenet of self-categorisation theory: Turner et al., 1987). For example, a female executive may define herself as a woman, as an executive, or as working for company X, depending on what is salient in a given context. Once a social identity is salient people are thought to automatically align the self with this social identity and conform to relevant group norms. However, depending on power relations, people may refrain from expressing some of these norms especially when they are punishable, even if they are salient (Reicher, Spears & Postmes, 1995). In early studies of this concept (Reicher & Levine, 1994a, b), group members were less likely to express adhesion to group norms (especially punishable ones) when they were identifiable to a powerful audience. This suggests that, over and above the more purely cognitive process of identity salience, there is also a motivational function providing room to "play" with group norms to accrue benefits for the group. This is the more strategic side to identity expression, or social identity performance (see also Barreto & Ellemers, 2003).

We have proposed that such strategic behaviour can fulfil two main functions: consolidation of one's identity, and group mobilisation. The first function relates to the fact that people seek to verify their identity in order to attain a secure and stable sense of self. To do so, they need their identities to be verified by others (Barreto & Ellemers, 2003; Chen, Chen & Shaw, 2004). The second function relates to the fact that by expressing their social identities in specific ways, people may seek to induce their audiences to collaborate in the achievement of projects they associate with their social identities. Lumumba's example can be readily interpreted in these terms: his use of stereotypes of the Congolese during the decolonisation of Congo can be understood to be aimed at influencing his audiences to support his political project (i.e. a unitary and independent Congo).

Thus, this approach allows us to contrast a purely cognitive view of stereotypes, depicting them as ideological tools in the service of reproducing the social system with a strategic perspective that views stereotypes as rhetorical tools used to mobilise audiences into supporting any political project, including those aimed at transforming the social system. Next, we shall consider whether sexual objectification can also be used in the same way for transforming social systems.

Sexual objectification and power relations

Philosophers since Kant have used the concept of objectification to refer to a mode of relation involving appraising others as objects (for reviews, see Gervais, Bernard, Klein & Allen, 2013; Papadaki, 2007). The concept has, however, been employed most notoriously in the context of gender studies (MacKinnon, 1987). One of the core goals of the feminist movement has been to confer upon women active roles in society and liberate them from their status as objects of male desire (see de Beauvoir, 1953). Sexual objectification is said to occur when a person's body parts or functions are separated from the person, reduced to the status of instruments, or regarded as capable of representing them (Bartky, 1990). Although, like stereotyping, the concept of objectification defined in this way could potentially target many social groups (e.g. manual workers, physically handicapped persons, ethnic minorities), most research on this topic has focused on women, and we shall therefore limit ourselves to this category.

Although they are clearly distinct, stereotypes and objectification bear many similarities. Researchers have focused on the processes as well as the content of both stereotyping and objectification. For example, some researchers have primarily focused on the process of stereotyping (Devine, 1989; Fiske & Neuberg, 1990; Lepore & Brown, 1997; see Macrae & Bodenhausen, 2000 for a review), such as attention to defining features, categorisation into a social category, stereotype activation, and stereotype application. Thus, in this perspective, stereotyping (and related self-stereotyping) is a cognitive process that involves appraising others by relying on mental representations of social groups. Likewise, much objectification research has focused on the cognitive processes involved in objectification (Gervais *et al.*, 2013; see also Bernard, Gervais, Allen, Campomizzi & Klein, 2012; Gervais, Vescio, Maass, Förster & Suitner, 2012), such as how a local appraisal of a person contributes to attention (e.g. the objectifying gaze) and recognition of women's bodies (e.g. reduction of women's bodies to their sexual body parts) as well as trait activation and application (or lack thereof). Hence, objectification (and related self-objectification) may be considered as a cognitive process as well, but not necessarily involving specific content. For example, if, as suggested by objectification theory, self-objectification involves adopting an observer's perspective on the self, this perspective may entail different traits or characteristics depending on which observer one has in mind. Considered in this way, the concept of objectification does not refer to the characteristics of the self that is being objectified, but only to the process per se.

Nevertheless, research on stereotyping process models has also been complemented by models of stereotype content (Devine & Elliott, 1995; Fiske *et al.*, 2002; Katz & Braly, 1933). These content-based models focus more on the specific substance of stereotypes rather than the processes underlying stereotyping. Likewise, objectification could also be considered as referring to a specific content: objects have different features than human beings (Haslam, 2006; Nussbaum, 1995). There may also be overlap between the content of stereotypes and the content of objectification. For example, objectification can also involve ascribing the characteristics of an object to another person, such as depriving another of agency or of personhood. One of the most essential aspects of stereotypes of women concerns passivity (Glick & Fiske, 1996): women are often viewed as passive and dependent relative to men. Self-objectification can be considered one psychological manifestation of this stereotype. The ultimate form of passivity involves considering one's own self as an object. Similarly, objectification is associated with stereotypes of hyper-sexualised women (e.g. the blonde stereotype, Rudman & Borgida, 1995).

Objectification theory (Fredrickson & Roberts, 1997) precisely argues that in male dominated Western cultures, the female body is continuously evaluated and women learn to adopt an observer's perspective on their own bodies. This leads to self-objectification with women coming to view themselves as men view them (i.e. as objects for the consumption of others). Fredrickson and Roberts theorised the negative consequences that such a self-view can produce: body shame, anxiety, and mental health disorders (see Moradi & Huang, 2008 for a review). Self-objectification can be beneficial to women to the extent that it helps them to navigate male-dominated environments in which physical appearance is a key to success (Wolf, 2002). However, such success comes at a dear price: it perpetuates a social system in which women are evaluated for their looks and may therefore contribute to disempowering them. Self-objectification leads women to focus on their own bodies rather than on factors that may advance the interests of their group as a whole, such as performing demanding intellectual tasks, or considering the plight of their group as a whole, thereby discouraging collective action.

Hence, it is probably safe to assert that self-objectification contributes to a form of false consciousness on the part of women. In support of this hypothesis, Calogero (2013) observed that women who self-objectified, either chronically or via an experimental manipulation, were less likely to engage in social activism on behalf of other women.

Whereas self-objectification has been at the forefront of social psychological research on gender for more than a decade now, its antecedent, objectification per se, has attracted interest only recently. Theorists have struggled to define exactly what it means to objectify another person. Indeed, this concept, which literally means treating a human like an object (Nussbaum, 1995), can be either considered a metaphor without clear psychological equivalents, or an actual psychological process, like stereotyping.

The philosopher Nussbaum (1995) described seven ways of treating someone like an object: instrumentalisation, denial of autonomy, passivity, interchangeability, violability, possession, and denial of subjectivity. Inspired in part by this list, a variety of indicators of objectification have been proposed: using the person as an instrument to achieve one's goals (Gruenfeld, Inesi, Magee & Galinsky, 2008), focusing on the person's appearance rather than personality (Heflick & Goldenberg, 2009) and on their sexual body parts rather than their faces (Gervais, Holland & Dodd, 2013), viewing a woman as a sum of parts rather than a whole human being

(Bernard *et al.*, 2012; Gervais *et al.*, 2012), associating women with dehumanizing traits (Vaes, Paladino & Puvia, 2011), or viewing a person as interchangeable with other people with similar body parts, regardless of their faces (Gervais, Vescio & Allen, 2012). Regardless of the criteria being used, this research has generally shown that women tend to be objectified more frequently and with greater intensity than men (see Bernard, 2013; Gervais *et al.*, 2013 for reviews). Thus, this suggests that objectification is not merely a metaphor but can be evidenced, like stereotyping, through empirically observable cognitive processes.

Whereas the automaticity of objectification has yet to be tested, it likely contains both automatic as well as controlled aspects. For example, Bernard *et al.* (2012) found that people tend to perceive bodies of women similarly to objects by capitalising on a well-known cognitive phenomenon. The latter, the inversion effect, involves two stages: in the first stage a stimulus is presented either in an upright or inverted (top down, rotated 180 degrees across the x-axis) position. In the second stage, the same stimulus and a distractor (e.g. a mirror image of the original stimulus) are presented. The participant's task is to identify the previously presented pictures. Earlier work on the inversion effect (Reed, Stone, Bozova & Tanaka, 2003) has shown that when the target is a human being or body, people recognise upright better than top down pictures. When the target is a physical object, people tend to perform equally well regardless of the stimulus orientation. Presenting a stimulus upside down disrupts the relation between the parts of the stimulus. If people attend to these relations rather than to the parts themselves, this presentation is likely to impair performance. Hence, these data suggest that human bodies or faces are perceived configurally, as "gestalts", whereas objects tend to be perceived in terms of their constituent parts (analytically). However, previous research had not examined the impact of the targets' gender on this effect. Bernard *et al.* (2012) did this using images of sexualised men vs. women and found an inversion effect for male but not female targets, suggesting an analogy between perceptions of sexualised women and objects. Note that this effect was found for both male and female participants. In a similar vein, Gervais *et al.* (2012, Experiment 1) showed male and female participants pictures of male and female bodies and, after each trial, asked participants to discriminate between two stimuli: a target and a foil. These two stimuli were either whole bodies or parts of the previously shown bodies (the foil was a slightly altered version of the original). Gervais *et al.* (2012) computed correct recognition scores and found that participants were better able to recognise parts of female bodies than whole female (but not male) bodies. Contrary to more overt measures of objectification (such as judging a female candidate for a job on her looks rather than on her skills), the present measures relied on perceptual measures that are unlikely to be under the participants' voluntary control. Objectification may plausibly occur automatically much like categorisation and stereotype activation (Devine, 1989). However, the influence of variables such as power (Gruenfeld *et al.*, 2008), global and local processing objectives (Gervais *et al.*, 2012, Experiment 2), or system justification motives (Calogero & Jost, 2011), suggests that more controlled processes may modulate objectification (see Macrae & Bodenhausen, 2000 for a similar consideration of stereotyping). Thus, the presence of such biases bears interesting parallels with stereotyping. In this perspective, an "authentic" perception of a woman would involve appraising her as a full-fledged person. Like stereotyping, objectification can be viewed as a curse that plagues us regardless of how we attempt to combat it, reinforcing a biased (and system justifying) view of women.

In addition, despite feminist scholarship suggesting that men are the sole perpetrators of objectification (Bartky, 1990), women are as likely to objectify women as are men (Bernard *et al.*, 2012). Thus, women rely on a mode of appraisal of other women that seems to contradict their interests. In this view, self-objectification discourages women from engaging in collective action. These elements suggest that objectification, like stereotyping, can be seen as a cognitive device that serves to maintain a form of false consciousness in women: it places women in a passive role, as the victims of the male gaze.

Having said that, we should consider an apparent cultural shift noted by a feminist writer (Gill, 2008), but largely overlooked in the social psychological literature, from passive to active sexuality. We shall now turn to this evolution and consider its implications for the role of objectification in the maintenance of gender inequalities.

Cultural shifts in sexualisation: women as sexual agents

In the past decade, the advertising media has tended to emphasise a view of women as powerful and in control of their sexuality (Gill, 2008). Purchasing specific products has been construed as an avenue for female consumers to assert independence from men.

> One of the most significant shifts in advertising in the last decade or more has been the construction of a new figure: a young, attractive, heterosexual woman who knowingly and deliberately plays with her sexual power and is always 'up for it'.
>
> *(Gill, 2008, p. 41)*

> Showing one's bare midriff or tattoos in suggestive parts of the body, is the most emblematic manifestation of women as agents of their sexuality, hence the term "midriff" to describe these women. These women "play" with male desire as the model in a Triumph advertisement stating "New hair, new look, new bra. And if he doesn't like it, new boyfriend" (p. 42). Thus, these women seem to reclaim a sense of power. The term "girl power" is used to describe this movement.
>
> *(Jackson, Vares & Gill, 2012)*

These women are not only virtual images in advertisements. Many Western teenage girls claim these identities (Jackson *et al.*, 2012). Girls and women may actually purposefully conform to these images and engage in behaviours that align with objectifying views of women. Self-sexualisation refers to any action taken by a woman that highlights her sexualised features (Allen & Gervais, 2012), and can be considered as an identity performance. Such a strategy is tempting because it carries the hope of greater power and more positive social relationships. For instance, a recent qualitative study showed that a full 33 percent of heterosexual women reported that they had kissed or made out with another woman at a party (Yost & McCarthy, 2012). The primary motive for such behaviour was to garner male attention. In a society that values agency, the midriff or hooking up with other women seems like an attractive ideal, much preferable to the mere sexual object.

The characterisation of this shift from objectification to self-sexualisation bears interesting parallels with the distinction between the cognitive and strategic aspects of stereotyping. Engaging in self-sexualisation (which comprises a largely intentional and often strategic component) does not *necessarily* involve cognitive self-objectification. However, self-sexualisation does involve intentionally playing with behavioural and appearance-related norms that are traditionally associated with objectification without necessarily endorsing them. Indeed, the (maybe illusory) promise of "girl power" is precisely that women may become active agents in their own sexuality.

Nevertheless, this strategy is not without its costs. Women featured in "midriff" advertisements are beautiful, sexy, sexually knowledgeable, and perceived as always willing to engage in sexual activity. Thus, the control accrued to women through such images often amounts to presenting themselves in ways that conform to traditional (sexually objectifying) male ideals. Similarly, of the women that publicly "hooked up" with other women, many reported feeling powerful from arousing sexual desire in men and engaging in sexual experimentation, but only 16 percent of women reported these powerful feelings in the absence of explicit pressure from others (usually men). Despite the fact that some feelings of agency were experienced during the public same-sex sexual encounters, many women (64 percent) reported that they also felt sexually objectified and degraded during these experiences and were contributing to the sexual objectification of other women (Yost & McCarthy, 2012).

Also, such images focus on the body rather than on other aspects of women as entire persons. Conforming to such ideals involves acknowledging that sex should play an important part in many social relationships (e.g. professional) in which its place is far from obvious. Besides, such messages are meant to induce the consumption of products allowing female consumers to achieve these ends. Hence, one can wonder whether women who actively advertise their sexuality, while experiencing a sense of agency, are not actually victims of this consumerism. Work reviewed by Allen and Gervais (2012) further suggests that actively conforming to these images may be detrimental to women's well-being. It may make them more vulnerable to sexual harassment and sexual violence. It may also make them more likely to be judged in terms of their sex-related characteristics.

Self-sexualisation and neoliberalism

Self-sexualisation can be viewed as a strategy of the weak, an individual response to lack of control, and reflects the old strategy of good looks that women have used to compensate for their lack of power. In support of this assumption, Allen and Gervais (2012) suggest that using self-sexualisation may be most effective for women in low status positions. In doing so, they would act consistently with their role prescriptions.

In such instances, women engage in individual forms of self-presentation aimed at garnering individual rewards (Jones & Pittman, 1982), a form of "personal identity" performance. To the extent that such behaviours correspond to objectifying ideals, however, they can be considered as perpetuating power relations (Klein & Snyder, 2003). Furthermore, they do so in a particularly pernicious way by conferring an illusory sense of agency. Note also that the examples of self-sexualisation we have reviewed so far are guided by purely individual goals (e.g. eliciting sexual attraction or attention from men). Indeed, implicit in "girl power" advertisements is the message that one needs to be more attractive or more sexually adventurous than other women. Such an emphasis on sexual attraction places heterosexual women in a competition with one another for access to men. The sense of agency conferred by the desired product may make women feel that they have an advantage in interpersonal and intragroup competition. It may thereby discourage women from pursuing group-based actions and undermine ingroup solidarity.

Such an observation resonates with research conducted by the French scholar Jean-Léon Beauvois (2004) showing that people are most likely to be influenced by a message to the extent that they feel free. This is what he calls "freely undergone submission"[5] (see also reactance theory, Brehm, 1966; self-determination theory, Ryan & Deci, 2000). In research on cognitive dissonance (e.g. Guéguen et al., 2013), asserting one's freedom before performing an unwanted behaviour (e.g. eating worms) makes people more likely to shift their attitudes to make them consistent with their behaviour (e.g. finding worms palatable: Comer & Laird, 1975). Since they were free, they feel bound and committed to the act: endorsing beliefs or attitudes that are consistent with the behaviour reduces dissonance. According to this logic, women who view their engagement in self-sexualisation as deliberate may be aware that this conforms to male ideals. However, because they have freely chosen to adopt these behaviours, they may come to endorse these ideals more than those of the past who conformed to male ideals out of (conscious) resignation. Beauvois sees this effect as an illustration of the neoliberal values governing Western societies. The widespread ideology that everyone is free actually makes people easier targets for manipulation. The empowerment that being an autonomous individual confers makes us more likely to blindly conform to cultural norms (Beauvois, 2004; see also Klein, 2009).

In Western market societies, there is a clear association between such neoliberal values and objectification. Thus, to a large extent freedom is thought to manifest itself in the capacity to purchase any product one aspires to (provided that the means are available). Living in a consumer market may affect social relationships in such a way that others are perceived only in terms of their instrumental value (Fiske, 1992). Obviously, the sexualisation of women plays a major role in this process as it serves to sell products that assuage male desires.

To summarise this section, we have gathered evidence that sexual objectification, in its passive form or in its more agentic version via self-sexualisation, seems to fulfil an ideological function. Leading women to conform to male ideals and/or to compete for access to men, by emphasising their physical appearance and sexuality to the detriment of less visible skills and psychological traits, discourages collective action, and legitimises the subordinate position of women. We came to a very similar conclusion when inspecting the existing literature on stereotypes, but we found that, viewed through the lens of social identity performance, social stereotypes could be used to transform social systems. Can a similar argument be proposed regarding sexual objectification? We now turn to examine this question.

Can sexualisation be used to transform social systems?

Although objectification research is recent, feminist movements have sought to address the phenomenon for many decades. In line with the view of objectification as an instrument of male domination, many feminists have resorted to forms of identity performance that contrasted with objectified body ideals. For example, some feminists have sometimes deliberately neglected their appearance, whereas others appropriated male dress in an effort to break the glass ceiling (for examples, see Scott, 2006).

Thus, they have resisted these stereotypes and the false consciousness they entailed in a way that may seem resonant of how Lumumba rejected paternalistic stereotypes endorsed by the Belgian colonisers when addressing Congolese audiences. Undermining a depiction of women that justified gender inequality allowed them to advance their political agenda.

In this context, it is interesting to consider the case of two recent movements which sought to advance feminist agendas while engaging in forms of identity performance that to a large extent outwardly conform to norms associated with sexually objectified women.

The first example of such a movement involves the Slutwalks, dozens of marches that started in Canada in 2011 to protest the declaration by a Toronto police officer that "women should avoid dressing like sluts", thereby seeming to legitimise sexual aggression against inappropriately dressed women. The (young) women participating in this movement marched dressed like "sluts", effectively engaging in the forms of dress associated with sexual objectification. In doing so, they asserted their right to dress as they wish without incurring the risk of sexual violence.

Another example, into which we shall delve more extensively, is the Femen movement that originated in Ukraine in 2008. It was initially composed of mostly female students. The goal of the movement was to advance the rights of women such as the legalisation of abortion and the prohibition of prostitution. The movement is particularly opposed to religious institutions (Islam and Christianity especially) limiting women's rights. To do so, members of this movement engaged in spectacular actions against symbols of male domination. For example, one of its members started stripping after a sermon by the Pope while waving a banner claiming "Freedom for women". In another action, Femen activists engaged in a topless demonstration at the London Olympic Games in 2012 against what they described as "bloody Islamist regimes" which were allegedly supported by the International Olympic Committee (*The Daily Telegraph*, 2012). They have performed dozens of such actions. The trademark of their action involves acting naked from the waist up and revealing feminist slogans tattooed on their skin, as noted in our introductory example.

These women seem to self-sexualise to advance political agendas. Like the "midriffs", they intentionally display sexual parts of their bodies. However, this form of identity performance is quite distinct from self-objectification as described by Fredrickson and Roberts (1997). Rather than being victims of the standards conveyed by the media, they actually instrumentalise the media's thirst for exposed female bodies, and they do so intentionally in the service of a collective political project aimed at the betterment of the conditions of women. In a paradoxical move, both movements use self-sexualisation to restore the agency of women. Deliberately exposing one's body to male eyes (or dressing like a "slut"), possibly conforming to their standards but doing so freely, appears as the supreme expression of women's agency. Thus, by instrumentalising one of the main channels of their objectification (the mass media), these movements demonstrate that they are not objects but agents.

In this respect, such a movement differs from the denunciation of system-justifying stereotypes by Lumumba and other leaders of oppressed groups. Indeed, these women do not, through their behaviour, attempt to contest sexually objectifying images of women. Rather, these images are a vehicle for attracting interest to their agendas.

Is such a strategy doomed?

We have shown that by conferring an illusory sense of power, self-sexualisation, like mixed self-stereotypes, may contribute to a form of false consciousness. Should we therefore consider self-sexualisation and power assertions of the Femen movement as manifestation of another illusion? Are the Femen another example of these revolutionaries who, in seeking to combat a social system, actually maintain it? There are grounds for drawing such criticisms.

The Femen are all young and slender. Thus, by exhibiting their body, they may actually contribute to perpetuating cultural standards for women's bodies. Their actions may seem to exclude women whose bodies do not correspond to these standards. Feminist writings (e.g. Wolf, 2002) have extensively emphasised that such standards exert formidable pressures on women and contribute to undermining their opportunities of upward social mobility. Although there do not seem to be formal barriers to membership in terms of age or body shape (Huon, 2013), their "commando" actions involve considerable physical activity. Hence a form of (self-) selection as a function of physical fitness seems to be present.

Second, like the midriffs, the Femens clearly claim a sense of agency related to their body. Especially, they claim a right to use their body as they choose. Superficially, this may seem to bear a resemblance to the advertising discourse on female sexual agency.

However, we believe that a clear distinction should be made between the form of agency claimed by the Femen movement and that of the "midriffs". Social identity theory (SIT: Tajfel & Turner, 1986) suggests that when people are faced with a negative social identity, they can engage in one of two types of strategies. Individual strategies generally involve trying to upgrade one's individual status by changing one's individual position in the social hierarchy (e.g. by moving to a more prestigious group). Although changing gender is rarely a plausible option for women, they may symbolically relinquish their femininity by emphasising aspects of their self that are not typically associated with gender (Pronin, Steele & Ross, 2004). The theory also suggests that people may shift their definition of themselves: in some cases they may define themselves in terms of their personal identity, whereas in other contexts their social or collective identity is more salient. Specifically, when faced with a negative social identity, distinguishing oneself from other members of one's own group to achieve a more satisfactory personal identity is a plausible option. Self-sexualisation, and conformity to the midriff ideal, can be appraised in this way. As we mentioned previously, self-sexualisation involves being sexier and more attractive to men than other competing, heterosexual women, a strategy that undermines the cohesiveness of women as a group. It may also involve fitting in with other women while at the same time distinguishing oneself from other women because sexiness is a stereotypically feminine trait, but not all women are (or can be) sexy (Allen & Gervais, 2012).

In contrast, the Femen movement clearly pursues a collective strategy. In the SIT sense, a collective strategy aims at upgrading the position of the ingroup in the social structure. It can be implemented through social competition (i.e. directly challenging the group on crucial dimensions of comparison) or social creativity (i.e. collectively redefining the identity of the group in more favourable ways). By directly contesting male domination in different areas (e.g. religion, sports, politics, and so on), the Femens seem to have used the social competition route, which contrary to social creativity, challenges the *status quo*. Their goal is to achieve not individual power, but collective power. Besides, their goal in exhibiting their body is clearly not to attract men individually, but to advertise that they are free to use their body as they wish, even if, paradoxically, this elicits the objectifying gaze.

The concept of social identity performance helps us appraise these differences. Whereas the Femen women use their naked body to present their collective identity as women to fulfil the goals of their movement, the midriffs sexualise their body to advertise their personal identity as attractive women. Although on the surface the behaviours may appear similar, the motivations are very different; the former behaviour is directed at social change while the latter is clearly not.

Even if the strategy of the Femen movement is opposed to that of the midriffs, there is no evidence that this strategy is successful. Indeed, whereas the strategies of the Femen movement have helped them garner attention to their cause, it remains unclear whether media attention has helped them convey their message efficiently. In October 2012 a German movement announced that all its members would demonstrate naked to support refugees (Kalbe, 2012). This announcement attracted much media attention, but when the media arrived to cover the demonstration, the women were clothed. They wished to demonstrate that the media's interest lies in the shock value of showing naked women rather than in conveying their message.

Second, it is doubtful that viewers are actually attentive to the message conveyed by the demonstrators. Nudity may divert attention from the message (Bushman & Bonacci, 2002). As an example, Glick, Chrislock, Petersik, Vijay and Turek (2008) showed that women advertising their sexuality by showing cleavage were perceived as less persuasive, at least when selling a "strong" product.[6] Feminists (e.g. Murphy, 2013) have actually criticised the Femen movement for falsely believing that the media were interested in anything other than their nudity.

However, for the Femens' slogans to have any effect, the demonstrations need to be available in the media in the first place. Competition for media space is particularly severe, and that places the Femens in a paradoxical situation. The belief that sex sells, which is commonly (albeit often erroneously: Glick *et al.*, 2008) held, made it possible for the Femen movement to access the global media. These actions have made it possible to highlight feminist issues in ways that more traditional actions may have failed to achieve.

Conclusion

We have sought to consider two phenomena that have generally been considered as ideological tools serving to preserve existing power relations: stereotyping and objectification. In relation to stereotyping, we have shown that stereotypes can serve an ideological function, and that this function is reinforced via three of their main features highlighted in the social psychological literature: they are thought to be automatically activated (sometimes even when the perceiver does not endorse them), they are considered to be biased, and they ascribe a group's current social position to stable dispositions thereby depriving groups of their history. We have suggested that this reflects a partial view of stereotypes. They can also be used by group leaders to define the ingroup's identities in ways consonant with projects of social transformation and in order to recruit audiences into supporting these projects. The counterpart to the automatic activation of cognitive representations lies in the strategic expression of stereotypes, a form of social identity performance. Stereotypes can serve utopias and not only ideologies. It is difficult to gauge the extent to which these tactics actually succeed in transforming power relations. It is obviously one of the chief tools political leaders can use to mobilise their constituencies against the *status quo* as it serves to define the identity of the ingroup. Work conducted in other contexts confirms that "self-category construction" indeed plays an important role in political mobilisation (see Reicher & Hopkins, 1996, 2001' Reicher, Hopkins & Condor, 1997). In Lumumba's case, this strategy seemed to have paid off, in terms of achieving independence from Belgium at least (although his political career was short-lived after independence).

We then turned to sexual objectification and found that, in many ways, a similar analysis could be performed. Self-objectification seems to justify the existing social order and to discourage collective action. We also considered a recent variant of self-objectification, self-sexualisation, which seems to restore a sense of agency to women. We suggested, however, that to the extent that it undermines solidarity and group cohesiveness, serves personal goals, and conforms to sexualised male ideals, such self-sexualisation reinforces the gender hierarchy. We contrasted such behaviour with the forms of collective self-sexualisation endorsed by the Slutwalks and the Femen movements, which we consider as a form of social identity performance. It is still uncertain how efficacious such movements can be. By using sexualisation to capture the attention of the media, they offer their feminist message a chance to be heard. However, if audiences fail to grasp the irony of these naked women harbouring a right to use their bodies as they wish, the result may, as is often the case for feminist endeavours, be backlash.

In sum, both stereotypes and objectification connect power and identity. On the one hand, they seem to reflect the texture of power relations as they emanate from these relations. In doing so, they describe or point to the identity of their target (for example, a social group or an individual woman) within the existing social structure. On the other hand, through rhetoric and social identity performance stereotypes and objectification can be used to transform these power relations by articulating views of the self or the ingroup with a utopia. The success of such endeavours may depend as much on the creativity and rhetorical skills of minority group leaders as on the "objective" factors traditionally studied by social scientists.

Notes

1   The work presented in this chapter was supported by grants from the FRS-FNRS (Belgian National Research Fund) to the first and third authors. We are very grateful to Manuela Barreto and Denis Sindic for their extensive, and constructive, feedback on earlier versions of this chapter.
2   Now the Democratic Republic of Congo.
3   Lumumba was sometimes portrayed as pro-Soviet or as promoting violence.
4   As clearly enunciated in the poem written in 1959 (Van Lierde, 1963) in which the history of "the Black man" is described as a "human livestock for millennia" who will now assert his pride and freedom.
5   "Soumission librement consentie" in French.

6 The product was a painkiller, which, based on charts shown to the participants, was efficient (70 percent more relief than a placebo). When the product was "weak" (9 percent more relief) the cleavage had no effect.

References

Allen, J. & Gervais, S.J. (2012) The drive to be sexy: Prejudice and core motivations in women's self-sexualization. In D.W. Russell and C.A. Russell (Eds), *Psychology of prejudice: Interdisciplinary perspectives on contemporary issues* (pp. 77−112). Hauppauge, NY: Nova Science Publishers.

Bagliano, A.P. (2006) "Le Pape, c'est le Christ sur Terre!" ["The Pope is the Christ on Earth!"]. *L'Histoire,* 305, 64.

Bargh, J.A. (1999) The cognitive monster: The case against the controllability of automatic stereotype effects. In S. Chaiken & Y. Trope (Eds), *Dual-process theories in social psychology* (pp. 361−382). New York: Guilford Press.

Barreto, M. & Ellemers, N. (2003) The effects of being categorised: The interplay between internal and external social identities. *European Review of Social Psychology,* 14, 139−170.

Bartky, S.L. (1990) *Femininity and domination: Studies in the phenomenology of oppression.* New York: Routledge.

Beauvois, J.-L. (2004) *Traité de la servitude libérale: Analyse de la soumission* [Treatise on liberal serfdom: An analysis of submission]. Paris: Dunod.

Bernard, P. (2013) *Gender and the objectification of sexualized bodies: Cognitive underpinnings and social consequences.* Doctoral dissertation. Université Libre de Bruxelles, Belgium.

Bernard, P., Gervais, S.J., Allen, J., Campomizzi, S. & Klein, O. (2012) Integrating sexual objectification with object versus person recognition: The sexualized body-inversion hypothesis. *Psychological Science,* 23, 469−471.

Brehm, J.W. (1966) *A theory of psychological reactance.* New York: Academic Press.

Bushman, B.J. & Bonacci, A.M. (2002) Violence and sex impair memory for television ads. *Journal of Applied Psychology,* 87, 557−563.

Calogero, R.M. (2013) Objects don't object: Evidence that self-objectification disrupts women's social activism. *Psychological Science,* 24, 312−318.

Calogero, R.M. & Jost, J.T. (2011) Self-subjugation among women: Exposure to sexist ideology, self-objectification, and the protective function of the need to avoid closure. *Journal of Personality and Social Psychology,* 100, 211.

Chen, S., Chen, K.Y. & Shaw, L. (2004) Self-verification motives at the collective level of self-definition. *Journal of Personality and Social Psychology,* 86, 77–94.

Code, L. (1995) *Rhetorical spaces: Essays on gendered locations.* New York: Routledge.

Comer, R. & Laird, J.D. (1975) Choosing to suffer as a consequence of expecting to suffer: Why do people do it? *Journal of Personality and Social Psychology,* 32, 92−101.

de Beauvoir, S. (1953) *The second sex.* New York: Random House.

Devine, P.G. (1989) Stereotypes and prejudice: Their automatic and controlled components. *Journal of Personality and Social Psychology,* 56, 5−18.

Devine, P.G. & Elliot, A.J. (1995) Are racial stereotypes really fading? The Princeton trilogy revisited. *Personality and Social Psychology Bulletin,* 21, 1139−1150.

Eagly, A.H. (1987) *Sex differences in social behavior: A social-role interpretation.* Hillsdale, NJ: Erlbaum.

Fiske, A.P. (1992) The four elementary forms of sociality: Framework for a unified theory of social relations. *Psychological Review*, 99, 689–723.

Fiske, S.T. (1998) Stereotyping, prejudice, and discrimination. In D.T. Gilbert, S.T. Fiske & G. Lindzey (Eds), *The handbook of social psychology*, Vols. 1 and 2 (4th ed.) (pp. 357–411). New York: McGraw-Hill.

Fiske, S.T., Cuddy, A.J., Glick, P. & Xu, J. (2002) A model of (often mixed) stereotype content: Competence and warmth respectively follow from perceived status and competition. *Journal of Personality and Social Psychology*, 82, 878–902.

Fiske, S.T., Lin, M. & Neuberg, S.L. (1999) The continuum model ten years later. In S. Chaiken and Y. Troppe (Eds), *Dual-process theories in social psychology* (pp. 231–254). New York: Guilford Press.

Fiske, S.T. & Neuberg, S.L. (1990) A continuum model of impression formation from category-based to individuating processes: Influences of information and motivation on attention and interpretation. In M.P. Zanna (Ed.), *Advances in experimental social psychology* (Vol. 3, pp. 1–74). San Diego, CA: Academic Press.

Fredrickson, B.L. & Roberts, T. (1997) Objectification theory: Toward understanding women's lived experiences and mental health risks. *Psychology of Women Quarterly*, 21, 173–206.

Gervais, S.J., Bernard, P., Klein, O. & Allen, J. (2013) Toward a unified theory of objectification and dehumanization. In S.J. Gervais (Ed.), *Objectification and Dehumanization* (pp. 1–23). New York, NY: Springer.

Gervais, S.J., Holland, A.M. & Dodd, M.D. (2013) My eyes are up here: The nature of the objectifying gaze toward women. *Sex Roles*, 69, 557–570.

Gervais, S.J., Vescio, T.K. & Allen, J. (2012) When are people interchangeable sexual objects? The effect of gender and body type on sexual fungibility. *British Journal of Social Psychology*, 51, 499–513.

Gervais, S.J., Vescio, T.K., Maass, A., Förster, J. & Suitner, C. (2012) Seeing women as objects: The sexual body part recognition bias. *European Journal of Social Psychology*, 42, 743–753.

Gill, R. (2008) Empowerment/sexism: Figuring female sexual agency in contemporary advertising. *Feminism and Psychology*, 18, 35–60.

Glick, P., Chrislock, K., Petersik, K., Vijay, M. & Turek, A. (2008) Does cleavage work at work? Men, but not women, falsely believe cleavage sells a weak product. *Psychology of Women Quarterly*, 32, 326–335.

Glick, P. & Fiske, S.T. (1996). The ambivalent sexism inventory: Differentiating hostile and benevolent sexism. *Journal of Personality and Social Psychology*, 70, 491–512.

Gruenfeld, D.H., Inesi, M.E., Magee, J.C. & Galinsky, A.D. (2008) Power and the objectification of social targets. *Journal of Personality and Social Psychology*, 95, 111–127.

Guéguen, N., Joule, R.V., Halimi-Falkowicz, S., Pascual, A., Fischer-Lokou, J. & Dufourcq-Brana, M. (2013) I'm free but I'll comply with your request: Generalization and multidimensional effects of the "evoking freedom" technique. *Journal of Applied Social Psychology*, 43, 116–137.

Haslam, N. (2006) Dehumanization: An integrative review. *Personality and Social Psychology Review*, 10, 252–264.

Heflick, N.A. & Goldenberg, J.L. (2009) Objectifying Sarah Palin: Evidence that objectification causes women to be perceived as less competent and less fully human. *Journal of Experimental Social Psychology*, 45, 598–601.

Hoffman, C. & Hurst, N. (1990) Gender stereotypes: Perception or rationalization? *Journal of Personality and Social Psychology*, 58, 197–208.

Huon, J. (2013) Avec les Femen, amazones de turbulence [With the Femen, Amazons of turbulence], *Le Soir*, May 24th, pp. 30–31.

Jackson, S., Vares, T. & Gill, R. (2012) "The whole playboy mansion image": Girls' fashioning and fashioned selves within a postfeminist culture. *Feminism and Psychology*, 23, 143–162.

Jones, E.E. & Pittman, T.S. (1982) Toward a general theory of strategic self-presentation. In J. Suls (Ed.), *Psychological perspectives on the self* (Vol. 1, pp. 231–262). Hillsdale, NJ: Erlbaum.

Jost, J.T. (1995) Negative illusions: Conceptual clarification and psychological evidence concerning false consciousness. *Political Psychology*, 16, 397–424.

Jost, J.T. & Banaji, M.R. (1994) The role of stereotyping in system-justification and the production of false consciousness. *British Journal of Social Psychology*, 33, 1–27.

Jost, J.T., Banaji, M.R. & Nosek, B.A. (2004) A decade of system justification theory: Accumulated evidence of conscious and unconscious bolstering of the status quo. *Political Psychology*, 25, 881–919.

Jost, J.T. & Kay, A. (2005) Exposure to benevolent sexism and complementary gender stereotypes: Consequences for specific and diffuse forms of system justification. *Journal of Personality and Social Psychology*, 88, 498–509.

Jussim, L. (2012) *Social perception and social reality: Why accuracy dominates bias and self-fulfilling prophecy*. New York: Oxford University Press.

Kalbe, U. (2012) Lockruf ins Protestcamp [Call of the protest camp]. *Neues Deutschland*. Retrieved from www.neues-deutschland.de/artikel/802781.lockruf-ins-protestcamp. html [Accessed 30th October 2012].

Katz, D. & Braly, K. (1933) Racial stereotypes of one hundred college students. *Journal of Abnormal and Social Psychology*, 28, 280–290.

Klein, O. (2004) L'expression des stéréotypes et des représentations groupales: Cognition, stratégie, politique [The expression of stereotypes and group representations: Cognition, strategy, politics]. *Perspectives cognitives et conduites sociales*, 9, 132–159.

——(2009) From Utopia to Dystopia: Levels of explanation and the politics of social psychology. *Psychologica Belgica*, 49, 85–100.

Klein, O. & Licata, L. (2003) When group representations serve social change: The speeches of Patrice Lumumba during the decolonization of Congo. *British Journal of Social Psychology*, 42, 571–594.

Klein, O., Marchal, C., Van der Linden, N., Pierucci, S. & Waroquier, L. (2011) Des "images dans la tête" à la "parole sauvage": Comment modéliser le rapport entre discours et cognition dans l'expression des stéréotypes? [From "pictures in the head" to "wild speech": How to model the relationship between discourse and cognition in the expression of stereotypes In L. Baugnet & T. Guilbert (Eds), *Discours en contextes* (pp. 125–155). Paris: Presses Universitaires de France.

Klein, O. & Snyder, M. (2003) Stereotypes and behavioral confirmation: From interpersonal to intergroup perspectives. In M.P. Zanna (Ed.), *Advances in Experimental Social Psychology* (Vol. 35, pp. 153–234). New York: Academic Press.

Klein, O., Spears, R. & Reicher, S. (2007) Social identity performance: Extending the strategic side of SIDE. *Personality and Social Psychology Review*, 11, 28–45.

Lepore, L. & Brown, R. (1997) Category and stereotype activation: Is prejudice inevitable? *Journal of Personality and Social Psychology*, 72, 275.

MacKinnon, C. (1987) *Feminism unmodified*. Cambridge, MA and London: Harvard University Press.

Macrae, C.N. & Bodenhausen, G.V. (2000) Social cognition: Thinking categorically about others. *Annual Review of Psychology*, 51, 93–120.

Mannheim, K. (1954) *Ideology and utopia: An introduction to the sociology of knowledge*. London: Routledge & Kegan Paul.

Marx, K. (1859/1979) *A contribution to the critique of political economy*. London: Progress.

Marx, K. & Engels, F. (1932/1998) *The German ideology*. London: Prometheus.

Moradi, B. & Huang, Y.-P. (2008) Objectification theory and psychology of women: A decade of advances and future directions. *Psychology of Women Quarterly*, 32, 377–398.

Murphy, M. (2013) There is a wrong way to do feminism. And Femen is doing it wrong. Blog post. Retrieved from http://feministcurrent.com/6619/there-is-a-wrong-way-to-do-feminism-and-femen-is-doing-it-wrong/ [Accessed 10 May 2013].

Nussbaum, M. (1995) Objectification. *Philosophy and Public Affairs*, 24, 249–291.

Oakes, P.J., Haslam, S.A. & Turner, J.C. (1994) *Stereotyping and social reality*. Chichester: Wiley-Blackwell.

Papadaki, E. (2007) Sexual objectification: From Kant to contemporary feminism. *Contemporary Political Theory*, 6, 330–348.

Poppe, E. (2001) Effects of changes in GNP and perceived group characteristics on national and ethnic stereotypes in Central and Eastern Europe. *Journal of Applied Social Psychology*, 31, 1689–1708.

Pronin, E., Steele, C.M. & Ross, L. (2004) Identity bifurcation in response to stereotype threat: Women and mathematics. *Journal of Experimental Social Psychology*, 40, 152–168.

Reed, C.L., Stone, V., Bozova, S. & Tanaka, J. (2003) The body-inversion effect. *Psychological Science*, 14, 302–308.

Reicher, S. (1996) Social identity and social change: Rethinking the context of social psychology. In W.P. Robinson (Ed.), *Social groups and identities: Developing the legacy of Henri Tajfel* (pp. 317–336). London: Butterworth.

Reicher, S.D. (2008) The psychology of crowd dynamics. In M.A. Hogg & S. Tindale (Eds), *Blackwell handbook of social psychology: Group processes* (pp. 182–209). Oxford: Blackwell Publishers.

Reicher, S. & Hopkins, N. (1996) Self-category constructions in political rhetoric: An analysis of Thatcher's and Kinnock's speeches concerning the British miners' strike (1984–5). *European Journal of Social Psychology*, 26, 353–371.

——(2001) Psychology and the end of history: A critique and a proposal for the psychology of social categorization. *Political Psychology*, 22, 383–407.

Reicher, S.D., Hopkins, N. & Condor, S. (1997) Stereotype construction as a strategy of influence. In R. Spears, P. Oakes, N. Ellemers & S.A. Haslam (Eds), *The social psychology of stereotyping and group life* (pp. 94–118). Oxford: Blackwell.

Reicher, S., Hopkins, N., Levine, M. & Rath, R. (2005) Entrepreneurs of hate and entrepreneurs of solidarity: Social identity as a basis for mass communication. *International Review of the Red Cross*, 87, 621–637.

Reicher, S. & Levine, M. (1994a) Deindividuation, power relations between groups and the expression of social identity: The effects of visibility to the out-group. *British Journal of Social Psychology*, 33, 145–163.

——(1994b) On the consequences of deindividuation manipulations for the strategic communication of self: Identifiability and the presentation of social identity. *European Journal of Social Psychology*, 24, 511–524.

Reicher, S.D., Spears, R. & Postmes, T. (1995) A social identity model of deindividuation phenomena. *European Review of Social Psychology*, 6, 161–198.

Ricoeur, P. & Taylor, G.H. (1986) *Lectures on ideology and utopia*. New York: Columbia University Press.

Rudman, L.A. & Borgida, E. (1995) The afterglow of construct accessibility: The behavioral consequences of priming men to view women as sexual objects. *Journal of Experimental Social Psychology*, 31, 493–517.

Ryan, R.M. & Deci, E.L. (2000) Self-determination theory and the facilitation of intrinsic motivation, social development, and well-being. *American Psychologist*, 55, 68–78.

Scott, L.M. (2006) *Fresh lipstick: Redressing fashion and feminism*. London: Macmillan.

Sidanius, J. & Pratto, F. (2001) *Social dominance: An intergroup theory of social hierarchy and oppression*. New-York: Cambridge University Press.

Tajfel, H. & Turner, J.C. (1986) The social identity theory of intergroup behavior. *The social psychology of intergroup relations*. Chicago: Nelson Hall.

Tayler, J. (2013) Why Femen is right. *The Atlantic*. Retrieved from www.theatlantic.com/international/archive/2013/05/topless-jihad-why-femen-is-right/275471/ [Accessed 1 May 2014].

The Daily Telegraph (2012, August 12) *Femen stage topless anti-Islamist protest in London*. Retrieved from www.telegraph.co.uk/sport/olympics/olympicsvideo/9447608/Femen-stage-topless-anti-Islamist-Olympic-protest-in-London.html [Accessed 6 August 2013].

Turner, J.C., Hogg, M.A., Oakes, P.J., Reicher, S.D. & Wetherell, M.S. (1987) *Rediscovering the social group: A self-categorization theory*. Oxford: Blackwell.

Vaes, J., Paladino, M.P. & Puvia, E. (2011) Are sexualized females complete human beings? Why males and females dehumanize sexually objectified women. *European Journal of Social Psychology*, 41, 774–785.

Van Lierde, J. (1963) *La pensée politique de Patrice Lumumba* [Patrice Lumumba's political thought]. Brussels, Belgium: Des Amis de Présence Africaine. Translated as Van Lierde J. (1972) Lumumba speaks. Boston: Little Brown.

Wolf, N. (2002) *The Beauty Myth: How images of beauty are used against women* (Reprint). Harper Perennial.

Yost, M.R. & McCarthy, L. (2012) Girls gone wild? Heterosexual women's same-sex encounters at college parties. *Psychology of Women Quarterly*, 36, 7–24.

Yzerbyt, V.Y., Rocher, S.J. & Schadron, G. (1997) Stereotypes as explanations: A subjective essentialistic view of group perception. In R. Spears, P. Oakes, N. Ellemers & A. Haslam (Eds), *The psychology of stereotyping and group life* (pp. 20–50). Oxford: Basil Blackwell.

6

EMPOWERMENT

The intersection of identity and power in collective action

John Drury, Atalanti Evripidou, Martijn van Zomeren

Collective action is a particularly fruitful area in which to study the intersection of power and identity. In the last twenty years, research on this topic—particularly research examining *crowd* events—has yielded a number of important insights into the nature of identity, the empowerment process and the relation between the two. This chapter will focus on social psychological accounts of subjective power in collective action, which explain how empowerment can operate as both "input" and "output" in such action.

The chapter begins by putting this theoretical work into historical context. The concept of empowerment originally belonged to activists, and it inevitably involves identity, for it raises the question of "power for *who*"? Social psychology has largely studied subjective power in collective action through the concept of group efficacy, which in recent models is linked to the social identity perspective. In the main part of this chapter, we describe the elaborated social identity model of crowd behaviour, from which we derive a series of novel implications and predictions for the causes of empowerment in collective action. Specifically, we will show three things: first that the basis of empowerment in collective action is the sense of unity, which is explained by common self-categorisation; second, that this psychological unity is the condition for expectations of support for action that instantiates a subordinated identity, something that cannot be achieved by individuals acting alone; and third, that this instantiation can transform the participants themselves and is a positive emotional experience. In the remaining sections of the chapter, we draw out some possible psychosocial consequences of empowerment in collective action, before examining the question of how collective actors deal with defeat.

Empowerment in history and theory

Scattered among historical, autobiographical and political accounts of struggles, strikes, riots and uprisings are stories of identity transformation. In these stories, the transformed identities are socially shared, newly confident and associated with positive emotion. The US urban riots of the 1960s provide some examples. Thus, Boesel, Goldberg and Marx (1971) quote a participant from the Plainfield rebellion, in which black residents usurped the power of the police, to illustrate their enhanced solidarity and sense of collective pride:

> You see how things are changing? It used to be that one black man couldn't stand to see another black man do something. We were all jealous of one another and each one tried to pull the other down ... But since the riots, we're not niggers any more. We're black men, and most of the people in the community have learned this.
>
> *(Quoted in Boesel et al., 1971, p. 82)*

Another example comes from the events in France in May 1968. A student protest over the closure of the University at Sorbonne culminated in a night of barricades and street-fighting with riot police. Soon, widespread occupations, wildcat strikes and huge demonstrations almost toppled the government of De Gaulle. One account states how "[w]ithin a few days, young people of twenty attained a level of understanding and a political and tactical sense which many who had been in the revolutionary movement for thirty years or more were still sadly lacking"; moreover, "[t]he tumultuous development of the students' struggle ... transformed both the relation of forces in society and the image, in people's minds, of established institutions and of established leaders" (Anon., 1968, p. 51). Occupying students displayed increased confidence in their own abilities and capacities: "The occupants of Censier suddenly cease to be unconscious, passive *objects* shaped by particular combinations of social forces; they become conscious, active *subjects* who begin to shape their own social activity" (Gregoire & Perlman, 1969, p. 37, emphasis in original); "people who have never expressed ideas before, who have never spoken in front of professors and students, become confident in their ability" (ibid., p. 41).

These examples of psychological transformation in collective action might be classed as examples of empowerment. One definition of empowerment is that it is "a process of awareness and capacity building leading to greater participation, to greater decision-making power and control, and to transformative action" (Karl, 1995, p. 14). The concept appears to have originated from movements like feminism and other struggles for civil rights and social change in the late 1960s. The concept of empowerment captures the idea of subordinated groups struggling to change their situation and in doing so becoming more conscious of the possibility of such change. Through their actions, subordinated groups come to see themselves as agents of their own transformation. The notion of empowerment thus implies that a group's liberation comes from itself, and is not given to it by other, dominant groups. The link between social change and changed identity is echoed in some contemporary accounts of empowerment in women's movements. Thus empowerment is conceptualised as a narrative of self-transformation (e.g. Britt & Heise, 2000), or as a set of skills (e.g. communication, organisation) that participants acquire through involvement in campaign activities (e.g. Salt & Layzell, 1985).

Today, however, most of the results of any internet search for "empowerment" do not refer to groups in struggle for social change, but to institutions, services, businesses and professional groups who make use of the term in ways that are quite different than its earlier usage as an activists' category. For example "empowerment" is now the slogan of the World Bank (2011). This co-option is also evident in academia—for example, in health psychology (e.g. Zimmerman, Israel, Schulz & Checkoway, 1992), community psychology (e.g. Ratna & Rifkin, 2007), social work (e.g. Thompson, 2008), and management studies (e.g. Spreitzer, 1995). In all these cases, the concept of empowerment has been detached from its links with social change. For example, whereas the activists' "empowerment" referred to a process of liberation and was politically potent, "empowerment" in management theory is essentially a tool for using others for management's own purposes. These current usages therefore are a world away from the exhilarating sense of possibility evident in our examples from uprisings and rebellions.

So, given this co-option, and indeed the ease with which the meaning has been debased, why would researchers of collective action persist with it? The short answer is that empowerment remains a meaningful concept to activists. Many of them still use the term because it captures something about their experience that other concepts do not (Drury, Cocking, Beale, Hanson & Rapley, 2005). Before outlining a model of empowerment in collective action, however, we first need to examine how most social psychologists have addressed the issue of subjective power in collective action, which is mainly through the concept of *efficacy*.

Subjective power in the social psychology of collective action: the concept of efficacy

In social psychology, research on collective action—including marches, demonstrations, boycotts, petitions and riots—has been flourishing in the past few years, with the publication of an increasing number of journal articles and special issues (e.g. Becker, 2012; Van Zomeren & Iyer, 2009; Van Zomeren & Klandermans, 2011). In these accounts, the concept used to refer to subjective power in collective action is not empowerment but efficacy. The advantages of the concept of efficacy include the fact that it is well-established outside of collective action research—it has proven utility in clinical and individual psychology more generally—and that it is a measurable construct, with robust measures and scales.

It is specifically the concept of *group* efficacy, based originally on Bandura's (1997) work, defined as the belief that a problem can be solved through group effort, that has been used in collective action research since the 1990s (e.g. Kelly & Breinlinger, 1995; Klandermans, 1997; Mummendey, Kessler, Klink & Mielke, 1999). The conclusion of these and many other more recent studies is that group efficacy beliefs are a key predictor of individuals' participation in collective action (e.g. Hornsey *et al.*, 2006; Tausch *et al.*, 2011, Van Zomeren, Spears, Fischer, & Leach, 2004). In a meta-analysis, Van Zomeren, Postmes and Spears (2008) found that group efficacy beliefs were a medium-strength predictor of collective action intentions ($r = .36$) and behaviour ($r = .25$). Alongside other key variables (identification and perceptions of injustice), efficacy predicted collective action, particularly against incidental disadvantages rather than against structural disadvantages. Efficacy and cognate concepts are therefore central to a number of models of collective action, including the dual-pathway model (Sturmer & Simon, 2004) and the social identity model of collective action (SIMCA; Van Zomeren *et al.*, 2008).

The concept of efficacy has therefore proved extremely useful in research on collective action. However, in relation to the question of the intersection of identity and power, there are two limitations in most of the existing work on group efficacy as an account of subjective power in collective action.

First, while group efficacy would seem to be a possible component of empowerment, the concept of empowerment is much broader than that of efficacy. Efficacy refers to a belief about a particular situation, agent or goal; empowerment encompasses this but also has other connotations. This is clear from the historical examples illustrated above, and from phenomenological research on empowerment amongst activists, in which positive emotion is to the fore in their accounts (Drury *et al.*, 2005; Drury & Reicher, 1999, 2005). The concept of empowerment captures the fact that world-changing collective action is a deeply desired goal, and so participation in it is a deeply positive, self-changing experience; participants' new understanding that the world is tractable, and that therefore they can change their position of subordination, is exciting and exhilarating. Empowerment refers to participants' understanding of their ability to transform social relations. If it is a cognition, it is a hot one.

A second limitation is that almost all group efficacy studies and models of collective action have examined subjective power only as an antecedent or predictor, or at best a mediator, of that action. Again, however, the historical illustrations and case studies of crowd events tell of the importance of subjective power also as an *effect* or outcome of collective action, both as arising within the event (Drury & Reicher, 1999) and as an enduring psychological after-effect (Drury & Reicher, 2005). The causal effects of collective action on the sense of group efficacy have also been demonstrated in the laboratory. For instance, in one experiment, participants confronted with an illegitimate outgroup action (e.g. genetically modified food) who signed a petition scored higher in collective efficacy than those who did not have the opportunity to sign the petition, or those who did have the opportunity but who did not sign it (Van Zomeren, Drury & Van der Staaij, forthcoming).

Arguably, therefore, some models of collective action, such as the SIMCA (Van Zomeren *et al.*, 2008), describe the predictive role of efficacy, but do not explain the process through which collective action itself can change this variable. Recently, however, more dynamic models have been developed which attempt to capture the way that subjective power can be "output" as well as "input" in collective action. For instance, Simon and Klandermans' (2001) model of politicised collective identity posits that, through political struggle, individuals achieve a sense of themselves as being collectively agentic. Thomas, McGarty and Mavor (2009) and Thomas, Mavor and McGarty (2012) add that intra-group discussions can create new, more efficacy-based, identities in collective actors.

Of these new models, Van Zomeren, Leach and Spears' (2012) dynamic dual pathway model provides the most detail on the dynamic psychological processes through which undertaking collective action changes levels of group efficacy. The model conceptualises collective action as a form of *approach coping* (Lazarus, 1991, 2001), meaning a form of action designed to alter one's circumstances. In this account, collective action is based on a process in which *primary appraisals* (notably perceptions of self-relevance of the collective action issue) determine whether one needs to cope in the first place; and *secondary appraisals* (such as perceptions of the self's coping potential) determine the most appropriate coping strategy. The model is psychologically dynamic because it makes explicit predictions regarding crucial feedback loops (e.g. from coping back to cognitive *re*appraisal). For instance, it predicts that undertaking collective action can lead to a change in the perceived relevance of identity as well as in perceptions of group efficacy. The perception of others' willingness to engage in collective action, which arises from participation itself, suggests stronger mobilisation resources that can therefore increase individuals' belief in group efficacy (Klandermans, 1997; Van Zomeren *et al.*, 2012). In other words, undertaking collective action can empower individuals through affecting their appraisal of the group's coping potential.

These models of collective action all employ key concepts from the social identity approach (Tajfel & Turner, 1979; Turner, Hogg, Oakes, Reicher & Wetherell, 1987). The same is true of the elaborated social identity model (ESIM; Drury & Reicher, 2000; Reicher, 1996a, 1996b; Stott & Reicher, 1998), which adds details of the *chronological* processes of change to the *psychological* processes described in the dynamic dual pathway model (Van Zomeren *et al.*, 2012). The social identity origins and similarity of scope of these models means that there is considerable overlap between them. However, there are two reasons for focusing on the ESIM for a fuller discussion of empowerment as the intersection of identity and power in collective action.

The first reason is that while most accounts of collective action refer just to the antecedents and a few refer also to the consequences, the ESIM does both of these things, as well as referring to what people actually *do* in that collective action. This is because the ESIM is an account of *crowd behaviour*. While not all forms of collective action involve crowds, the crowd is nevertheless an important form of collective action both politically—social change is often visible through the crowd (Ackerman & Kruegler, 1994)—and theoretically—the crowd is a privileged arena for the understanding of a range of phenomena in social science (Reicher, 2011). The second reason for focusing on the ESIM is that, in contrast to the other models, the empirical and theoretical work surrounding it has explicitly set out to examine empowerment as such, rather than just efficacy.

A dynamic intergroup account of empowerment in collective action

In this part of the chapter, we will first outline the ESIM and then develop its key claims about the process of empowerment in collective action. The ESIM developed from the observation by Reicher and colleagues of a common pattern across a variety of crowd events, including a student protest (Reicher, 1996b), a mass demonstration against local taxation which became a riot (Stott & Reicher, 1998), and cases of football crowd "disorder" (Stott, Hutchison & Drury, 2001). In essence, the pattern was as follows. Events would begin with a relatively heterogeneous crowd, the majority of which defined themselves as moderates, and a minority who were more radical and sought conflict. However, crowd members were *perceived* as homogeneous and dangerous by the authorities (notably the police) and *treated* as such—that is, they were denied the ability to act in a way they saw as legitimate. This then led to a radicalisation among moderate crowd members who joined with the radicals in challenging the police. It also changed their views about the authorities and indeed their own identity in relation to the authorities.

In explicating this pattern, the ESIM involves three elements: *concepts, conditions* and *dynamics* (Drury & Reicher, 2009). First, in terms of *concepts*, social identity is seen as the way in which people understand how they are positioned relative to others, along with the forms of action that make sense from that position; and context is understood as the identity-based action of those forces external to actors which enable or constrain their action (Reicher, 1996a). This point can be illustrated by studies of the 1990 London poll tax riot (Stott & Drury, 1999, 2000; Stott & Reicher, 1998). Here, the context for protesters was the actions of the police—who formed cordons, initiated baton charges and so on. However, such actions were at the same time the expression of the police's identity-based understanding of their relationship to the protesters—as a dangerous and hostile crowd.

Second, the ESIM suggests that the *conditions* necessary for the emergence and development of crowd conflict are two-fold. The first condition is an *asymmetry of categorical representations* between crowd participants and an outgroup such as the police. For example, during the poll tax riot, where crowd members understood their behaviour of sitting down in the road as "legal and legitimate protest", police defined it as a "threat to public order"; and where police understood their own action as a defensive response to a situation of growing threat from the crowd, the crowd understood the police action as unprovoked and "heavy handed". The second condition is *an asymmetry of power* such that the (police) outgroup is able to impose its definition of legitimate practice on the ingroup of crowd participants— for example, through having the technology, organisation and strength in numbers to form cordons, coordinate baton charges and thereby constrain the physical movement of the crowd.

Third, there is a *dynamic*. Police practices which impose a common fate on all crowd members can transform a relatively heterogeneous crowd into a homogeneous one. Moreover, to the extent that this police action is seen as not only *indiscriminate* (i.e. perceived as affecting everyone) but also *illegitimate* (e.g. denying the right to protest and using offensive tactics to disperse the crowd) then the entire crowd will unite around a sense of opposition to the police.

The dynamic therefore entails a social *re*positioning through which a number of dimensions of psychological change occur (Drury & Reicher, 2000; Reicher & Drury, 2011). First, there is change in the *content* of identity ("who we are"). Those who initially saw themselves as moderates change their understanding of their relationship with the authorities and hence there is change in their identity; being positioned as radicals, they come to understand themselves as radical. Second, if "who we are" changes, there may be corresponding change in the definition of *legitimate group aims* and the criteria for success (e.g. from "protesting peacefully against the poll tax" to "overcoming the police"). Third, there are changes in the *boundaries* of the collective self—i.e. in who counts as ingroup and who counts as outgroup. Fourth, where these boundaries become more inclusive, and where the ingroup-outgroup distinction is highly salient, there are feelings of consensus and hence expectations of mutual support; this *empowers* crowd members to express their radical beliefs and confront the outgroup. These four dimensions of identity change are derived from the original statements of social identity theory (Tajfel & Turner, 1979) and self-categorisation theory (Turner *et al.*, 1987). While the dimensions are clearly interlinked, most of the research carried out, and the focus here, is on the dimension of empowerment. This research falls into two areas: the role of perceived support and the process of collective self-objectification.

Perceived support for group-normative action

The basis for empowerment in collective action is participants' understanding that there is unity, which is a function of people defining themselves as members of the same group (common self-categorisation) rather than as individuals. All else being equal, the more people there are who define themselves in the same way, the greater the sense of unity.

There are a number of possible antecedents of common self-categorisation (Turner *et al.*, 1987). However, in many of the crowd studies, it was found that common self-categorisation and hence unity was a function of common fate; as specified in the ESIM, indiscriminate outgroup action caused individuals and previously separate subgroups to see themselves as part of a single crowd and hence as "the same people". For example, a study of a demonstration at a local council meeting showed that before the event participants were initially part of small, exclusive groups of friends, but they came together as a united force through their shared experience of illegitimate exclusion from the council meeting (Drury & Reicher, 1999). The new sense of crowd unity was evident in participants' behaviour, as they oriented together, focusing on the same targets, sang and chanted together, and pushed in unison, rather than remaining in small subgroups. However, participants also explicitly reported *feeling* more togetherness with the crowd as a whole. Their subsequent empowerment was evident in both the observed and self-reported increases in the boldness of their actions aimed at disrupting the meeting.

The reason that being part of a wider social group in which there is agreement about who "we" are and what "we" should do is a component of empowerment is that it is the basis of expectations of support for group-normative action. If there is a common self-categorisation and hence a sense of unity, then participants know they will be backed up if they act; they feel more able to act as they know that others are or will be acting in the same way, and they also feel that others won't criticise or stop them and will come to their aid if those they oppose attack them.

This is a *cognitive* process—in the sense that I *know* that I will be supported if I perceive: (a) that others self-categorise in the same way as me; and (b) that these others see me as a group member (meta-perception; Neville & Reicher, 2011). It is also "cognitive" in the sense that the perception of support need not map exactly onto reality to provide encouragement.

However, the process also has an important *strategic* dimension, in two senses. The first sense in which the process is strategic is the fact that shared identification allows effective coordination of action. If we know that others are relatively similar to us on a relevant dimension, there is a basis for discussion about the right thing to do for us as a group, in terms of our values and aims in relation to the enemy or target (Klein, Spears, & Reicher, 2007; Reicher & Levine, 1994). The second sense in which the process has a strategic dimension is evident in attempts at mobilisation: we seek to gain social support for our cause by construing the ingroup category inclusively (Reicher & Hopkins, 2001). The strategic dimension to empowerment is examined in more detail below ("Dealing with defeat").

Collective self-objectification

When we believe we have collective support for our aims, what do we do? When our fellows are around us, and when we are not outnumbered or otherwise prevented from overcoming our foes, we try to *enact* those aims. More specifically, for subordinate groups in struggle—and most crowds in struggle are from subordinate groups—the aim is to enact a group value which is normally impossible to enact for individuals acting alone. Since the subordinate group's identity is defined in opposition to the powerful other and the (illegitimate) world they represent, acting tangibly upon the world in a way that embodies the subordinate group's definition of legitimate practice means *changing* the world. This enactment itself can be empowering and is a positive emotional experience. In the ESIM, we use the term *collective self-objectification* (CSO)[1] to refer to this joyful self-transforming process whereby participants perceive their collective action to realise (objectify, make concrete) their social identity over and against the power of dominant outgroups (Drury & Reicher, 2005).

What are the conditions for this process? Not all collective action participation empowers. There are many cases of collective action that are not empowering; and some collective actions actually leave participants feeling disempowered (Drury *et al.*, 2005). The outcome or effect of the action as successful seems to matter (Becker, Tausch, & Wagner, 2011); it's not just the taking part. However, this raises the question of what constitutes "success" psychologically. Just as the particular form of crowd action—the targets, contours and limits—reflects a particular definition of identity (Reicher, 1984), so the definition of success is also a function of identity definition. That is, in collective action, the experience of "success" is a matter of actions that serve to create a world which is organised on the basis of ingroup beliefs, values and understandings, over and against the power of the outgroup. Thus, one can only determine what is a success or a failure—and hence know what does or does not lead to experiences of empowerment—by understanding the significance of outcomes in relation to the specific understandings associated with a given social identity. Indeed, what might look like failure to outsiders may constitute a success from an ingroup perspective.

Based on Marx's concept of labour (1932/1975) as self-producing activity,[2] we argue that collective action can empower to the extent to which it expresses the collective definition of how the world should be, over and against that of dominant forces. Collective action empowers participants when it turns a *subjective* imperative into an *objective* feature of the world. In realising the collective's (hitherto subordinate) identity, such an action-impact thereby *evidences* to participants, tangibly, through what they see as the transformed context, that their collective self is indeed an active and powerful subject. In short, collective self-objectification refers to the process whereby self-transformed social context tells us about our own collective agency. Powerlessness is a negative experience (Reicher & Haslam, this volume; Sindic, this volume), and the reversal of this through empowerment and collective self-objectification is therefore experienced positively (Drury *et al.*, 2005).

Central to the concept of collective self-objectification are claims about the critical role of identity-*congruence* in collective action. These claims can be organised into (at least) four areas: the empowering effects of identity-congruence in collective action-impacts; the disempowering effects of action-impacts antithetical to the collective identity; changing definitions of success; and the endurance of feelings of empowerment.

The identity-congruence of collective action-impact empowers

Collective action can be empowering through impact that is *immediate to the action* or through impact that is *mediated*. Forms of mass direct action fit the first description, as when an animal rights crowd closes down a factory farm for the day through force of numbers. "Mediated" impact is where the mobilisation has such effects in later days or even months—such as when the factory farm eventually closes, and this closure is perceived as an effect of the animal rights campaign.

Depending on their definition of "politics", participants might understand the mobilisation itself as a successful impact (Hornsey *et al.*, 2006). Put differently, means can also be experienced as ends in themselves. Thus the aim may be to build the movement. This can be achieved through a display (to one's own group and to others outside the group) of the support for, and power of, the group—as measured by the perceived relative size, coherence, and organisation of the crowd on the streets. In such cases, the demonstration itself—the march and rally, the banners, flags and chants, and the flooding of the streets with "our people"—represents a tangible imposition of our identity on the world. It therefore has empowering effects over and above the effects of expectations of mutual support within the crowd. Thus, interviews with activists show that some feel uplifted and encouraged by big demonstrations, and may regard them as a result or achievement in their own right (Drury *et al.*, 2005; Evripidou & Drury, 2013).

Action-impacts antithetical to our identity disempower us

By the same principle that successful collective action provides evidence that our group is powerful, successful *out*group action against us can provide counter-evidence to this self-perception. Defeats, or collective actions in which the identities of others antithetical to us are instantiated and hence where there is re-imposition of outgroup values, are experienced as *dis*empowering. Again, there are different forms of such antagonistic identity instantiation, broadly corresponding to the opposite of the empowering congruent action-impacts described above.

First, there are those events where the preconditions for collective self-objectification are insufficient. An example is a May Day demonstration march against austerity held in Greece in 2012 where numbers and organisation were both regarded as poor, and hence where some participants felt disempowered by their own event (Evripidou & Drury, 2013)—particularly those participants who defined their political practice in terms of this kind of large-scale movement-building.

Second, there are cases where exemplars of the dominant group actively defeat the collective during the mobilisation itself and impose themselves. An example would be the case of the crowd that tried to prevent the removal of a tree in an anti-roads campaign, but who were forcefully swept aside by police so that the tree could then be felled (Drury & Reicher, 2000, 2005).

Third, because there may be different definitions of appropriate conduct and political aims, it is possible that participation in the same collective action may be experienced as empowering by some participants but disempowering by others. At a mobilisation against the UK governing party's annual conference, both socialists and direct-action anarchists assembled in the same space. Police pre-emptively arrested some of the anarchists, who were then reduced to "marching from A to B" with the socialists instead of actively disrupting the conference as they had hoped. The socialists described the event as empowering and self-affirming, due to the numbers and determination of the crowd. The anarchists described it as disempowering and demoralising; over and above the police intervention itself, the consequent lack of support for their aims, the pouring rain and the other factors which contributed to their miserable experience, what depressed them was the form of the mobilisation itself, which they regarded as politically alien (Drury *et al.*, 2005).

The role of identity-congruence in empowerment and disempowerment has also been demonstrated experimentally. In one study, the example of the Greek May Day demonstration described above was used in a vignette (Evripidou & Drury, forthcoming, Study 2). In one condition the event was presented as successful, whereas in the other condition it was presented as unsuccessful. The basic finding, that participants reported more collective joy and group efficacy for the successful than the unsuccessful version of events, was moderated by identification with the Greek anti-austerity movement; low identifiers were indifferent to the outcomes, whereas high identifiers felt joyful and efficacious in response to the successful mobilisation (when congruence can be presumed to be high), but unhappy and powerless in relation to the unsuccessful mobilisation (when congruence can be presumed to be low). Moreover, subjective reports of congruence were found to mediate these effects of congruent versus incongruent scenarios.

However, there was a possible confound in this study. We didn't simply vary the outcome of the event (building vs. not building the movement); we also described the collective activity itself differently for each condition (a well-organised vs. a poorly organised demonstration). Therefore, in a second study we kept the form of the collective activity constant and just manipulated the identity-congruence of outcome. We also improved on the design by apparently getting the participants to undertake collective action, rather than using a vignette. In this experiment (Drury, Choudhury, Van Zomeren & Sumner, 2012, Study 3), we first imposed two plausible identities on Sussex University students by telling one half of the sample that previous research had found that Sussex students rated value for money above other issues when it came to the campus shops, and telling the other half that Sussex students rate "fair trade" values most highly. We then asked all participants to take part in a survey that would supposedly inform the students' union in making a decision about their policy for the campus shops in the coming year. Two weeks later, participants were first given (false) feedback on their own responses on the survey, to reaffirm which group they were in (value for money or fair trade). Then, half of each group were told that the survey had found in favour of their group's view, while the other half of each group were told that the survey had found in favour of the opposite view. Thus all participants had taken part in the same collective decision-making mechanism (the survey), but for half of them the outcome of their action was identity-congruent while for the other half it was identity-incongruent. As expected, participants in the congruent conditions reported greater positive emotion than in the incongruent conditions, and this was the case irrespective of identity-content (fair trade or value for money). Subjective perceptions of success were found to mediate this effect of congruence on positive emotion. In line with predictions, there was an indirect effect of congruence condition on efficacy through perceptions of success: congruence condition was associated with success and the latter with efficacy.

Definitions of success can change in and through collective action

Definitions of success for a collective mobilisation can vary not only "horizontally" (when there are different subgroups in the same mobilisation) but also chronologically. In some events, there is evidence of a process whereby participants come to *redefine* aims and definitions of success over time. One example is the case of animal rights activists trying to close down an animal laboratory who had to overcome a police presence to do so; the aim of the action then became that of defeating the police; and when the group succeeded this was a cause of joy and enhanced confidence in the group, irrespective of the direct effects on the animal laboratory (Drury et al., 2005). Means were transformed into ends.

In that particular example, the group already had particular ideas about the role of the police in society and the legitimacy of conflict with them. However, other transformations within collective action entail a more profound and enduring psychological change in relations with other groups and hence in the content of identity itself. For example, in an anti-roads campaign, the original aim of some of the campaigners was simply stopping construction taking place in their local area. Later, the aim became to expose the illegitimacy of the authorities; protestors saw a set-piece eviction as a great success due to the widespread negative publicity given to police dragging protestors from precarious perches on the roofs of the condemned buildings (Drury & Reicher, 2000). Linked to that, the aim extended from the local campaign to opposing the national roads programme and injustice more broadly (Drury, Reicher & Stott, 2003). For this group, *what it meant to be an anti-roads campaign participant* changed; and indeed many participants changed towards seeing themselves as "activists" (Drury & Reicher, 2000).

As outlined above, the ESIM specifies the conditions and dynamics for such identity transformations to occur. According to the ESIM, it is a self-changed context, in which one is now positioned differently in relation to others, that changes self. This point is derived from the tenet of self-categorisation theory, that (variable) social context defines identity (Turner et al., 1987). Analysis of this process in crowd settings elucidates the dynamic and novel potential of identity variability. Thus, for example, for those who changed from saving the local green to opposing the police, it was their own action in coming together as "peaceful protesters" that (inadvertently) changed the context through which they defined themselves. Their participation in the mobilisation took place in an intergroup context, where the police had a different understanding of legitimate conduct than the crowd *and* had the power to act upon this understanding. The police response (violent eviction) served to change the comparative context from "locals, activists vs. road-builders" to "campaigners vs. police" (Reicher & Drury, 2011).

Extent of endurance of empowerment

There are a number of possible conditions for a sense of empowerment to endure after the event that gave rise to it and to feed into future actions. One is whether the support evident in the collective action is perceived as representative of a wider movement, both horizontally and chronologically (Drury & Reicher, 1999). Thus the perception at the time that there is a high level of unity, and that others are determined, predicts reports of subsequent involvement (Drury *et al.*, 2003, 2005).

The endurance of feelings of empowerment can also be explained by the concept of collective self-objectification. That is, the endurance of an empowered collective self reflects the extent to which context, changed tangibly by collective action to reflect the group's values, is itself perceived to endure. Again, this point is in line with the tenet of self-categorisation theory that just as variability in self-categorisation is a function of variability of context, so the persistence of particular self-stereotypes reflects situations in which the context is relatively stable (Oakes, Haslam & Turner, 1994).

Psychosocial consequences of collective empowerment

If collective action can produce feelings of empowerment as an outcome, then the psychological importance of subjective power extends beyond what happens within a single crowd event. Such feelings can have a number of psychosocial consequences subsequently.

First, feelings of empowerment may affect participants' motivation for involvement in subsequent collective action. Being inspired by collective action, and having more confidence in the movement and in themselves as movement actors, can lead to more participation in the future. For instance, interviews with thirty-seven activists about empowering actions found that they referred to "confidence" (in the collective and personally), "pride", "enthusiasm", "joy", "feeling good" and being "on a high" (Drury *et al.*, 2005). Twenty-one stated that their involvement increased due to their positive emotional experiences (and eight of these cited more than one case of increased involvement).

This example suggests that it is not only emotions previously regarded as "negative" (in particular anger) that predict collective action (Van Zomeren, Spears *et al.*, 2004; Van Zomeren *et al.*, 2012); certain positive emotions can also drive people to act. However, since empowerment consists of a variety of affective and cognitive components, what needs to be established is whether it is the empowerment experience as a whole or just certain of its components, perhaps in a particular sequence, that makes the difference. Thus, it could be that overcoming a powerful other is a positive emotional experience, but it is the *knowledge* of that overcoming rather than the emotion itself that leads to further collective action. The motivational role of one particular positive emotion (pride) following a successful collective action was examined in a two-stage survey of student protests against tuition fees by Tausch and Becker (2013). This study found that pride at success in the first phase exerted a significant indirect effect on action intentions via increased efficacy perceptions, over and above baseline efficacy and action intentions.

As a second kind of psychosocial consequence, the empowerment that arises from collective action may affect people's personal lives outside the protest event. Research on experiences in the women's movement shows that campaigning can lead to greater personal self-confidence (Agronick & Duncan, 1998; Harford & Hopkins, 1984). Similarly, there is a fascinating literature on women's experiences of the 1984–5 UK miners' strike, which shows how some of them developed a new confidence in themselves as women that then influenced their choices in terms of education, career and relationships (e.g. Salt & Layzell, 1985). Much of this change was due to their taking roles involving responsibility for the campaign, while some other types of change, such as politicisation, were clearly linked to picket-line conflicts with police.

A third possible psychosocial consequence of empowerment relates to mental and physical health. Collective action can be physically demanding for participants. Participation in a demonstration march can lower the immune system; there may be tiredness, lack of food or water, stress and worry from police coercion and the threat of arrest, and the greater likelihood of injury. Furthermore, over the long term, activists often suffer burnout. Yet research has also found that successfully fighting back benefits mood, self-reported wellbeing and other indicators (Barreto, 2012; Evripidou & Drury, 2013; Foster, 2013), that activists lead more fulfilled lives compared to non-activists (Klar & Kasser, 2009), and that activists also have greater happiness and fewer personal worries later in life (Boehnke & Wong, 2011).

Since activists usually participate collectively, these instances suggest that (empowering) collective action can be good for you. Though individual action may also be beneficial, there seems to be something qualitatively distinct about the wellbeing benefits of collective action. First, to the extent that we identify with the collective, we can benefit from our group's successes, even if we are not involved. Second, the practice or self-objectification of the lone individual is inherently limited. As an individual you can complain about injustice, but as a group you can change it. It may be that the bigger the identity-congruent action-impact, the greater the sense of agency and joy; and hence perhaps the positive effects of action are greater for collectives than for individuals. These arguments are in line with, but also extend, the recent work on "the social cure", showing that membership of psychological groups can enhance wellbeing in a number of ways (Jetten, Haslam & Haslam, 2012).

Dealing with defeat

A final important question about empowerment in collective action arises from the above discussion, especially in the present economic and political context. The question concerns how participants (particularly activists) cope with defeat (Milesi & Catellani, 2011). If defeat is disempowering, how do activists deal with those negative feelings and beliefs? In the context of working class retreat and austerity, when collective actions end in disappointment, how is hope still possible (Cohen-Chen, Halperin, Saguy & Van Zomeren, 2013)? Many activists do continue despite the set-backs. Given what we have shown about the important motivating effects of empowerment, this activist resilience is clearly something that requires explanation. The question therefore is: under what conditions do collective actors continue following a failure to objectify the collective self?

Addressing this important question, however, is also an opportunity to foreground a key point in the account of collective self-objectification that has largely been only implicit until now. This point is that all the different dimensions of impact discussed above are potentially contestable. That is, there is a vital *strategic* dimension to the process, at every stage. Consider the following questions: what kinds of evidence do participants select to determine whether the action is successful or unsuccessful? Just how important do participants regard the methods of the campaign—can they be construed as achievements in themselves? What do people define as the group aims in this context? More generally, do participants agree that the action-impact is necessarily (in)congruent with the group identity? More generally still, what is the group identity anyway? The underlying point here is that, while the world is structured by groups (Oakes *et al.*, 1994; Turner *et al.*, 1987), the identity-contents and boundaries of those groups can be reconstrued— something which is particularly evident in the political realm (Reicher & Hopkins, 2001). Thus, one thing that would-be leaders of movements try to do is to define goals and hence the scope of collective self-objectification such that the actions of the group are understood as both successful and identity-relevant (Drury & Reicher, 2009). The leader is not just an identity-entrepreneur but an identity-engineer, insofar as the structures and social realities created by a leader must be *seen as* objectifications of the collective identity (Haslam, Reicher & Platow, 2011). Thus, not only is the construal of categories key to mobilisation (Reicher & Hopkins, 2001), it is also crucial to dealing with defeat. Here we briefly examine two of the crucial conditions determining the scope for dealing with defeat through construal: *affordances of context* and *identity resources*.

Affordances of context

We have seen that an important reason why material victories feel good and are inspiring is precisely because of their tangible nature. The fact that the world is now perceptibly different, that it has actually changed in line with our values and through our action, is the objective evidence of our collective agency. The objective effects of our action are the basis of beliefs about ourselves. However, by the same token, this objectivity sets a constraint on what can be claimed.

Thus, strategic arguments that an outcome is a "moral victory" may not always achieve their intended effects. For example, Arthur Scargill, leader of the UK miners' union, claimed a moral victory over the government when the miners were forced back to work having failed to prevent any of the pit closures they were striking against. The argument may have conferred legitimacy and "the moral high ground", but it did not feel good to the miners or their supporters. It did not *feel* like a victory, and it did not make the end of the strike empowering.

The idea that "material" victories are more immediately empowering than "moral" ones was tested in an experiment. In a vignette study, two outcomes for the Occupy campaign in St Paul's, London were presented (Drury et al., 2012, Study 3). In the first, the Occupiers managed to continue their occupation of the area next to St Paul's Cathedral in the City of London, which a spokesman characterised as a "material victory"; in the second scenario, they were brutally evicted by police, which a spokesman said was a "moral victory" because it showed the world the illegitimacy of those they were fighting against. Participants reported greater joy and efficacy in the "material victory" condition, with joy moderated by identification (low identifiers were unaffected by the manipulation). In line with collective self-objectification, the most joyful people were those in the congruent ("material victory") condition who were strong believers that eviction was incongruent with group aims.

In the field study on which this vignette was based, the claim that the violent, distressing eviction and demolition by the police of the chestnut tree symbolic of the campaign was a "moral victory" was accepted intellectually, but the overriding emotions among participants were grief and despair, not joy (Drury & Reicher, 2005). There was no evidence of a positive effect on group efficacy. Yet, importantly, the "moral" aspect of what happened was the basis of subsequent discussions around the aims and legitimacy of campaign action, which in turn served to broaden the base of the campaign and so eventually increased group power (an example of mediated impact). The illegitimate eviction enhanced the participants' sense both that they were right and, eventually, that they were part of a wider movement against forms of injustice. A key point here, however, is that the radicals' arguments about the wider (political) significance of the campaign only became persuasive when, through the reconfigured relationship with the police, these radicals became positioned as fellow ingroup members rather than "outsiders" (Drury et al., 2003). In short, the context constrained interpretations of the campaign.

Identity resources

The re-framing of negative events, as in the last example, may be an attempt to resolve the cognitive dissonance or other aversion felt in defeat (Blackwood & Louis, 2012; Einwohner, 2002). Whether or not there is such a cognitive need for consistency, the point we want to make is that it is much easier to argue that an event has positive qualities when there are the discursive resources available to make such an argument. Thus a re-evaluation of the meaning of actions may be easier for some groups than for others, due to their access to such resources. For instance, one interview study found that experienced activists have certain identity-based discursive strategies available to them that could be used to counter the de-motivating effects of (apparent) failure (Drury et al., 2005). These strategies included being able to place experiences in a wider context (e.g. "just one battle within a long-term war"), activists reminding themselves of successful struggles ("some you win, some you lose"), or characterising particular defeats as "learning experiences" from which they could develop. Each of these strategies was linked to the activists' knowledge of the history of their campaign.

Being an experienced activist means not only having certain knowledge and arguments, but also being part of a milieu and hence being able to access discursive resources from others (i.e. in meetings, groups, social centres, publications etc.). These resources would not be easily accessible to political neophytes and those not socialised into the activist culture. Therefore, while experienced activists might feel philosophical after a set-back, the neophyte might instead feel defeated and demoralised (Drury *et al.*, 2005). Both identity-based interpretative strategies and the social relations with the group giving support to such interpretations can therefore be understood as forms by which shared identity operates as a resource to provide continued motivation.

These ideas were examined in the context of the G8 protests at Gleneagles in 2005 (Barr & Drury, 2009). While those with less political experience found the protests disappointing and uninspiring, the more seasoned activists (re-)interpreted potentially disempowering events positively. An example was the re-evaluation of the role of the protest campsite, which came to be seen by activists as the central achievement instead of just a basis for the direct action.

Conclusion

Subjective power is a crucial dimension of collective action and is recognised in different ways by a variety of theoretical perspectives. This is not to say that an account of empowerment is a complete account of the social psychology of collective action itself. (For recent review articles covering other relevant factors in collective action, see Drury, Reicher & Stott, 2012, Thomas *et al.*, 2012, and Van Zomeren *et al.*, 2012.) However, while a consideration of subjective power may not be sufficient in understanding the nature of collective action, we suggest that it is necessary for two reasons.

The first reason is that subjective power is an essential dimension of identity itself. This has been an underlying argument throughout this chapter. To be a subject—a self—entails some sense of one's ability to put one's intentions into practice. Put differently, identity is in part a definition of possible action (Reicher & Drury, 2011). In line with the literature, we have argued in this chapter that collective action is based on shared social identity. This means that collective action requires not only a definition of who "we" are but also an understanding of what "we" can do.

The second reason that subjective power is necessary to the understanding of collective action should also be clear from what we have argued in this chapter. Empowerment—that positive social psychological transformation that takes place for members of subordinated groups who overturn existing relations of dominance (Drury & Reicher, 2009)—can be an exhilarating, life-transforming and emotional experience for collective actors. This is evident in historical examples; and it is what collective actors talk about passionately when they are surveyed and interviewed about their participation. Empowerment is the link between the phenomenological and the political in the collective action process. It matters to collective actors involved in trying to create social change, and therefore it should matter to those of us who study collective action.

If subjective power is necessary to the understanding of collective action, it is also the case that collective action helps us understand empowerment. In this chapter we have shown that the study of collective action, particularly in the form of crowd events, can provide new insights about the intersection between power and identity. Crowd events have features that make them different from other group contexts or collective actions: they are unstructured, often less predictable and liable to change. It is these qualities, among others, that make crowd events especially useful for the study of identity and power. Specifically, crowds provide their members with the means to enact otherwise subordinate identities. As we have described, when people share an identity in a crowd, they perceive support for ingroup-normative actions, and hence they are able to act and to coordinate. Their collective actions are attempts to make the values shared in the crowd an objective, tangible reality. In successful collective action, a world in which the identity is subordinate to that of other groups is transformed into one in which that identity has recognition, agency and power. Hence, through identity enactment, crowds can alter the social relations on which those identities are based. This is what we meant by saying that empowerment can operate as both "input" and "output" in collective action. This chapter has indicated some of the processes, both psychological and chronological, through which this dynamic operates.

Notes

1   This same concept has been referred to in some places as "collective self-realization" (e.g., Reicher & Haslam, 2010). Reicher (2012) argues that collective self-objectification refers to enactment that involves overcoming another group, whereas collective self-realization does not, hence the latter is a more appropriate term for collective enactment in such events as religious ceremonies. Pehrson, Stevenson, Muldoon and Reicher (2013) add that the concept of collective self-objectification can also be usefully applied to non-conflictual crowd events, such as parades, where there are dominant and subordinate groups.

2   "if one was to single out the most fundamental idea in *The German Ideology*, which is discovered in the 1844 Manuscripts and is assumed by Capital, it would be that man [sic] produces himself through labour … There is … a dialectically conceived relation between his nature as determined by the conditions of his life, and the practical transformation of those conditions. The link between the two is labour—in the broadest sense." (Arthur, 1970, p. 21; emphasis in original). The notion of alienated labour—labour which, since it is for an alien subject (capital), denies our subjectivity, interests and being—is therefore based on the notion of free labour, i.e. that which affirms us as human subjects. In each case, our own activity makes our subjectivity.

References

Ackerman, P. & Kruegler, C. (1994) *Strategic nonviolent conflict: The dynamics of people power in the twentieth century.* Westport, CT: Praeger.

Agronick, G. & Duncan, L. (1998) Personality and social change: Individual differences, life path, and importance attributed to the Women's Movement. *Journal of Personality and Social Psychology,* 74, 1545–1555.

Anonymous (1968) *Paris: May 1968.* London: Solidarity.

Arthur, C.J. (1970) Editor's introduction. In C.J. Arthur (Ed.) K. Marx & F. Engels *The German Ideology.* London: Lawrence & Wishart.

Bandura, A. (1997) *Self-efficacy: The exercise of control.* New York: Freeman.

Barr, D. & Drury, J. (2009) Activist identity as a motivational resource: Dynamics of (dis) empowerment at the G8 direct actions, Gleneagles, 2005. *Social Movement Studies,* 8, 243–260.

Barreto, M. (2012, February) *The costs and benefits of confronting prejudice.* Seminar given at the School of Psychology Colloquium, University of Sussex, UK.

Becker, J.C. (2012) Virtual special issue on theory and research on collective action in the European Journal of Social Psychology. *European Journal of Social Psychology,* 42, 19–23.

Becker, J.C., Tausch, N. & Wagner, U. (2011) Emotional consequences of collective action participation: Differentiating self-directed from outgroup-directed emotions. *Personality and Social Psychology Bulletin,* 37, 1587–1598.

Blackwood, L.M. & Louis, W.R. (2012) If it matters for the group then it matters to me: Collective action outcomes for seasoned activists. *British Journal of Social Psychology,* 51, 72–92.

Boehnke, K. & Wong, B. (2011) Adolescent political activism and long-term happiness: A 21-year longitudinal study on the development of micro- and macrosocial worries. *Personality and Social Psychology Bulletin,* 37, 435–447.

Boesel, D., Goldberg, L.C. & Marx, G.T. (1971) Rebellion in Plainfield. In D. Boesel & P.H. Rossi (Eds), *Cities under siege: An anatomy of the ghetto riots, 1964–1968* (pp. 67–83). New York: Basic Books.

Britt, L. & Heise, D. (2000) From shame to pride in identity politics. In S. Stryker, T.J. Owens & R.W. White (Eds), *Self, identity and social movements* (pp. 252–268). Minneapolis: University of Minnesota Press.

Cohen-Chen, S., Halperin, E., Tamar Saguy, T. & Van Zomeren, M. (2013) Beliefs about the malleability of immoral groups facilitate collective action. *Social Psychological and Personality Science.* Advance online publication. doi: 10.1177/1948550613491292.

Drury, J., Choudhury, S., Van Zomeren, M. & Sumner, H. (2012, August) *Explaining why undertaking collective action can empower participants: Some laboratory paradigms.* Paper presented at the British Psychological Society Social Psychology Section Annual Conference, St Andrews, UK.

Drury, J., Cocking, C., Beale, J., Hanson, C. & Rapley, F. (2005) The phenomenology of empowerment in collective action. *British Journal of Social Psychology,* 44, 309–328.

Drury, J. & Reicher, S. (1999) The intergroup dynamics of collective empowerment: Substantiating the social identity model. *Group Processes and Intergroup Relations,* 2, 381–402.

——(2000) Collective action and psychological change: The emergence of new social identities. *British Journal of Social Psychology,* 39, 579–604.

——(2005) Explaining enduring empowerment: A comparative study of collective action and psychological outcomes. *European Journal of Social Psychology*, 35, 35–58.

——(2009) Collective psychological empowerment as a model of social change: Researching crowds and power. *Journal of Social Issues*, 65, 707–725.

Drury, J., Reicher, S. & Stott, C. (2003) Transforming the boundaries of collective identity: From the 'local' anti-road campaign to 'global' resistance? *Social Movement Studies*, 2, 191–212.

Drury, J., Reicher, S. & Stott, C. (2012) The psychology of collective action: Crowds and change. In B. Wagoner, E. Jensen & J. Oldmeadow (Eds), *Culture and Social Change: Transforming society through the power of ideas* (pp. 19–38). Charlotte, NC: Information Age Publishing.

Einwohner, R.L. (2002) Motivational framing and efficacy maintenance: Animal rights activists' use of four fortifying strategies. *The Sociological Quarterly*, 43, 509–526.

Evripidou, A. & Drury, J. (forthcoming) Identity-congruent collective action empowers but identity-incongruent collective action disempowers: Activists and (dis)organization on a movement-building demonstration. Manuscript in preparation.

——(2013) This is the time of tension: Collective action and subjective power in the Greek anti-austerity movement. *Contention: The Multidisciplinary Journal of Social Protest*, 1, 31–51.

Foster, M. (2013) Everyday confrontation of discrimination: The well-being costs and benefits to women over time. *International Journal of Psychological Studies*, 5, 135–154.

Gregoire, R. & Perlman, F. (1969) *Worker-student action committees: France May '68*. Detroit: Black and Red.

Harford, B. & Hopkins, S. (Eds) (1984) *Greenham Common: Women at the wire*. London: The Women's Press.

Haslam, S.A., Reicher, S.D. & Platow, M.J. (2011) *The new psychology of leadership*. Hove, UK: Psychology Press.

Hornsey, M.J., Blackwood, L., Louis, W., Fielding, K., Mavor, K., Morton, T., … White, K. M. (2006) Why do people engage in collective action? Revisiting the role of perceived effectiveness. *Journal of Applied Social Psychology*, 36, 1701–1722.

Jetten, J., Haslam, C. & Haslam, S.A. (Eds) (2012) *The social cure: Identity, health, and wellbeing*. Hove, UK: Psychology Press.

Karl, M. (1995) *Women and empowerment: Participation and decision-making*. UN NGLS: Zed Books.

Kelly, C. & Breinlinger, S. (1995) Identity and injustice: Exploring women's participation in collective action. *Journal of Community and Applied Social Psychology*, 5, 41–57.

Klandermans, B. (1997) *The social psychology of protest*. Oxford, UK: Blackwell.

Klar, M. & Kasser, T. (2009) Some benefits of being an activist: Measuring activism and its role in psychological wellbeing. *Political Psychology*, 30, 755–777.

Klein, O., Spears, R. & Reicher, S. (2007) Social identity performance: Extending the strategic side of SIDE. *Personality and Social Psychology Review*, 11, 28–45.

Lazarus, R.S. (1991) *Emotion and adaptation*. New York: Oxford University Press.

——(2001) Relational meaning and discrete emotions. In K.R. Scherer, A. Schorr & T. Johnstone (Eds), *Appraisal processes in emotion* (pp. 37–67). Oxford, UK: Oxford University Press.

Marx, K. (1975) Economic and philosophical manuscripts. In *Early Writings*. Harmondsworth, UK: Penguin. (Trans. G. Benton. Original work published 1932.)

Milesi, P. & Catellani, P. (2011) The day after an electoral defeat: Counterfactuals and collective action. *British Journal of Social Psychology*, 50, 690–706.

Mummendey, A., Kessler, T., Klink, A. & Mielke, R. (1999) Strategies to cope with negative social identity: Predictions by social identity theory and relative deprivation theory. *Journal of Personality and Social Psychology*, 76, 229–245.

Neville, F. & Reicher, S. (2011) The experience of collective participation: Shared identity, relatedness and emotionality, *Contemporary Social Science*, 6, 377–396.

Oakes, P.J., Haslam, S.A. & Turner, J.C. (1994) *Stereotyping and social reality*. Oxford: Blackwell.

Pehrson, S., Stevenson, C., Muldoon, O.T. & Reicher S. (2013) Is everyone Irish on St Patrick's Day? Divergent expectations and experiences of collective self-objectification at a multicultural parade. *British Journal of Social Psychology*. Advance online publication. doi: 10.1111/bjso.12029.

Ratna, J. & Rifkin, S. (2007) Equity, empowerment and choice: From theory to practice in public health. *Journal of Health Psychology*, 12, 517–530.

Reicher, S.D. (1984) The St Pauls' riot: An explanation of the limits of crowd action in terms of a social identity model. *European Journal of Social Psychology*, 14, 1–21.

Reicher, S. (1996a) Social identity and social change: Rethinking the context of social psychology. In W.P. Robinson (Ed.), *Social groups and identities: Developing the legacy of Henri Tajfel* (pp. 317–336). London: Butterworth.

——(1996b) 'The Battle of Westminster': Developing the social identity model of crowd behaviour in order to explain the initiation and development of collective conflict. *European Journal of Social Psychology*, 26, 115–134.

——(2011) Mass action and mundane reality: An argument for putting crowd analysis at the centre of the social sciences. *Contemporary Social Science*, 6, 433–449.

——(2012, June) *The four transformations of collective psychology*. Paper presented at the First International Conference on Social Identity and Health, Exeter, UK.

Reicher, S. & Drury, J. (2011) Collective identity, political participation and the making of the social self. In A. Azzi, X. Chryssochoou, B. Klandermans & B. Simon (Eds), *Identity and participation in culturally diverse societies: A multidisciplinary perspective* (pp. 158–176). Oxford, UK: Wiley-Blackwell.

Reicher, S. & Haslam, S.A. (2010) Beyond help. In S. Stürmer & M. Snyder (Eds), *The psychology of prosocial behavior: Group processes, intergroup relations, and helping* (pp. 289–309). Oxford, UK: Wiley-Blackwell.

Reicher, S. & Hopkins, N. (2001) *Self and nation: Categorization, contestation and mobilization*. London: Sage.

Reicher, S. & Levine, M. (1994) On the consequences of deindividuation manipulations for the strategic communication of self: Identifiability and the presentation of social identity. *European Journal of Social Psychology*, 24, 511–524.

Salt, C. & Layzell, J. (1985) *Here we go! Women's memories of the 1984/85 miners' strike*. London: Co-operative Retail Services.

Simon, B. & Klandermans, B. (2001) Politicized collective identity: A social psychological analysis. *American Psychologist*, 56, 319–331.

Spreitzer, G.M. (1995) Psychological empowerment in the workplace: Dimensions, measurement, and validation. *The Academy of Management Journal*, 38, 1442–1465.

Stott, C. & Drury, J. (1999) The intergroup dynamics of empowerment: A social identity model. In P. Bagguley & J. Hearn (Eds), *Transforming politics: Power and resistance* (pp. 32–45). London: Macmillan.

——(2000) Crowds, context and identity: Dynamic categorization processes in the 'poll tax riot'. *Human Relations*, 53, 247–273.

Stott, C., Hutchison, P. & Drury, J. (2001) 'Hooligans' abroad? Inter-group dynamics, social identity and participation in collective 'disorder' at the 1998 World Cup Finals. *British Journal of Social Psychology*, 40, 359–384.

Stott, C. & Reicher, S. (1998) Crowd action as inter-group process: Introducing the police perspective. *European Journal of Social Psychology*, 28, 509–529.

Sturmer, S. & Simon, B. (2004) Collective action: Towards a dual pathway model. In W. Stroebe & M. Hewstone (Eds), *European review of social psychology* (pp. 59–99). Hove, UK: Psychology Press.

Tajfel, H. & Turner, J.C. (1979) An integrative theory of intergroup relations. In S. Worchel & W.G. Austin (Eds), *Psychology of intergroup relations* (pp. 33–47). Monterey, CA: Brooks-Cole.

Tausch, N. & Becker, J.C. (2013) Emotional reactions to success and failure of collective action as predictors of future action intentions: A longitudinal investigation in the context of student protests in Germany. *British Journal of Social Psychology*, 52, 525–542.

Tausch, N., Becker, J., Spears, R., Christ, O., Saab, R., Singh, P. & Siddiqui, R.N. (2011) Explaining radical group behavior: Developing emotion and efficacy routes to normative and nonnormative collective action. *Journal of Personality and Social Psychology*, 101, 129–148.

Thomas, E.F., McGarty, C. & Mavor, K.I. (2009) Aligning identities, emotions, and beliefs to create commitment to sustainable social and political action. *Personality and Social Psychology Review*, 13, 194–218.

Thomas, E.F., Mavor, K.I. & McGarty, C. (2012) Social identities facilitate and encapsulate action-relevant constructs: A test of the social identity model of collective action. *Group Processes & Intergroup Relations*, 15, 75–88.

Thompson, N. (2008) *Anti-discriminatory practice* (4th ed.). Oxford, UK: Blackwell.

Turner, J.C., Hogg, M.A., Oakes, P.J., Reicher, S.D. & Wetherell, M.S. (1987) *Rediscovering the social group: A self-categorization theory*. Oxford, UK: Blackwell.

Van Zomeren, M., Drury, J. & Van der Staaij, M. (forthcoming) Undertaking collective action increases empowerment. Manuscript submitted for publication.

Van Zomeren, M. & Iyer, A. (Eds) (2009) Special issue on social and psychological dynamics of collective action. *Journal of Social Issues*, 65, 4.

Van Zomeren, M. & Klandermans, B. (Eds) (2011) Special Issue: Innovation in theory and research on collective action and social change. *British Journal of Social Psychology*, 50, 573–791.

Van Zomeren, M., Leach, C.W. & Spears, R. (2012) Protesters as 'passionate economists': A dynamic dual pathway model of approach coping with collective disadvantage. *Personality and Social Psychology Review*, 16, 180–199.

Van Zomeren, M., Postmes, T. & Spears, R. (2008) Toward an integrative social identity model of collective action: A quantitative research synthesis of three socio-psychological perspectives. *Psychological Bulletin*, 134, 504–535.

Van Zomeren, M., Spears, R., Fischer, A.H. & Leach, C.W. (2004) Put your money where your mouth is!: Explaining collective action tendencies through group-based anger and group efficacy. *Journal of Personality and Social Psychology*, 87, 649–664.

World Bank (2011) What is empowerment? Retrieved from World Bank website: http:// web.worldbank.org/V45HD4P100 [Accessed 2 September 2014].

Zimmerman, M.A., Israel, B.A., Schulz, A. & Checkoway, A. (1992) Further explorations in empowerment theory: An empirical analysis of psychological empowerment. *American Journal of Community Psychology*, 20, 707–727.

7

MAY THE FORCE BE WITH YOU

Social identity, power and the perils of powerlessness

Stephen Reicher and S. Alexander Haslam

It is now over a decade since we conducted the BBC Prison Study—a ten-day field investigation that was designed to revisit Zimbardo's classic Stanford Prison Experiment (SPE) by dividing men into prisoners and guards within a simulated prison environment.

The Stanford study is well known for the fact that the guards rapidly became brutal, the prisoners became passive and increasingly disturbed, and overall, behaviour became so extreme that things had to be brought to an end after six days rather than fourteen days as originally scheduled. Delve deeper, however, and it is clear that this narrative is overly simple. Certainly some guards were brutal and some prisoners were passive, but equally, as can be seen from Zimbardo's own video of the study (Zimbardo, 1989), some guards resisted their role and were fair (or even sided with the prisoners) while some prisoners also resisted their subordination even to the very end of the study. Any adequate account or explanation of what happened must look at both conformity and resistance, at domination and rebellion.

Our aim was specifically to address issues of identity, power and resistance in such a context because, we felt, these were missing from Zimbardo's analysis. More generally, we wanted to reopen research and debate into the question of when people succumb to tyranny and when they challenge it. Given the depressingly and continually topical nature of such issues, our hope and our aim was to provoke debate in popular as well as academic domains.

In both respects we can claim some success. The original study was televised as four hour-long documentaries on BBC television (Koppel & Mirsky, 2002) which since have been aired in countries around the world. More particularly, the study has become a core part of the psychology syllabus in the UK and also in other countries such as Denmark and Australia. In addition, our website on the study (www.bbcprisonstudy.org) now attracts over twenty thousand unique visitors each month and has recently registered its millionth visitor.

As concerns our academic impact, we have now published ten articles in refereed international journals. Some of these provide an overview of our findings (Haslam & Reicher, 2004, 2006a, 2012a, b; Reicher & Haslam, 2006a) and others address specific topics such as the bases of human brutality (Haslam & Reicher, 2007a), leadership (Haslam & Reicher, 2007b; Reicher, Haslam & Hopkins, 2005), and well-being (Haslam & Reicher, 2006b; Reicher & Haslam, 2006b). In addition to this, we have written three articles for journals and magazines aimed at a more general audience (Haslam & Reicher, 2003, 2005; Reicher, Haslam & Platow, 2007). Finally we have written four book chapters—or rather five, including this one (Haslam & Reicher, 2007c, 2012c; Reicher & Haslam, 2006c, 2012).

And yet, for all this, we still feel that we have hardly scratched the surface of what we observed during those ten long days back in December 2002. In part this is because of the sheer volume of data. We have continuous video recordings of the entire study from two different cameras (i.e. nearly five hundred hours of footage). We have continuous audio recordings from every single participant and also from ourselves. We have psychometric data taken from every participant on every day. We even have daily cortisol readings derived from saliva swabs which the participants took on each day of the study. There is a room in the depths of the psychology department at Exeter University filled from floor to ceiling with this material.

But our sense that there is still more to say is not related simply to the amount of material that we still have to analyse. It also has to do with the nature of a field study like this, and of what happens when one studies the interactive dynamics of social behaviour over time—notably in terms of predictability and complexity. So, although we made a number of theoretically informed interventions over the course of the study, although we had clear predictions as to what effect they would have, and although, in the main, these predictions were upheld (see Reicher & Haslam, 2006a), that is not to say that the study was without surprises. Moreover, the diverse nature of our data sources, which did not limit us to information concerning constructs that we had decided, a priori, were of relevance, allowed us to observe and analyse phenomena (and interactions between phenomena) which, at the start, had not even occurred to us to be of interest. To borrow from Donald Rumsfeld, unknown unknowns became known unknowns, and sometimes even known knowns. Furthermore, to extend the point, it can be argued that one of the most elusive and most important goals of science must be to bring the things we didn't even know we didn't know into the ambit of enquiry—and one of the greatest strengths of rich, extended and immersive field studies like ours is precisely that they allow you to elucidate unknown unknowns.

In effect, ours was a study of two halves. The first half was conducted on our terms—with participants acting in terms of the Prisoner and Guard categories to which they had been randomly assigned, and within the broad framework that those categorical relations envisaged. Participants oriented to the system that we had devised, to a greater or lesser extent they oriented to the categories into which we had assigned them, they responded to the interventions that we had designed (see Reicher & Haslam, 2006a), and overall, they taught us a great deal about the conditions under which people do or do not resist a system of inequality (see Haslam & Reicher, 2012a). Indeed, if anything, what happened demonstrated that we hadn't taken our own counsel concerning the importance of resistance seriously enough—for not only did the prisoners come to resist their subordination, but so too the guards resisted the exercise of domination. As a result, mid-way through the study our system of inequality collapsed in a night of dizzy rebellion.

The second half was then conducted on the participants' terms. They created their own democratic system, their own categories, their own interventions. Gradually, however, that system collapsed. As we looked on with some horror (it seemed to us like watching a slow-motion version of Berthold Brecht's fable on the rise of Hitler, *The Resistable Rise of Arturo Ui*), our participants lost their faith in democracy, some assumed the role of new guards, and at the point that we terminated the study they were on the brink of creating a new regime of inequality. The nature of this regime was clearly characterised in a conversation between the self-appointed cadre of guards:

PB: *I'm going in the box tomorrow and I'm gonna say, "Listen, we want to be the guards".*
PP: *Yeah, good idea.*
PB: *And fucking make them toe the line.*
PP: *Yeah.*
PB: *I mean, on the fucking line.*
PP: *Yeah mate, yeah yeah.*
PB: [As if talking to prisoners] *"No fucking talking while you're eating. Get on with your food and get the fucking hell back to your cell."*
PP: *I agree, I totally agree.*
JE: *Yeah, I'll have some of that* [all three shake hands].

So we are left with a complex story and a seeming paradox: our participants, who chafed under a relatively mild system of inequality at the start, and who showed great determination and ingenuity in challenging it, ultimately created a far more draconian system of inequality for themselves. This leaves us with a plethora of questions about how people were able to challenge inequality, why they wanted to challenge inequality, and when they would accept inequality. Is it possible to offer a parsimonious account of the relevant processes that can account for all these phenomena?

Sometimes it is only with distance that one can spot the larger patterns. It takes a long time to get from complexity to simplicity. Now, some ten years after the study was conducted, we feel that we are in a position to offer an integrated account of the BBC Prison Study that centres on the importance of the relationships between shared identity, power and powerlessness. First, though, it is necessary to provide some theoretical background which explains how we came to undertake the study in the first place, and then to say something about the study itself and what happened in general terms.

FIGURE 7.1   PB, BG, JE and PP meet and agree to set up a new Guard regime.

Social identity and collective action

In Spring 2001 the BBC contacted us, asking if we wanted to be involved in a replication of the Stanford Prison Experiment. Actually they approached quite a few people, and we, like the others, said no. However, we did say that we would be interested in revisiting the Stanford Prison paradigm, in order to gain new insights into the dynamics between unequal groups.

Our motivation for this was rooted in what we saw as two important gaps in the literature. On the one hand, there was a gap between the 'official version' of the SPE and the details that emerge when one looks more closely into what happened in that study. The story that we all know and which features in our textbooks tells us how the Guards and Prisoners accepted their respective roles, how the Guards became brutal and the Prisoners became passive, and how, as a result, the system became so toxic that the experiment had to be ended early. However, this ignores how many Guards were reticent about their authority to the very end of the study, how some sided with the experimenters, some were firm but fair, and only a few became tyrannical (indeed, we only have clear evidence of one Guard, the one dubbed 'John Wayne', exemplifying the brutal role; see Zimbardo, 1989). It also ignores how many of the Prisoners challenged the Guards, how at the end of the first day they were in the ascendancy, and how, even to the very end of the study, some refused to knuckle under (Zimbardo, 1989, see also Reicher & Haslam,

2006a). So, as we intimated at the start, the SPE is as much a story of resisting as of accepting one's place. It is therefore necessary to address when resistance happens as much as when acceptance happens. Such a study would be new and significant. That was our pitch to the BBC, and that was the pitch that the BBC bought.

On the other hand, there is a gap between the ongoing impact of the SPE as a story and the anachronism of its underlying theory. Thus, Zimbardo's study is the last of a series of classic field studies (following Sherif and Milgram) which transformed social psychology in the post-war period (Smith & Haslam, 2012). By creating and manipulating immersive social worlds, they demonstrated the power of social relations in transforming perceptions and actions. They showed how authority relations and group memberships have a profound effect on what we do. At the same time, however, they proposed (or at least implied) that we always accept the positions to which we are assigned, and we always act to reproduce these relations. This is what has been referred to as 'conformity bias' (Moscovici, 1976; see also Haslam & Reicher, 2012a; Reicher & Haslam, in press).

In Zimbardo's case, this is quite explicit. He and his colleagues argued that guard aggression "was emitted simply as a 'natural' consequence of being in the uniform of a 'guard' and asserting the power inherent in that role" (Haney, Banks & Zimbardo, 1973, p. 12). People, they suggest, cannot help but accept their roles in society. The group is inherently a force of conservatism.

But this position has come under increasing challenge over recent years, most directly from research in the social identity tradition (for an overview see Reicher, Spears & Haslam, 2010)—work which, over the decades, has come to constitute the dominant approach to group processes in social psychology (see Haslam, Ellemers, Reicher, Reynolds & Schmitt, 2010). Specifically, Tajfel and Turner's social identity theory starts by noting that group members seek a positive definition of their group (social) identity by differentiating themselves from relevant outgroups. Beyond this, though, they set out to ask what happens when people find themselves within groups that are negatively valued in our stratified and unequal world. When do they accept the inequality and try to manoeuvre around it? When do they question or even challenge the inequality (Tajfel & Turner, 1979)?

The answer given by Social Identity Theory comes in two stages. The first turns on the issue of permeability. If people see the social system as permeable (that is, if they can move through the system despite their group membership), they will use individual strategies of advancement, seeking to downplay their group membership or even distancing themselves from other members of their own group. However, when they see the system as impermeable (such that there is an absolute barrier to movement premised on their group membership) they will identify with their group and use collective strategies of advancement.

The second stage, which has to do with the type of collective strategy that group members use in impermeable social systems, turns on the issue of security. If people see the system of structural inequality between groups as secure (either because they see it to be legitimate or because they cannot conceptualise an alternative to it, or both) their collective endeavours will be aimed at improving their lot within the system (for instance, by creative strategies aimed at re-evaluating distinctive group characteristics) rather than acting to change the system. If, however, they see the existing system as insecure (both because it is illegitimate and because cognitive alternatives exist) then they will confront the dominant group and seek to overturn their dominance.

For the present purposes, there are three key elements of this approach that we wish to emphasise. The first is that people don't necessarily accept the social categories into which they are thrust: black people in a racist society or women in a sexist society may sometimes insist that they are not seen in terms of 'race' or gender (Barreto & Ellemers, 2003). The second is that when people do accept category memberships—or at least when people accept subordinate group memberships—it is often in order to contest their social position rather than to accept it. Third, and linked to this, shared social identification in a group is the basis for people reaching agreement, coordinating their activities and thereby achieving the social power which is necessary for members of subordinated categories to effect change. In the terms of the old Trades Union saying, the power of the powerless lies in their combination.

There is a range of research to support both the general contention that shared social identity in a group provides the power to effect social change (e.g. Drury & Reicher, 1999, 2009) as well as the specific hypotheses of social identity theory concerning the roles of permeability, legitimacy and cognitive alternatives in shaping group strategies (e.g. see Ellemers, 1993; Ellemers, van Knippenberg, De Vries & Wilke, 1988; Ellemers, van Knippenberg & Wilke, 1990; Ellemers, Wilke & van Knippenberg, 1993). However, for all its conceptual clarity, tight design and consistent results, this work lacks the scope, scale and drama of Zimbardo's study. The studies might provide theoretical tools to make sense of struggles between groups, but they don't in themselves embody that struggle. In large part this is because in the laboratory—unlike in Zimbardo's prison—the blood, sweat, and tears are missing. Furthermore, because it lacks this immediacy and intensity, the work also fails to grab (and constrain) our imaginations in quite the same way as the SPE.

Any attempt to develop our understanding of domination and resistance cannot therefore ignore Zimbardo's work; rather, it must be confronted head on. This was what we sought to do through the BBC Prison Study. In short, we wanted to create an environment in which we could interrogate intergroup struggles through a social identity lens.

So, in its conception, our study was intended and designed to marry together the heroic scale of the classic field studies with the conceptual precision of contemporary social psychology (and of the social identity tradition in particular). We set our focus wide enough to pick up signs of conformity and resistance, and, as we have already intimated, at various stages of the study we introduced a series of theoretically informed interventions designed to impact on the balance between conformity and resistance. Then we used the various data sources outlined above in order to examine the antecedents of group identification and also its consequences for both intra- and inter-group processes. Full details of both the study design and the study findings can be found elsewhere (Haslam & Reicher, 2002; Reicher & Haslam, 2006a). For now, we will simply outline the elements that are necessary to frame a discussion of the interrelationship between identity, power and powerlessness.

A narrative of the BBC Prison Study

Set up

We ran the BBC Prison Study as we would any other study: we were responsible for designing it, operationalising it, taking it through normal University ethical procedures, running it, analysing it, and defining the story to be told from it. For this, the BBC had to cede a measure of editorial control, with their role being focused on building the prison set, filming the study, managing the very complex logistics, and assembling the material so as to tell our story in the most compelling way. This was a difficult and controversial decision for them. Critically, though, it distinguished our project from 'reality TV' where academics are invited in to comment on an entertainment devised by television producers. It made our project unique then and, we believe, still now. In essence, this was an experiment televised, not a confection with an academic veneer.

Our first task was to select our participants. They were rigorously screened to ensure that they were neither a danger to themselves nor to others. They were then divided into two groups—five Guards and nine Prisoners—in such a way as to ensure that they were matched on key psychological dimensions such as authoritarianism and level of social dominance. Any differences we found later would therefore have to be attributed to the dynamics of the study rather than to the nature of the participants (although, as in any study, there might always be unforeseen factors which were not matched and which might be of importance).

The Guards were briefed in advance and told that their task was to run the 'prison' as efficiently as possible. Beyond that, they were given no instructions as to how to achieve this goal. They were given various tools with which to enforce their authority. These included surveillance systems, keys to control space, and the ability to provide incentives and punishments. However, even here, to avoid promulgating implicit norms, the Guards were told that whether, how and when to use these tools was entirely up to them. It should be added that all was done within strict ethical limits (for a discussion of the ethical dimension, see Haslam, Reicher & McDermott, in press).

The Guards also had a series of privileges—the ability to wear their own clothes in leisure periods, their own 'mess', a comfortable dormitory, good food. In contrast, the Prisoners were housed in small three-person cells with basic bunks, locked up for long periods of the day, obliged to do tedious chores, given a basic diet, and with limited privileges (granted at the Guards' discretion).

FIGURE 7.2 Meal-time for Prisoners in the BBC Prison Study.

Of course, the participants knew that they were not in a real prison. Nevertheless, the inequalities between them were real, and the inequality chafed from the start. This is exemplified by an exchange on the first evening, when, after they had eaten an unappetising meal and were locked in their cells for the night, the Prisoners in one of the cells were discussing their fate:

PP: [The Guards] *come up with all these excuses as to why I can't have a fag, and they're all sittin' out there wafflin'.*

JE: *I think it's part of the test.*

PP: *No, but you see, it's wrong, because I'm the only one that this part of the test is being formulated on!*

JE: *No, no. I'll tell you what, Paul, I think you're falling for it, mate.*

PP: *I am falling for it hook, line, and sinker. It wasn't in the fucking contract that I can't have a snout [a cigarette] when I want a snout.*

How, then, would they respond? Would they acquiesce or revolt? Would factors such as permeability, legitimacy and cognitive alternatives be of importance in determining the answer? To address this, we told participants that they had been divided into Prisoners and Guards on the basis of our psychometric tests. The Guards were selected for their qualities such as reliability and trustworthiness. But, we said, no tests are perfect, so we would be observing the Prisoners and if anyone showed the requisite qualities there was provision for one of them to be promoted to be a Guard. In this way, we sought to make the system *permeable* (i.e. the promotion meant that it was possible to pass through the group boundary by virtue of one's individual efforts) and *secure* (there were legitimate reasons for the allocation to groups and, what is more, there were no obvious cognitive alternatives to the Prisoner/Guard system).

On Day 3 a Prisoner was promoted to be a Guard, and after this we announced that there were to be no more changes. This made the system *impermeable* since participants were now locked into their group memberships. It also began to undermine the legitimacy of the system by implying that, even if the Prisoners did show 'Guard qualities' (and even if the Guards did not), they would remain in their groups. On Day 5 we then introduced a new Prisoner who was as naive to our hypothesis as the other participants, but whose history as a Trades Unionist would, we believed, lead him to introduce new ways of looking at the system and challenge not only the authority of the Guards but also of the experimenters. In particular, we envisaged that he would strengthen the Prisoners' sense of *illegitimacy* and provide *cognitive alternatives* to the existing system.

In line with social identity theory, then, our prediction was that on Days 1 to 3 there would be little concerted resistance from the Prisoners. They would generally acquiesce to Guard authority in order to stand a chance of being promoted. On Days 3 to 5 we would see that acquiescence end—the Prisoners would begin to act collectively, to challenge Guard authority, and start to create their own alternative culture. After Day 5 we therefore anticipated that the level of direct confrontation would increase dramatically.

As for the Guards, our predictions were less precise. We thought that as members of a positively valued group (due not only to their privileges but also to the positive qualities which, we told them, defined group membership), they would identify highly, act together to impose their authority, and use their resources to push back at any resistance. We expected an intergroup struggle and were intrigued to see how it would play out. What techniques and tactics of struggle would be used by either side in the effort to prevail?

Findings

In broad terms, we have already foreshadowed what actually happened. However, now it is time to shade in some more detail (see Reicher & Haslam, 2006a). Over the course of the study our predictions concerning the Prisoners were increasingly confirmed, while our predictions concerning the Guards were increasingly disconfirmed. Thus, at the start the Prisoners were divided. They certainly took seriously our promise that they might be promoted if they showed the requisite qualities. While some sought to comply with the Guards in order to gain advancement, others shunned the idea of promotion and challenged the Guards. However, they were divided; they failed to develop a shared sense of Prisoner identity and they didn't mount a collective challenge. This much was more or less as expected. Unexpectedly, though, the Guards were also divided. Some sought to impose their authority, but others were uncomfortable with a position of power. This meant that they too failed to develop a shared sense of identity. However, in these early stages, where challenges to their authority were relatively sporadic, even a divided group of Guards was able to keep their regime afloat.

Once the promotion took place and the system became impermeable, all this changed. The Prisoners almost immediately cohered as a group. They identified together and worked together. Moreover, the reticence of the Guards to exercise their authority had already largely undermined the notion that they had special qualities that legitimated their position. So the Prisoners moved directly from compliance to challenging the system. This only became more acute after the new Prisoner had been introduced and further exposed both the weakness of the Guards and the possibility of alternatives to the status quo.

Under the mounting challenge of the Prisoners, the Guards became even more divided. In the face of ever-greater rule transgression by the Prisoners, the split between those who wanted to exert their power and those who were afraid of seeming authoritarian became more evident. Moreover, a divided group of Guards became ever less able to contain the Prisoners; they became bitter and recriminatory towards each other, and this further undermined any sense of identity they might have had.

In sum, we witnessed two contrasting spirals for the two groups in our study. The Prisoners as a whole identified with their group and this made them more united and more effective in challenging the Guards. Their successes were experienced very positively and this led to stronger identity and more radical plans for challenging the Guards. Conversely, while some individual Guards identified themselves as such, others did not. That is, they lacked a *shared* identity and this made them less united and less effective in containing the Prisoners. Their failures were experienced very negatively. This led to weaker identity and increasing despondency about their ability to maintain the system.

Analytically, then, this raises three issues. The first has to do with the antecedents of shared identity: what have we learned about when people do and when they do not form a sense of themselves as a psychological group? The second has to do with the ways in which shared identity leads to enhanced coordination between group members and hence to group power. The third has to do with the way in which group power is experienced and the nature of its consequences for group identification.

However, our study also raised another issue, which has to do with the consequences of powerlessness. The processes we have described thus far made the Prisoner/Guard system untenable. In effect, most of the Guards withdrew from the exercise of power. This meant that on the night of the Prisoners' rebellion they sat in their quarters, leaving a single Guard to deal with an incessant stream of challenges which he could not cope with alone. Ultimately the Prisoners broke out of their quarters, took control of the prison, and the system collapsed.

The participants then set up their own system—an egalitarian structure in which everyone came together in what they described as a self-governing, self-disciplining commune. Many participants were deeply invested in this system, and initially they worked very hard to make it function, putting far more effort into their chores than ever before. However, there were dissidents who didn't want to work. The committed 'Communards' felt powerless to deal with them. Moreover, one day the breakfast was (unintentionally) particularly bad. The participants took this as a sign that we, the experimenters, disapproved of the Commune, and that we would effectively starve them into submission if they persisted with it. This added to the Communards' sense that they were powerless to defend the system.

In this context, even erstwhile supporters lost faith in the Commune, and their levels of authoritarianism rose until they were statistically indistinguishable from those of the core dissidents—who at this point developed a proposal to impose a quasi-fascist regime (complete with uniforms, rules and formal manifesto). Was there a link between powerlessness and the slide to tyranny? That is the last of the four questions that we will now consider.

Four facets of identity, power and powerlessness

The antecedents of shared identity

As we have seen, in the case of the Prisoners our study served largely to support the classic predictions of social identity theory (which, after all, focus on the reactions of subordinate group members to their plight). We don't automatically identify with the groups to which we are assigned; we do so only when this makes sense in the context at hand. In this regard, the clearest finding was that identification with a devalued group depends upon the impermeability of the social system. Indeed, the Prisoners banded together within minutes of the promotion, almost as if a switch had been flicked. At this point one of our perverse pleasures was to see BBC executives—who had tolerated but not been entirely convinced by our theoretical discussions—walking around and expostulating about permeability and impermeability. Illegitimacy and cognitive alternatives were also clearly important, although these emerged out of the intergroup dynamic itself and we did not have to impose them through external interventions as originally intended.

However, our work did not just confirm pre-existing theory. It also extended our understanding in two important ways—and here the metaphor of a 'switch' may be somewhat misleading, for context did not automatically shape how participants thought and acted. It wasn't the case that at the start every Prisoner was compliant and wanted promotion. Rather, there was diversity: some were and did, others weren't and didn't. What is more, the Prisoners were quite happy to respect each other's different stances and to act differently. All this is exemplified by a conversation between three Prisoners which took place on the night that the promotion was being decided:

JE: *What would you do? Would you rather be Prisoner then to be promoted or vice versa, what would, I mean, obviously.*

KM: *I'd rather start as a Prisoner.*

JE: *Absolutely.*

PP: *I just want to stay like this, man, I'm not interested in …*

PP: *Nah.*

JE: *Well, I tell you what, I am, I am. I'd like a few luxuries, thank you.*

KM: *I just want experience.*

PP: *Typical, see that's just, see, that's you angling and that's us two saying yeah, yeah, you don't want to be, don't want to be a Guard and all that, and then as soon as you get a chance …*

JE: *No, I'm not being funny. No, no, you guys can do what you like, but I'd, I'd like to be a Guard because they get all the luxuries and we, we're not.*

PP: *Fair comment, John. Fair comment, mate.*

After the promotion, however, things were very different. There was still some level of diversity, but at the same time there was an expectation that the Prisoners should take the same position and act together. This could be seen when the three Prisoners we have just discussed hatched a plot to trap one of the Guards in his cell:

JE: *Hopefully we'll get Mr Quarry in. That's the person, he's the target.*

KM: *No. I mean, obviously I think it's going to be a lot of fun for us to do this, but I don't think Mr Quarry … I feel so … I just feel …*

PP: *Listen, listen mate, I, you've got to, you've got to start forgetting about other people's feelings and what they're doing, because the days when you're sitting here starving hungry and you've got fuck all and you've got nothing, mate, and you've got a ratty little bed and a stupid little blanket to sit under and they're under there in their duvets, they've got everything they want and they're not giving two fucks about you. So—think on and fuck them.*

KM: *I think they do care about us. But guys, I'm going to back you all the way. You should no' doubt me. Just, you can't stop thinking, perhaps Mr Quarry will have a fucking breakdown or something because of this.*

The effect of impermeability, then, is not to shift everyone from one position to another, nor indeed to shift people from heterogeneity to homogeneity. Rather, it is to instigate a process whereby people believe that, as members of a common group, they should agree. As a consequence they pick up on points of agreement (rather than disagreement) in what others say, thereby gradually moving towards actual consensus (see Haslam, Turner, Oakes, McGarty & Reynolds, 1998). However, the nature of this consensus is dependent not only on the prevailing social structure but also on the availability of voices to make sense of that structure and help clarify how to respond to it. That is, social reality is not transparent, it still needs analytic and normative interpretation (explaining how things are and how one should respond). Here it is telling that PP, who was a lone voice before the promotion, becomes a source of group influence afterwards. His narrative of intergroup antagonism gains plausibility and traction as the Prisoner/Guard divide becomes structurally entrenched.

But even accepting that identification involves an interaction between social structure and the availability of influence sources, we still have to explain why people are willing to take on group identities when it would seem to go against their interests to do so, or else why they are unwilling to do so when it would seem to be in their interests. Why did PP embrace his Prisoner identity even when he could have chased promotion? Why did several of the Guards reject the group even when it brought them status and rewards? This brings us to our second area of theoretical elaboration, which concerns the issue of multiple identities and the impact of surveillance on their respective relevance.

The key point here is that each of us has a variety of different social identities. Thus our participants may have been Guards and Prisoners in the study, but outside they had occupational, political, religious and other identities. Social identity theorists, who have been concerned with the dynamics of identity in context, have tended to proceed as if, in any given context, only one of these identities will be salient and relevant to what we think and do. However, this is not always true. An academic may act differently when they are a football fan on the terraces than when they are a lecturer in class. Nevertheless, he or she is likely to be aware that behaviour at a match can impact on one's academic career and hence hold back from doing anything that might have an adverse impact (e.g. getting arrested). This will be particularly true if the person knows that behaviour in one context will become known to those in the other context (e.g. because they go to the match with colleagues).

To put it more technically, the constraints that multiple identities put on us will be a function of: (a) the compatibility between the values and norms of the different groups; and (b) the degree of visibility between the different contexts in which different identities are expressed (Emler & Reicher, 1995). In our study, PP was a reformed drug addict who worked with young people. His credibility with them came from the fact that he wasn't a conventional authority figure, and hence to seek out a position of authority—and to appear for all to see on national television as doing so—would undermine this identity. Equally, our most troubled Guard, TQ, ran a non-hierarchical IT company and was concerned lest he be seen as an authoritarian figure by other members of this organisation. This made him profoundly reluctant to embrace or exercise power, since to identify as a Guard would be at odds with his professional identity.

In both cases, high incompatibility and high visibility between identities impacted on their identification in our study. However, while visibility was relatively constant across groups and participants (all were being televised), incompatibility was most certainly not. On the one hand, in contemporary Western liberal democracies the position of the authority figure is generally more frowned upon than that of the rebel (Ent & Baumeister, 2014). Hence it is more likely that a Guard identity will be at odds with other valued identities than will a Prisoner identity. This, in part, helps to explain the non-identification of our Guards.

On the other hand, the combination of social identities will be unique for each individual. If Guard TQ was concerned about how being a Guard in the study would mesh with being an egalitarian in the workplace, this was not a concern for one of the more enthusiastic Guards, BG, who was employed as a security officer. In this way our analysis provides a parsimonious and non-reductionistic account of both group-level and individual differences in identification (see Haslam & Reicher, 2010). Altogether, social structure, social influence and the existence and visibility of identity incompatibilities go a long way towards explaining when people identify together as group members.

Shared identity and group power

Whatever the reasons why Prisoners formed a sense of *shared* identity and Guards did not, the consequences of this for their coordination, power and effectiveness were readily apparent. Indeed, possibly the clearest finding to emerge from the entire study was that shared identity created group power, while a lack of shared identity undermined group power.

In accounting for this, we can point to two core transformations that occur when people adopt the same social identity. First, shared social identity results in cognitive alignment. Group members begin to act with reference to the same collective beliefs and priorities, they expect to agree with each other, and thereby they are better able to form a consensus as to how general beliefs translate into specific actions within a given context (Haslam, Oakes, Reynolds, & Turner, 1999; Turner, 1991).

Second, shared social identity results in relational intimacy. Those who see others as ingroup members are more likely to respect, cooperate and trust others (Tyler & Blader, 2000). They are more likely to give support to and expect support from others (Haslam, Reicher & Levine 2011; Levine, Prosser, Evans & Reicher, 2005).

The combination of these cognitive and relational transformations empowers group members to enact group beliefs and priorities even against the opposition of outgroups (Drury & Reicher, 1999, 2009). They don't just agree on what should be done, they also coordinate their efforts in order to get it done. By contrast, when people lack shared identity, when they have different values and priorities, they might show just as much individual effort, but to the extent that effort is exercised towards different ends, it fails to aggregate and can even be cancelled out by the efforts of others. Multiple forces deployed against each other produce no net result.

The plight of the Guards in our study is a powerful illustration that collective failure cannot be related to individual contributions. One of the most striking aspects of the whole study was their complete failure to develop any workable form of organisation—despite the fact that we recommended them to do so. For example, instead of creating a shift system in which some Guards rested while others were on duty, all of them worked from the time that they awoke to the time they went to bed. This was not so that they could support each other, but rather precisely because they lacked the trust that would make support effective. Some Guards feared that others would be too punitive if left alone (and vice versa), so they had to keep an eye on each other, they had to be ready to intervene and rectify any 'misbehaviour' by the others. Our psychometric evidence shows how this resulted in an increasing level of burnout over time (Haslam & Reicher, 2006a). The Guards worked ever harder to ever less effect, and the ineffectiveness of their efforts left them exhausted and with a deep sense of lack of accomplishment (Haslam & Reicher, 2006b).

Turning from the quantitative to the qualitative data, the dynamics we have been describing are illustrated perfectly by the first major confrontation between Prisoners and Guards on the day after the promotion. It started with Prisoner JE throwing his food to the ground. Guard FC responded by ordering all Prisoners into their cells. He was immediately contradicted by Guard TA, who ordered JE not to go to his cell. The Guards then argued with each other as to how to respond. As they were doing this, the Prisoners from JE's cell (including the previously reticent KM) all decided to defy the Guards by refusing to return to their cell. Moreover, they supported each other by coming up with a succession of excuses to challenge Guard authority: Prisoner KM declared that his shoes were causing blisters and he needed treatment, while Prisoner PP demanded the right to smoke a cigarette before returning to his cell. The Guards then fell to arguing once again about whether to grant PP's wish. Several were against this, until Guard TQ decided unilaterally to give him what he wanted:

PP$_P$: *No, no, because by the time I get back in there, mate, that's it, you're going to lock down and I ain't going to get nothing, and I want my fag.*

FC$_G$: *Could you come over here and talk to me?*

JE$_P$: *No, you've got to give him his cigarette now. I mean, if you don't give him a cigarette now,*

TQ$_G$: *Listen, we know what's happening here. We talked about it earlier. You're testing the boundaries, you've made your point, we know this is …*

JE$_P$: *Forget that! Forget that! Give him his cigarette, and nothing said, no more said, yeah, because once we get back into that cell you can do what you want then. Now, so now we're out here, let him have his cigarette.*

PP$_P$: *Let's have a cigarette, have a snout, and we'll go back in our cell.*

KM$_P$: *Yeah, done.*

TQ$_G$: *That's it. We've reached an agreement.*

[BG gives PP a lighter and cigarette]

BG$_G$: *That was handled totally wrong there, Tom. Totally.*

FIGURE 7.3   Altercation between Prisoners and Guards on day 3.

This process of mutual support among the Prisoners combined with mutual disagreement among the Guards can be seen to reverse the formal power relations of the prison and allow the Prisoners to prevail. In microcosm, it describes the entire dynamic which led the prison system to collapse. It is a potent demonstration of the links between shared identity, coordination of effort and empowerment.

The experience and consequences of group power

It is illuminating to stick with this incident a little longer and examine what happened next as the Prisoners retired to their cell and the Guards to their quarters in order to reflect on what had just happened. The Prisoners were self-evidently exhilarated. On film they can be seen whooping, laughing and literally dancing with delight:

KM_p: *Hey!*

PP_p: *That was fucking sweet!*

JE_p: *You were acting quality, man, I thought he was going to go off, I really thought he was going to go off.*

PP_p: *I was like, "Don't fucking ..."!* [Indicates how he confront the Guards]

JE_p: *I thought he was going to go off, you know.*

PP_p: *This is just the start, mate, this is just the start.*

Even if the written text is only a pallid representation of the scene, it still conveys the point that we cannot understand what is going on simply by looking at the cognitive and relational transformations that take place in groups. As is becoming increasingly recognised, we must also look at emotional transformations (e.g. Smith & Mackie, 2003). However, in contrast to most of the work on group emotions which focuses on the emotional consequences of particular types of action, our focus is more on the oft-remarked emotionality of group experience in general. We suggest that the development of group power and the ability to enact group norms even against the opposition of the outgroup—what we call collective self-realisation (Reicher & Haslam, 2006b)—is in itself exhilarating. Another way of looking at this is in terms of collective agency. Most of the time we live in a world made by others, where we have to act in terms set by others. To be able to act in one's own terms, to determine one's own history, to impose oneself over others is a joyous experience. It is all the more joyous for those in subordinated positions who are imposed upon in everyday life (see Reicher & Stott, 2011).

However, as is also clear, collective joy is not simply an end in itself. It is another link in a spiral of processes. People who experience such pleasure want more of it. They become more committed to a group which allows them to shape their own social reality. What is more, they become bolder in their plans to change the world in which they live. As PP$_p$ puts it: "this is just the start". In somewhat more formal terms, we propose a 'virtuous circle of social identification' (Reicher & Haslam, 2006a) whereby shared identity leads to organisation, which creates group power, which enhances the possibility of collective self-realisation which, finally, creates both positive affect and enhanced identification.

This can be contrasted to a 'vicious cycle of social atomisation' which we can illustrate by turning from the Prisoners in their cell to the Guards in their quarters as they reflect on the events of the previous day. They sit despondently and bicker with each other:

TA$_G$: *Today's only Day 4. Now, once, after, they can see what's happened today, and they can, now they know they can do whatever they want.*
BG$_G$: *No. That's wrong.*
TA$_G$: *Yes! Anytime they're out of their cell, they can start effing and blinding* [A colloquial term meaning 'swearing'] *to each other. They can do whatever they want and there's nothing we can do about it. Now, if we for a minute think that we have to endure this, for the next ten days, then we have to seriously consider changing the way we work ...*
TQ$_G$: *We won't, we won't.*
TA$_G$: *... the way we act. There are issues here, because it's happened, yeah? I mean, come on. You know what that's just done, that's just lit the fuse on Bimpson's arse.*

Once again, the words are a pallid representation of the scene. They don't convey the downcast eyes, the resigned tones, the resentful glances. Nevertheless, they do convey something of the negative affect, the increased divisions, the sense of ineffectiveness in the present and hopelessness about the future. Atomised identity, disorganisation, and the inability to impose one's position (a sense of collective impasse) result in negative affect and further reductions in shared identification.

Even at this stage of the study, however, we observed further effects resulting from feeling incapable of controlling one's own fate—of the Guards' helplessness and powerlessness in the face of the Prisoners. Towards the end of the original regime the Guards became simultaneously willing to cede control to the Prisoners to secure a stable and manageable system, while also becoming increasingly callous towards them. Once again this is reflected both quantitatively (on the callousness sub-scale of our burnout measure; see Haslam & Reicher, 2006b) and qualitatively, in the conversations between Guards:

TQ$_G$: *I'm not going to give him* [one of the Prisoners] *the steam off my shit. He can basically...*

TA$_G$: *You know what they are? They're nothing but piss, no, no, they're nothing but the bubbles of your piss.*

However, the toxic effects of powerlessness became even clearer in the second stage of the study, as participants lost faith in their ability to make the self-created Commune work.

Powerlessness and the appeal of tyranny

It bears repeating, indeed underlining, that in the final stages of our study, levels of authoritarianism (supposedly a stable individual difference variable that shapes an individual's attitude to, and exercise of, power) rose significantly among supporters of the Commune (Reicher & Haslam, 2006a). Their conversations and comments help us to understand why. First, they were well aware that the Commune was failing. A number of people were ignoring or else ostentatiously flouting collective agreements: not doing the tasks allocated to them, breaching rules, taking more than their fair share of resources. Second, they felt helpless, not even knowing what to do. Just before the end of the study one of the Commune's staunchest supporters reflected plaintively: "*Where did it all go wrong? Where did it all go wrong?*" The chief architect of the Commune's downfall, PB, responded sardonically: "*God must sit up there sometimes and think that.*" Third, the failure was particularly difficult given the fact that participants themselves were responsible for making the system work. As the Communard NP put it, it was deeply dispiriting to put so much effort into creating something one believed in, only for it to come to nothing. This was the context in which our erstwhile democrats began to believe in hierarchical leadership, and, moreover, in which they saw some attraction in handing over the responsibility for making things work to someone else.

Once again, however, participants did not automatically change their views as a function of circumstances and experience. Leadership, influence and the need for someone to theorise the nature and implications of social reality were all critical. Thus a cadre of 'new Guards' led by PB were a necessary element in the dynamics of emergent tyranny. We can illustrate their role by elaborating upon an incident that has already been mentioned—one that might appear trivial but which became a turning point in the history of the Commune.

On the Commune's second morning (Day 6 of the study), breakfast comprised a bowl of overly thick and overly salty porridge. We explained how—albeit incorrectly—this was taken as a sign that the experimenters would not tolerate an egalitarian system. However, the participants did not come to this conclusion on their own. Rather, BG, who had just been recruited by PB as one of the 'new guards', planted the idea that this was the writing on the wall for the Commune: "*This is deliberate. This is deliberate now, isn't it? So that means that if we don't do anything, we're going to get food that we can't eat, or no food at all.*"

Shortly after this PB made the message even clearer. He convened a meeting of all participants—himself speaking, his would-be guards circling, everyone else seated. He began by repeating BG's message that the Commune couldn't work: "*Right, what this situation is, we're sitting here eating shit, and we're eating fucking shit because the regime of yesterday doesn't work. Irrespective your fucking beliefs, a little bit of moderate force does work.*" He then went on to argue for the need for strong forceful leadership to control those who were breaking the rules, alternatively berating the Communards in violent terms for not standing up to the miscreants and offering himself as the man to restore order: "*What do you think a leader should be? Yeah? He's got to be strong. And do you know why he's got to be strong? Cause you got to tread on a few of you fucking arseholes to make you fucking realise you need rules.*"

PB had offered himself as an individual messiah once before in the study, when he had proposed leading the Prisoners in rebellion against the Guards. At that point, however, he had been comprehensively rejected, because the Prisoners preferred to act together (Haslam & Reicher, 2007b). Therefore, clearly his relative success at this later stage cannot be attributed to his personal qualities or his message alone. Rather, there is again an interaction between circumstances and the influence of different leaders. More specifically, we see here that under conditions of powerlessness and group failure, people are more willing to leave it up to a leader to solve their problems rather than acting together in order to create a solution for themselves.

The evidence to support this claim is both quantitative and qualitative. On the one hand, as we have already described, those who supported the Commune become more authoritarian towards the end of the study. On the other hand, they expressed both a helpless dismay at the failure of a system they believed in and a reluctant concession that, perhaps, authoritarian leadership is required to achieve order. In this they echo PB himself, who confided that: "*since I've been filling in your psychological profile forms, I've found myself going towards strong leaders. You need strong leaders. You do need a certain amount of force to impose rules.*"

Since PB's proposal for a takeover was consciously based on fascist precedents (notably, he proposed a uniform of military dress, black berets and black sunglasses) it is appropriate to invoke the conditions under which such seizures of power have been successful. Thus Abel (1938/1986) cites the words of a German high school teacher, reflecting on the failure of the Weimar republic: "I reached the conclusion that no party, but a single man could save Germany. This opinion was shared by others, for when the cornerstone of a monument was laid in my home town, the following lines were inscribed on it: 'Descendants who read these words, know ye that we eagerly await the coming of the man whose strong hand may restore order'" (p. 151).

More generally, Eric Hobsbawm describes the context of helplessness and hopelessness which facilitated the rise of the Nazis. This consisted of: "an old state and its ruling mechanisms which could no longer function; a mass of disenchanted, disoriented and disorganized citizens who no longer knew where their loyalties lay; strong socialist movements threatening or appearing to threaten social revolution, but not actually in a position to achieve it ... These were the conditions that turned movements of the radical right into powerful, organized and sometimes uniformed and paramilitary force" (1995, p.127).

Conclusion

We are now in a position to integrate the lessons on identity, collectivity, power and powerlessness that we have learned from the BBC Prison Study.

First, people do not necessarily accept the groups and associated social identities to which they are assigned. Whether they do so depends upon a complex arrangement of macro- and micro-social factors in interaction with their own unique configuration of group memberships.

Second, shared identity in a group is a source of social power due to the combination of cognitive alignment and mutual support.

Third, where social power enables members to enact their group norms and priorities (i.e. where it leads to collective self-realisation), this is a profoundly positive and reinforcing experience which further enhances shared identification and group power. Conversely, lack of power and failure of collective self-realisation is a profoundly negative experience.

Fourth, leadership is a key element, both in the creation of shared identity and in the definition of group identity. That is, leadership is critical both to the formation and the exercise of collective power. Conversely, however, leadership is dependent upon conditions conducive to the creation of shared identity.

Fifth, group power may be exercised in many different ways, to both confirm and resist the status quo (as a function of group position), and to both impose and depose systems of inequality.

Sixth, under conditions of powerlessness and group failure, people are more likely subsequently to embrace groups that are hierarchical, undemocratic and brutal, and which exercise their power in anti-social ways.

This last lesson embodies a paradox which, we believe, is the legacy of traditional theorising and constituted the tragedy of our Communards. Their sense that groups and the exercise of group power is always bad for you meant that they were not prepared to act collectively in order to protect the norms and practices of the Commune. They only kept half of their promise to us in creating a self-governing, but not a self-disciplining regime. They could not defend this regime from subversion, and in their helplessness they helped in the creation of something far worse. These decent democrats became complicit in the creation of a tyranny.

We can sum this up in a metaphor that struck us each time we stepped outside the George Lucas Studios where the BBC Prison Study was being conducted. In the parking lot were the full-size Star Wars Starfighters left over from the original films. If there had been a voiceover, it might well have proclaimed *"May the Force be with you"*. To this we might add *"... and may you use it well"*. Because if you don't, others will use it against you and for ill.

References

Abel, T. (1938/1986) *Why Hitler Came to Power*. Cambridge, MA: Harvard University Press.

Barreto, M. & Ellemers, N. (2003) The effects of being categorised: The interplay between internal and external social identities. *European Review of Social Psychology*, 14, 139–170.

Drury, J. & Reicher, S.D. (1999) The intergroup dynamics of collective empowerment: Substantiating the social identity model of crowd behaviour. *Group Processes and Intergroup Relations*, 2, 381–402.

——(2009) Collective psychological empowerment as a model of social change: Researching crowds and power. *Journal of Social Issues*, 65, 707–726.

Ellemers, N. (1993) The influence of socio-structural variables on identity enhancement strategies. *European Review of Social Psychology*, 4, 27–57.

Ellemers, N., van Knippenberg, A., De Vries, N.K. & Wilke, H. (1988) Social identification and permeability of group boundaries. *European Journal of Social Psychology*, 18, 497–513.

Ellemers, N., van Knippenberg, A. & Wilke, H. (1990) The influence of permeability of group boundaries and stability of group status on strategies of individual mobility and social change. *British Journal of Social Psychology*, 29, 233–246.

Ellemers, N., Wilke, H. & van Knippenberg, A. (1993) Effects of the legitimacy of low group or individual status on individual and collective identity enhancement strategies. *Journal of Personality and Social Psychology*, 64, 766–778.

Emler, N. & Reicher, S.D. (1995) *Adolescence and Delinquency*. Oxford: Blackwell.

Ent, M.R. & Baumeister, R.F. (2014) Obedience, self-control, and the voice of culture. *Journal of Social Issues*, 70, 574–586.

Haney, C., Banks, C. & Zimbardo, P. (1973) A study of prisoners and guards in a simulated prison. *Naval Research Review*, 9, 1–17 [Reprinted in E. Aronson (Ed.), *Readings About the Social Animal* (3rd ed., pp. 52–67). San Francisco, CA: W.H. Freeman].

Haslam, S.A., Ellemers, N., Reicher, S.D., Reynolds, K.J. & Schmitt, M.T. (2010) The social identity perspective today: The impact of its defining ideas. In T. Postmes & N.R. Branscombe (Eds), *Rediscovering Social Identity: Core Sources*. New York: Psychology Press.

Haslam, S.A., Oakes, P.J., Reynolds, K.J. & Turner, J.C. (1999) Social identity salience and the emergence of stereotype consensus. *Personality & Social Psychology Bulletin*, 25, 809–818.

Haslam, S.A. & Reicher, S.D. (2002) *A User's Guide to The Experiment: Exploring the Psychology of Groups and Power*. London: BBC Worldwide.

——(2003) Beyond Stanford: Questioning a role-based explanation of tyranny. *Dialogue* (Bulletin of the Society of Personality and Social Psychology), 18, 22–25.

——(2004) A critique of the role-based explanation of tyranny: Thinking beyond the Stanford Prison. *Revista de Psicologia Social,* 19, 115–122.

——(2005) The psychology of tyranny. *Scientific American Mind,* 16, 3, 44–51.

——(2006a) Debating the psychology of tyranny: Fundamental issues of theory, perspective and science. *British Journal of Social Psychology.* 45, 55–63.

——(2006b) Stressing the group: Social identity and the unfolding dynamics of stress. *Journal of Applied Psychology,* 91, 1037–1052.

——(2007a) Beyond the banality of evil: Three dynamics of an interactionist social psychology of tyranny. *Personality and Social Psychology Bulletin,* 33, 615–622.

——(2007b) Identity entrepreneurship and the consequences of identity failure: Three dynamics of leadership in the BBC Prison Study. *Social Psychology Quarterly,* 70, 125–147.

——(2007c) Social identity and the dynamics of organizational life: Insights from the BBC Prison Study. In C. Bartel, S. Blader & A. Wrzesniewski (Eds) *Identity and the Modern Organization* (pp. 135–166). New York: Erlbaum.

——(2010) The requirement for a non-individualistic psychology of individual differences: Evidence from studies of tyranny and oppression. *European Review of Personality,* 24, 492–494.

——(2012a) When prisoners take over the prison: A social psychology of resistance. *Personality and Social Psychology Review,* 16, 154–179.

——(2012b) Contesting the 'nature' of conformity: What Milgram and Zimbardo's studies really show. *PLoS Biology,* 10 (11): e1001426.

——(2012c) Tyranny: Revisiting Zimbardo's Stanford Prison Experiment. In J.R. Smith & S.A. Haslam (Eds), *Social Psychology: Revisiting the Classic Studies* (pp. 126–141). London: Sage.

Haslam, S.A., Reicher, S.D. & Levine, M. (2011) When other people are heaven, when other people are hell: How social identity determines the nature and impact of social support. In J. Jetten, C. Haslam & S.A. Haslam (Eds), *The Social Cure: Identity, Health and Well-being* (pp.157–174). London: Psychology Press.

Haslam, S.A., Reicher, S.D. & McDermott, M.R. (in press) Studying harm-doing without doing harm: The case of the BBC Prison Study. In R.J. Sternberg & S.E. Fiske (Eds), *Principles and Case Studies in Ethics for the Behavioral and Brain Sciences.* Cambridge: Cambridge University Press.

Haslam, S.A., Turner, J.C., Oakes, P.J., McGarty, C. & Reynolds, K.J. (1998) The group as a basis for emergent stereotype consensus. *European Review of Social Psychology,* 8, 203–239.

Hobsbawm, E. (1995) *Age of Extremes: The Short Twentieth Century 1914–1991.* London: Abacus.

Koppel, G. & Mirsky, N. (2002) *The Experiment.* London: British Broadcasting Corporation.

Levine, M., Prosser, A., Evans, D. & Reicher, S.D. (2005) Identity and emergency intervention: How social group membership and inclusiveness of group boundaries shape helping behavior. *Personality and Social Psychology Bulletin,* 31, 443–453.

Moscovici, S. (1976) *Social Influence and Social Change.* London: Academic Press.

Reicher, S.D. (2011) Mass action and mundane reality: An argument for putting crowd analysis at the centre of the social sciences. *Contemporary Social Science,* 6, 433–450.

——(2012) Crowds, agency and passion: Reconsidering the roots of the social bond. In R. Parkin-Gounelas (Ed.), *The Psychology and Politics of the Collective* (pp. 67–85). London: Routledge.

Reicher, S.D. & Haslam, S.A. (2006a) Rethinking the psychology of tyranny: The BBC Prison Study. *British Journal of Social Psychology, 45,* 1–40.

——(2006b) Tyranny revisited: Groups, psychological well-being and the health of societies. *The Psychologist, 19,* 146–150.

——(2006c) On the agency of individuals and groups: Lessons from the BBC Prison Experiment. In T. Postmes & J. Jetten (Eds), *Individuality and the Group: Advances in Social Identity* (pp. 237–257). London: Sage.

——(2012) Change we can believe in: The role of social identity, cognitive alternatives and leadership in group mobilization and social transformation. In B. Wagoner, E. Jensen & J. Oldmeadow (Eds), *Culture and social change: Transforming Society Through the Power of Ideas* (pp. 53–73). London: Routledge.

——(in press) Towards a 'science of movement': Identity, authority and influence in the production of social stability and social change. *Journal of Social and Political Psychology.*

Reicher, S.D., Haslam, S.A. & Hopkins, N. (2005) Social identity and the dynamics of leadership: Leaders and followers as collaborative agents in the transformation of social reality. *Leadership Quarterly, 16,* 547–568.

Reicher, S.D., Haslam, S.A. & Platow, M. (2007) The new psychology of leadership. *Scientific American Mind, 17,* 22–29.

Reicher, S.D., Haslam, S.A., Spears, R. & Reynolds, K.J. (2013) A social mind: An appreciation of John Turner's work and its influence. *European Review of Social Psychology, 23,* 344–385.

Reicher, S.D. & Hopkins, N.P. (2001) *Self and Nation.* London: Sage.

Reicher, S.D., Spears, R. & Haslam, S.A. (2010) The social identity approach in social psychology. In M. Wetherell & C.T. Mohanty (Eds), *The Sage Identities Handbook* (pp. 45–62). London: Sage.

Reicher, S.D. & Stott, C. (2011) *Mad Mobs and Englishmen? Myths and Realities of the 2011 Riots.* London: Constable and Robinson.

Smith, E.R. & Mackie, D.M. (2003) *From Prejudice to Intergroup Emotions.* New York: Psychology Press.

Smith, J.R. & Haslam, S.A. (2012) *Social Psychology: Revisiting the Classic Studies.* London: Sage.

Tajfel, H. & Turner, J.C. (1979). An integrative theory of intergroup conflict. In W.G. Austin & S. Worchel (Eds), *The Social Psychology of Intergroup Relations* (pp. 33–47). Monterey, CA: Brooks/Cole.

Turner, J.C. (1982) Towards a cognitive redefinition of the social group. In H. Tajfel (Ed.) *Social identity and intergroup relations* (pp. 15–40). Cambridge: Cambridge University Press.

——(1991) *Social influence.* Milton Keynes: Open University Press.

——(2005) Explaining the nature of power: A three-process theory. *European Journal of Social Psychology, 35,* 1–22.

Turner, J.C., Hogg, M.A., Oakes, P.J., Reicher, S.D. & Wetherell, M.S. (1987) *Rediscovering the Social Group: A Self-Categorization Theory.* Oxford: Blackwell.

Turner J.C. & Reynolds, K. (2010) Self-categorization theory. In P. Van Lange, A. Kruglanski & T. Higgins (Eds), *Handbook of Theories in Social Psychology.* London: Sage.

Tyler, T.R. & Blader, S.L. (2000) *Cooperation in Groups: Procedural Justice, Social Identity, and Behavioral Engagement.* New York: Psychology Press.

Zimbardo, P. (1989) *Quiet rage: The Stanford prison study video.* Stanford, CA: Stanford University.

8

POWER BY THE PEOPLE AND FOR THE PEOPLE

Political power and identity in the separation and integration of national states

Denis Sindic

On the 18th September 2014, Scotland held a referendum about whether or not it should become an independent country. Although secession from the UK was rejected by the majority of voters, there is no doubt that the movement for secession is far from being marginal. For several decades Scottish independence has consistently received support from a large proportion of the population, with figures varying between 20 to 40 percent, and reaching 45 percent in the referendum. There is also no doubt that the issues at stake—as with any separatist movement—place the questions of (national) identity and (political) power in the foreground. Indeed, the kernel of contention, debated by citizens and political actors alike, is whether or not a difference in nationality should be enshrined in a difference of government; that is, whether being a nation with a distinct identity should mean the possession of autonomous institutions of political power.[1] A similar question obviously arises in the context of the European Union, since the legitimacy of supranational political institutions is bound up with the legitimacy of disentangling political sovereignty from existing patterns of national identities.

My goal in this chapter is not to provide an in-depth enquiry into the roots and consequences of Scottish separatism and European integration per se, but rather to use some aspects of those debates as thinking ground for a more conceptual reflection on the nature of political power and its relationship to identity. In the first part of this chapter, I argue that, at least within the social psychological literature, our existing conceptual tools are insufficient to capture the specificity of political power, in particular its group-based dimension. I then examine the consequences of this reflection for the relationship between political power and identity, and argue that: (a) identity is essential to the constitution of political power; and (b) political power constitutes the means through which identity and the vision of social life it entails are actualised in practices and institutions. In the second part I illustrate both of these points using interviews with Scottish politicians on the subjects of Scottish independence and of Britain/Scotland's membership of the European Union. I conclude by examining the epistemological and political consequences of our views about political power.

Power in theory

Let us start by considering some definitions of power that have been offered by key authors in the relevant social psychological literature.

- "Power is generally viewed as a relational construct that describes a social relationship in which one party has, or is perceived to have, the ability to impose its will on another to achieve desired outcomes" (Simon & Klandermans, 2001, p. 322).
- "We can define social power as fate control: person A has power over person B when A controls B's outcomes (...). In turn, power relations can be conceived as asymmetrical outcome-dependency situations" (Fiske & Dépret, 1996, pp. 55–56).
- "Power: The process that results in a person or group having (or being perceived to have) control over the behaviour and circumstances of others by virtue of the reward- and punishment-related resources at their disposal" (Haslam, 2001, p. 385).

These definitions are generic definitions of social power insofar as they focus on the power of people over other people rather than things. While they do not target political power specifically, there is no doubt that political power can be seen as a particular case within that category. Thus the possession of political power could be defined as the ability to determine the behaviour, outcomes and fate of other people in matters that fall under political jurisdiction, through (for instance) the control of the allocation of "reward- and punishment-related resources". However, my purpose in this section is to show that such a view of political power, while not necessarily inaccurate, is limited in that it misses some of its essential characteristics.

   To achieve that purpose, an examination of the above definitions and of their (in)adequacy to capture the specificity of political power may be used as a springboard to help pinpoint what is missing. It should be stressed, however, that some of the authors of these definitions have themselves questioned the representation of social power that they offer in subsequent work[2] (e.g. Simon & Oakes, 2006; Haslam, Reicher & Platow, 2011), and that this work constitutes one of the main bases of my own critical examination. The focus on these definitions is therefore openly partial, but is nevertheless far from representing a straw man argument. Indeed, the view of social power that they convey forms the basis of the most frequent operationalisations of power in social psychological research (for a review, see Guinote & Vescio, 2010), a large proportion of which is meant to be applicable to (or even directly targeted at) our understanding of power in a political sense. Perhaps few of those who rely on these definitions would claim that they capture all elements of political power, but what is left out, which may be most crucial, is generally left unspecified. The result is that the specificities of political power may be perceived as secondary to what it shares with other forms of power, which, as I shall argue, deprives us of a richer view of what political power is about.

Political power as a productive force

My first line of argument can be applied to all forms of power, but is particularly relevant to its political variety. According to the above definitions, power is to be conceived as a repressive force that is exercised upon others, preventing or allowing them to act as they would have otherwise. Power therefore necessarily establishes a relationship of dominance between A and B, and power equates to a form of (non-physical) violence since both act as forces to control and coerce others. This view also implies that power dynamics are characterised by a constant struggle for power that acts as a zero-sum game (i.e. A has power over B who is therefore powerless, or vice-versa). Applied to political power, one could summarise such a perspective by turning around Clausewitz's famous statement and saying that politics is the continuation of war by other means.

What can be questioned here is the assumption that power is always a "negative" force, and one that is necessarily exercised over others. Certainly in everyday language the word "power" is often used in that sense, but it is also frequently used to designate a "positive" force, i.e. a force that is not limited to the prevention (or permitting) of actions which would have taken place if power had not been applied, but to the production of actions made possible through power. In more technical terms, this can be captured by the famous distinction between *power over* and *power to* (Pitkin, 1972). Whether we see these two forms of power as related (e.g. Allen, 1999) or as entirely separate (e.g. Wartenberg, 1990), the fact remains that conceiving power as exclusively about "power over" provides us with a partial view of the concept. As one author of one of the above definitions stressed in a later paper:

> (…) too often, and certainly within social psychology, power has been portrayed as the brake rather than the accelerator in the social vehicle, as 'something which denies, forestalls, represses and prevents' (Clegg, 1989: 152). Controlling resources endows some with *power over others* (…) but it says nothing about the way in which the coordination of human activity (…) is fundamental to the *power to* achieve anything as a society (…) Thus the critical point is not so much that people and their outcomes are *affected*, but rather that projects are *effected*.
>
> *(Simon & Oakes, 2006, p. 113, emphases and citation in the original)*

A similar view was advocated by Foucault (1975/1995) when he stressed that "we must cease once and for all to describe the effects of power in negative terms: it 'excludes', it 'represses'... In fact, power produces; it produces reality" (p. 194; see also Haugard, 1997; Hindess, 1996). Even where the goal is the control of others, power can and often must be exercised in other ways than the mere repression of their actions for that control to be achieved. Indeed, the whole thrust of Foucault's work was to show how new modes of thinking and acting have been created and promoted (through the production of institutions, practices and discourses) in order to facilitate such control.

Perhaps this point is even more clear if we look at it the other way around. Indeed, equating power with power *over* others logically leads to what can be called the "paranoid fallacy", i.e. to embrace the concomitant assumption that "powerlessness results from domination—that when people lack power, it can only be because of the machinations of the powerful" (Lukes, 2005, p. 68; see also Morriss, 2002; Dowding, 1996). Contrary to the idea of power as a zero-sum game, however, even our common intuition as to the possible sources of powerlessness suggests that one can be powerless for a variety of reasons that have nothing to do with being dominated by others. For instance, a lack of internal consensus and organisation within a group may lead the group to be powerless in achieving its goals even in the absence of another group trying to actively prevent it.

The point, then, is that power over others is generally achieved through the deployment of productive as well as repressive forces, through creation as well as coercion. Furthermore, power over others is itself but a limited application of that productive power. Of course, one might question whether power that is not power *over* other people is still social power, since it is not necessarily targeted at dominating others. However, such power may still be social in another and perhaps more fundamental sense, namely the extent to which it depends on others for its very existence. In other words, the *power to* act and achieve anything may be crucially dependent on what can be termed *power with* others, which is particularly important to consider in the case of political power since it constitutes one of its most defining features.

Political power as a group property

My second and most important line of argument concerns the fact that, according to the above definitions, power is to be conceived as a property that can belong indifferently to individuals or to groups. Indeed, there is nothing that prevents either groups or individuals from possessing the ability to control "reward- and punishment-related resources" or "to impose its will on another to achieve desired outcomes". Whether it lies in the hands of individuals or groups, the nature of that power remains essentially the same. However, putting both individual and group power into the same basket may prevent us from enquiring about the specificity of the latter, a point stressed by Turner (2005) in his seminal work on power:

> (...) power belongs to things as well as people and affects things as well as people (...) but there is also a kind of power which *only* emerges from human social relationships, from the capacity of people to organize themselves into groups, institutions and societies. People acting in concert, cooperating, coordinating, and unifying their actions (...) are able to have an impact on both the physical and social worlds through their interrelatedness that would be impossible if they were purely individual beings.
>
> *(p. 6, emphasis in the original)*

The idea that group power can differ in key respects from individual power can also be found in the work of some earlier political theorists, in particular in the work of Hannah Arendt (1972; see also Parsons, 1967, 1969), who went as far as arguing that the term "power" should be exclusively reserved to designate the capacity of groups to act together:

> *Power* corresponds not just to the human ability to act but to act in concert. Power is never the property of an individual; it belongs to a group and remains in existence only so long as the group keeps together. When we say of somebody that he is "in power", we actually refer to his being empowered by a certain number of people to act in their name.
>
> *(p. 143, emphasis in the original)*

Setting aside the ambition to limit the usage of power to its group-political form, Arendt's views also take us back to the association of political power with the coercive force of violence. Indeed, she stresses that precisely because of its group-based nature, political power and violence are not only different but in direct opposition to each other—and consequently that politics is not the continuation of war but its opposite. Whereas political power cannot exist without the support of other human beings, violence only requires the possession of the tools of violence, which can potentially lie within the hands of a single individual. As she puts it: "The extreme form of power is All against One, the extreme form of violence is One against All" (Arendt, 1972, p. 141). Of course, political power and violence can be, and often are, used in combination, but the predominance of violence over political power often marks the failure to address issues of societal organisation through the latter—in the same way that the emergence of war represents the failure to solve political crises through political means. Both violence and war, then, constitute the last resort of the "powerless", that is, of those who can no longer rely on political power and the support of others to achieve their desired ends.

Paul Ricoeur (1990/1992) refers to this power that uniquely belongs to human groups as "power-in-common". He stresses that such power is a more fundamental force than domination or coercion, in that it constitutes the basic foundation of political institutions as well as the source of their legitimacy. That is, political institutions represent the attempt to formalise and objectify the will "to act and live together" (p. 197) of a community, and while they constitute a necessary step to both actualise and stabilise that will, the power they provide is but the reflection of the power of the initial group consent that led to their creation.

However, because political institutions build their own inertia, and end up being affected by other forces such as domination, the power-in-common that lies at their root is typically forgotten or confused with them. This is why the difference between the two appears more clearly when the "will to act and live together" and political institutions cease to act in unison and enter into conflict with one another. The movement of non-violent resistance initiated by Gandhi can be seen as an example of this. Since the power of that movement was disentangled from both violence and the "power" of official institutions, it illustrates the existence of power-in-common as a force in its own right. The movement has also shown that relying on power-in-common can be extremely effective as a political strategy—though its success in India also depended on a loss of power-in-common on the colonial side. That is, while the colonial administration had not lost the resources of its political institutions or its means of violence, it had already lost the unwavering support of people at home, who had started to wonder whether they really still wanted to be a colonial power (see Arendt, 1972).

Ricoeur's claim also implies that in order to capture the dimension of power-in-common that lies at the root of political power, we need to question the way in which political power is frequently reduced to the formal power of institutions, which provide the objective tools of control and decision. This is the point I shall now address.

Beyond the objective tools of political power

Coming back to the above definitions, and with the possible exception of the first one, we can describe them as being representative of what has been termed the "dependence model of power" (Simon & Oakes, 2006). In that view, A has power over B because B is dependent on A to achieve certain outcomes, obtain rewards or avoid punishments. By this it is generally understood that the power of A lies in its ability to control the allocation (or deprivation) of objective resources such as money or other material goods (e.g. Sachdev & Bourhis, 1985, 1991).

However, as Turner (2005) points out, this notion of social power constitutes a reification, insofar as it represents power as "some abstract commodity which exists in principle outside of social relationships" (p. 19). Power is based on securing resources that are deemed independent of human interactions for their existence. It also turns the problem of social power upside down, since in that view power is first obtained through the control of resources and then used to establish a pattern of social relationships (e.g. dominance), rather than power depending on success in establishing a pattern of social relationships (e.g. securing one's dominance) that may then be used to obtain the control of resources.

Within social psychology, the tendency to conceive social power in those terms can perhaps be explained by the advantages it offers for experimental research. It makes power a variable that can be manipulated easily (by varying the objective structure of dependence between individuals or groups), and the effects of power become a variable that can be measured unambiguously (e.g. the numerical results of money distribution), thereby facilitating the identification of causal mechanisms.

The payback, however, is that the very situation of outcome dependency is taken for granted as a point of departure and remains unquestioned as to its origin. One could argue that, outside of the laboratory, power may be as much the cause as the result of outcome dependency (Simon & Oakes, 2006)—i.e. it is typically those who already have power that will end up controlling the resources, as much as vice versa. However, this argument can also be applied to the laboratory itself. Within experimental situations, the establishment of a structure of outcome dependency is set up by the experimenter who is the real person in charge (Billig, 1976; Spears & Smith, 2001). The ability to control resources, possessed by some of the participants, is granted by the experimenter and is therefore but a derivation of the experimenter's power. In turn, the power of the experimenter does not primarily exist because of a situation of outcome dependency, but because of the implicit contract that takes place between the experimenter and the participants when the latter accept to take part in the study and offer their willing obedience. It flows from the experimenter being endowed with a specific identity ("scientist") that entitles him or her to make that contract with the "participants", in which their willing obedience is defined as a legitimate expectation. Thus, even within the confines of the laboratory where the control of objective resources constitutes the apparent locus of power, power depends for its existence on the establishment of a specific set of social relationships.

The tendency to identify power with its objective tools can also be found in parts of the sociological and political science literature. Indeed, a popular conception of political power in those fields is its definition in terms of the control of the decision-making process, a conception that is even more directly relevant to the specific case of political power and its role in the issues of state separation and integration. In fact there are important similarities between this approach and the idea of power as control over resources. First, controlling the distribution of resources can be seen as a specific case of controlling the decision-making process, since the former can be rephrased as the ability to decide how resources are distributed. Second, although the decision-making approach has generally been used to study power in more naturalistic contexts, its methodological rationale is similar to the resource approach. Indeed, in the words of its most famous proponent (Dahl, 1957), looking at power in terms of decision-making outcomes constitutes "the best way to determine which individuals and groups have 'more' power in social life, because direct conflict between actors presents a situation most closely approximating an experimental test of their capacities to affect outcomes" (p. 18). That is, looking at power in those terms offers the same methodological advantages as its operationalisation in terms of resource control: the outcomes of particular decisions can be identified easily (there are clear-cut winners and losers), the opposing forces in the struggle leading to that outcome can be measured objectively (e.g. by counting votes), and thus the relative power of different parties can be accurately weighted. The consequence is therefore a similar focus on capturing power through its objective indicators, with the control of votes replacing the control of money as the paradigm case. For that reason, the decision-making approach is open to a similar criticism of reification. In particular, and as I will demonstrate in more detail later, one can challenge the fact that the number of votes constitutes an undisputable indicator of power.

Political power and identity

To summarise, my point is that in order to pay closer attention to the specificity of political power, we need to give due consideration to: (a) political power as a productive/expressive as well as a repressive force; and (b) the fact that political power ultimately belongs to groups, meaning that political actions undertaken by individuals derive their power from the group. This in turns implies that: (c) the objective tools of political power should be seen as but the reification of that expressive group power, which is more fundamentally based on social relationships.

My contention is that conceiving political power in those terms implies that political power is necessarily linked with issues of collective identity. Conversely, it is by looking at the relationship between political power and identity that one can further specify how the concept of group-based political power should be understood. More specifically, I shall now underline two aspects of that relationship that emerge as corollaries of the above argument, which I will subsequently illustrate.

Power by the people: identity as a condition for political power

The first point is that thinking of political power as a group property implies that a shared group identity is a key necessary condition for political power to exist. Simply put, speaking of group power logically presupposes that there is actually a group to speak of, rather than a mere collection of individuals. Psychologically, this requires that individuals see themselves and others as belonging to the same meaningful category, to which political power can then be attributed or denied. According to Social Identity Theory (Tajfel & Turner, 1979) and Self-Categorisation Theory (Turner, 1985, 1987; Turner, Oakes, Haslam & McGarty, 1994), it is social identity that provides that psychological cement. More specifically, it is when membership into a specific social category is incorporated as part of the self that psychological group formation ensues, others being included along with the self into a meaningful whole. Only when this psychological sense of "us" develops does it become possible for the actions of particular individuals to be construed in group terms, i.e. for their actions to turn into "our" actions and for the effects of such actions to be seen as reflecting "our" power.

The most relevant consequence of that argument for the present discussion concerns the notion of political representation in electoral politics, which arguably constitutes the axis of political power in modern democracies. If political power ultimately belongs to groups, then speaking of elected individuals as having political power should, as suggested above, constitute a derivative use of the term. That is, one needs to show that their "power" does not merely stem from possessing the objective tools of office, which they hold as individuals, but reflects the fact that they have been bestowed with the ability to wield those tools on behalf of others—to represent, decide and act in their name. My claim is that the connection between those who represent and those who are represented, without which genuine political power cannot exist, is established on the basis of a shared identity.[3] Furthermore, since the legitimacy of the power wielded by political representatives depends on that connection, a shared identity is therefore also the source of that legitimacy.

Power for the people: political power as identity in action

My second point relates to political power as an expressive force, i.e. as the ability to actualise the "will to act and live together" in common institutions and practices. To be more specific, political power is, in that view, directed towards the realisation of an ethical vision of what the "good life" as a society should be (Ricoeur, 1990/1992). Since conceptions of what life as a society should consist of are inextricably intertwined with understandings of the self (Taylor, 1989; Reicher & Hopkins, 2004), this creates another connection between political power and identity. By defining who we are, we also define what kind of society we should have—a society that allows us to be ourselves and to act as a function of the aspirations and dictates of our identity. Thus, identity also occupies a pivotal place in providing the substance of what political power should be used for. Political power represents the ability to concretise identity into a *way of life*, i.e. to build a society characterised by institutions and practices that reflect and allow the expression of identity-based values and norms (Sindic & Reicher, 2009). In other terms, it is the means through which what has been referred to as collective self-realisation (Haslam & Reicher, 2006; Reicher & Haslam, 2006a) or collective self-objectification (Drury, Cocking, Beale, Hanson & Rapley, 2005; Drury, Evripidou & Van Zomeren, this volume) can be achieved.

Giving primacy to that expressive dimension over the repressive aspects of political power is not to deny the importance of the latter—which is certainly highly relevant to the debates on separatism. Rather, it is to reframe its meaning in relation to identity expression. The repressive effects of political power are a by-product of the processes of collective self-realisation, which emerges when (what are perceived to be) different identities, or different conceptions as to how to actualise that identity, clash against each other in their respective realisation. This implies that autonomous political power is not sought after merely on the basis of identity difference, but on the basis of an incompatibility in their practical actualisation (Sindic & Reicher, 2009). It also implies that the repressive use of political power to prevent the realisation of other's identities is itself identity-driven.

Power in practice: the case of Scottish separatism and European integration

In this section I illustrate the above arguments using data from interviews with Scottish political candidates about the issues of Scottish independence and the UK's membership in the EU. Specifically, I focus on how the candidates address the question of power and how their arguments at that level relate to identity (for a more complete analysis, see Sindic, 2010).

Given the nature of the debates, it is no surprise that power was indeed a major issue in the respondents' arguments. In particular, their focus was on the question of whether "we", as a subgroup (Scotland/UK), are powerful or powerless within the superordinate group (UK/EU), and whether "we" would become less or more powerful by leaving the superordinate group. As can be expected, those arguing for separation claimed that "we" are powerless within the superordinate group (and therefore that "we" need to separate to regain control over our fate), while integrationists not only denied this claim but stressed that being part of the larger group actually enhances "our" power (so that separation would make "us" powerless).

These diverging arguments can be taken as a starting point from which two further questions can be asked of the data, corresponding respectively with each of the points made above. The first concerns the basis on which those arguments about power can be made; i.e. what does it take to say "we are powerful" or "we are powerless"? In that respect, I argue that this question cannot be answered without making implicit assumptions about and/or explicit references to a shared identity. The second question concerns the reasons why power is sought—i.e. why, after all, does it matter to have power? In that respect, I argue that power is not wanted so much as an end in itself as it is wanted for reasons that have to do with the realisation and enactment of identity.

Consider the following two extracts, which concern the question of whether or not Britain is powerless in Europe:

> Gradually, Britain's sovereignty is eroded (…) If everyone in Britain agreed, within a federal Europe on, you know, a particular point, and then say that's important to us, we want to do that, everyone here said that, but the rest of Europe didn't want to do that from a federal state, that would be it, we couldn't do it. And that's that kind of loss of identity, that I think it's unnecessary to go down that route (…) We have our different identities, and we're quite proud of it, and they're proud of theirs and you can't destroy that, it's the freedom of choice to act in our own way.
>
> *(Conservative candidate, anti-Europe)*

I suppose when you say Europe might impose, it's like, well, who are these people that are imposing on us? But if you're part of the debate, and part of forming what direction the European parliament is going to take (...) then you're part of it, I don't kind of see this isolationist approach that, you know, *they*'re doing this to *us*.

(Labour candidate, pro-Europe; emphatic stress by the candidate)

In the first extract, the Conservative candidate clearly designates the loss of power (here in terms of a loss of sovereignty) as the key issue about Europe, pointing out that membership in the EU entails that Britain can be prevented from doing anything it wishes to do by other European countries. However, this argument relies on the assumption that it makes sense to speak of "we" when referring to Britain and of "them" when referring to the other European countries, in the specific context of attributing power. That is, it presupposes not only treating them as clearly separable entities, but also that these are the relevant entities to consider when deciding whether or not "we" are powerful. It is countries (not isolated individuals, or Europe as a whole) who are the "subjects" of power and who should possess the freedom to act in their own way. It is countries who can therefore be said to be powerful or powerless as a function of whether they can or cannot do so.

The fact that this use of "we" and "them" goes beyond a mere linguistic convention and reflects a particular way to frame the issue with its particular assumptions can be shown in at least two ways. First, the above extract is actually one instance where, rather than being taken for granted, the basis of this separation between "we" and "them" was made explicit. Specifically, it is rooted in the existence of distinct identities, which, as the candidate argued elsewhere, are themselves based on differences in language, culture etc. Second, a comparison with the second extract shows that, as a particular framing of the issue, it can be challenged. Thus the Labour candidate's rejection of the idea that "they" (Europe) impose on "us" (Britain) is done by challenging the very categorisation "we" vs. "them" on which the question itself relies as a premise. If "we" are part of "them", then "they" are not really "them" since "they" overlap with "us". The purpose of the vocal emphasis on these two pronouns ("*they*'re doing this to *us*") is precisely to caricature the representation of the issue in those terms as an abusive simplification. Consequently, the power of the EU is "our" power as well as "theirs" and allows "us" (as that candidate argued later on) to do things that could not be done otherwise (e.g. addressing crime, the environment etc.).

The next example of diverging arguments addresses even more directly the issue of control over the decision-making process, this time in the context of Scotland's power within Britain:

I mean, if you look at it logically, the idea was we're partners, Scotland and England are equal powers and equal partners. Well, how many companies or businesses do you know where one equal partner has only seventy-three votes, and the other equal power has, what, over five hundred votes? It's not very equal.

(Scottish Nationalist Party candidate, pro-independence)

I think it's rubbish (…) that feeling that we're being ruled by a distant parliament (…) because there is so many Scots who are prominent within the UK government, for me that kind of takes away the feeling that these are distant politicians. The Chancellor is Scottish, and I think that Gordon Brown's policies are just like Scottish policies as much as anything else.

(Labour candidate, pro-UK)

The reverse of this argument is, well, you know, most of the Cabinet is Scot. I would say, well they've probably forgotten that. I think it is the seduction of Westminster, that they're wanting to be this big fish in the big pond (…) because in order to win a general election, you have to win the English folk (…) so you've got to play to them, you've got to put in the policies, you've got to look to the economy of what is politely called Middle England, which means you've got to cut away from your own background in order to appeal to these people.

(Scottish Nationalist Party candidate, pro-independence)

In the first extract, the pro-independence candidate from the Scottish Nationalist Party (SNP) stresses the powerlessness of Scotland by pointing out the numerical inequality of votes that Scotland and England possess in the British Parliament. In the second extract, the Labour candidate rejects this conclusion by putting the emphasis on the quality of the Scottish voices over their sheer quantity (i.e. they carry more weight). In the third extract, this argument is in turn countered by the SNP candidate, who questions the credentials of those pre-eminent Scots to actually represent the interests of the Scots. Not only have they been "corrupted" by the "seduction of Westminster", but the very system of which they are a part makes it impossible for them not to become corrupted, for any Scot who would stay faithful to Scottish interests would simply lose in the general election and thus would not be in the Cabinet in the first place.

This third extract is particularly revealing, for by directly challenging the assumptions present in the second extract, it brings them to light. The Labour candidate's argument could be seen as simply stating an "objective" fact in support of the idea that Scotland is not powerless, but this argument can only work if one also accepts the implicit assumption that those members of Parliament that are of Scottish nationality are thereby legitimately able to represent Scottish interests. By challenging that assumption, the SNP counter-argument shows that the ability to speak for Scotland does not merely depend on administrative nationality but also on identity credentials. Those Scottish MPs who cut themselves off from their background are those who do not remember who they are and where they came from, and therefore they cannot legitimately represent Scotland. Likewise, while the SNP argument in the first extract would still work even without any assumptions about the representative capacity of Scottish MPs, it could not work without making the parallel assumption that the English members, by virtue of being English (and not, say, British), cannot represent the Scottish interest because, being English, they are bound to have different interests.

A similar point can be made on the basis of the three following extracts that address the question of "would an independent Scotland be less or more powerful in Europe?"

> I don't have a problem with the UK being at the big table so it speaks on behalf of Scotland, because the UK is such a major player within Europe. I think for Scotland to be a small independent nation, especially with the enlargement of Europe, the SNP fantasies that we're gonna be this strong country who will be better heard, I think are a wee bit misplaced. I don't see how it will be better heard with a reduced number of votes.
>
> *(Labour candidate, pro-Britain)*

> But at the end of the day, is it not better to have seven votes acting in your interest than having twenty-nine acting against your interest? (…) The whole point is, at present, we have no power at all.
>
> *(Scottish National Party candidate, pro-independence)*

> But if you don't actually feel that power is being exercised on your behalf, then you don't have the power, do you? And so I think that, that however much you practically and objectively get from Europe, the key thing will be (…) I mean not just a totally self-deluding power, but the key thing will be the extent to which you feel there's some way in which your will is being expressed, and in that sense, there'll be more people feeling power and they will be more confident in trying to express their aspirations.
>
> *(Scottish Socialist candidate, pro-independence)*

This time it is the Labour candidate in the first extract who supports her argument by relying on the sheer number of votes—in this case, those that Britain possesses at the European level. In contrast, the two other candidates question the fact that having an objectively higher number of votes necessarily means more power if those votes are not "our" votes. For them, power that is not "our" power is no power at all, since it is not exercised on "our" behalf and does not represent "our" aspirations. However, this point of view is in fact implicitly shared in the first extract, since the Labour argument relies on the assumption that British votes are the extension of Scotland's will (as well as the rest of Britain's). In other words, all candidates agree on the importance of establishing that power is "our" power; their only difference is on the question of whether or not British votes can be construed in those terms, i.e. as representing the Scots.

These extracts therefore show us that the attribution of power cannot be done by relying merely on its "objective" or "subjective" bases. Rather, an interplay between the two is always involved. On the one hand, some of the arguments rely on pointing out facts (e.g. the sheer number of votes, the higher representation of Scots in the Cabinet) which can be deemed "objective", in the sense that it would be very difficult to dispute them directly—and indeed none of the above respondents did. These "objective" facts may not always be explicitly mentioned in other extracts, but they do provide the focus points around which the question of power revolves and put constraints on the counter-arguments deployed. Those who wish to question the conclusions drawn by their adversaries on the basis of these facts are forced to shift the attention to and unfold the more implicit and more debatable elements on which these conclusions also rely. Such argumentative work may end up altering altogether the meaning of the "objective" facts, but it would be unnecessary if those facts did not matter.

On the other hand, relying on "objective" facts is not enough to settle the debate. One can disagree on which of these facts have to be taken into account, which are the most important to consider, or on their meaning and implications. In particular, the political and practical meaning of the "objective" facts depends on whether or not representatives are in a social relationship with the represented of such a nature that they are able to legitimately speak for them and represent their interests. In turn, this crucially depends on whether or not they are construed as part of the group and as embodying its identity. This "subjective" facet of political power may sometimes be taken for granted, but in all cases the arguments deployed cannot work without relying on it. It is only when both the "objective" features of the structure of decision making and the "subjective" aspect of identity-based social relationships are joined together that a definite answer to the question about whether a particular group of people can be considered as having power emerges.

Let us turn now to the idea that political power is sought as the means for the realisation and enactment of identity. This point can be addressed by looking at how the question "Why do we need power?" is answered by the candidates. The above extracts already contain some examples of these answers. Notably, in the very first extract, the Conservative candidate stressed the reason why a loss of British sovereignty is to be avoided, by equating it with a loss of identity. For him, to be sovereign is important because it is the means through which we maintain "the freedom of choice to act in our own way", i.e. our ability to enact our specific identity within our practices (later on he gave a series of examples, such as the right to make and label food the way we like it, to have a tax system and working regulation that suit "us" and "our" particular needs, etc.). Likewise, in the very last extract, the Scottish Socialist candidate described power as a good to be pursued insofar as it will make people "more confident in trying to express their aspirations", with the understanding that those are distinct in Scotland compared to the rest of Britain.

Both extracts therefore allude to the practical realisation of a distinct identity as the endgame of political power. But let us finish by considering one additional extract that perhaps best encapsulates this idea. The extract is from the SNP candidate who elaborates on the argument that an independent Scotland would be more powerful in Europe:

> What it would do, it's giving us more confidence, inasmuch as we would now know that we have direct access to, you know, the smoky corridors and boardrooms and committee chambers. And we would have more confidence, because we would know that we would be able to directly input, would be able to say, yes that's good, no that's not so good. (...) I think that is the biggest difference that it would make as an independent member. Confidence, self-belief, being able to be part of it. At the moment, I suppose it's like being, being the perpetual, perpetually on the substitutes' bench. You know you're a good player, and you had plenty of practice with your mates, but you never get the opportunity to actually go out there and show what you can do. Being an independent member of the European Union would give us a chance to get up off the substitute bench, and show what we can do.
>
> *(Scottish Nationalist Party candidate, pro-Europe)*

The general idea, and even the vocabulary, are similar to the Scottish Socialist extract, with its emphasis on (self-)confidence. However, the added analogy with the substitute player makes the relation with identity more explicit. It implies that Scotland has undeniable qualities (it is a "good player"), but does not have the means and opportunity to express those qualities in practice (to "show what it can do")—a metaphor which echoes the SNP's main slogan within that particular electoral campaign, i.e. "Release our potential". Borrowing from Taylor (1989), one might say that both extract and slogan rely on the common modern image of the self as possessing hidden depths that one needs to express in order to be truly oneself (a view that Taylor coins *expressivism*). At the same time, the first part of the extract also refers to a more down-to-earth concern for access to the "smoky corridors and boardrooms and committee chambers". Taken in isolation, this statement could even suggest a concern for power that is unrelated to identity. However, through the relation that is established between such access and the improvement of Scotland's confidence, the practical concern for institutionalised forms of power is not contrary to, but consonant with the concern for identity. Having access to the objective tools of power is construed as what will enable Scotland more generally to express her hidden potential and distinct qualities. It is the mean and necessary condition to the possibility of collective self-realisation.

Power by the people and for the people

The main goal of this foray into the debates on Scottish separatism and European integration was to illustrate the fact that political power is essentially related to the question of power-in-common (or *power with*) and thereby to issues of collective identity. This was done by showing that collective identity is always at play in discussions about where political power lies, even in cases where one might think that using the "objective" tools of power (such as the number of votes in decision-making processes) as indicators might suffice to settle the question. Certainly, the question of whether or not groups possess political power is tied up with whether or not they possess its objective tools, but it also depends upon the identity-based relationship that is constructed between the individuals who use the tools and those on behalf of whom they are supposed to do so. Moreover, the ability to realise the group's identity through the possession of political power is constructed as the ultimate goal for which these objective tools are sought.

Importantly, this double reliance on identity characterises both the arguments in favour of separation and those that support the status quo. Separatist movements are often perceived as the only side that plays identity politics, but this impression stems from the fact that those supporting the status quo can more easily take for granted the particular identities on which their arguments depend, thereby making such reliance less readily apparent. This is corroborated by survey data that questions the idea that identity matters only to separatists (Brown, McCrone, Paterson & Surridge, 1999; Sindic & Reicher, 2009). More generally, it is in line with the concept of banal nationalism (Billig, 1995).

Of course, this does not mean that group members will necessarily agree with claims made by political representatives that they embody their collective will and therefore empower them. As a matter of fact, the above respondents themselves systematically contested the legitimacy of such claims when they were made by their opponents. Nevertheless there is a point on which they all agree, which is precisely that a shared identity is the basis on which that legitimacy is established. To contest the legitimacy of one particular claim of representation is to contest the existence of a particular identity-based relationship, thereby confirming the importance of establishing that relationship. Likewise, respondents across the political spectrum agreed that the reason why political power is important is because it constitutes the ability to protect and promote an identity-based way of life. Whether or not group members agree with their arguments about the particular ways in which that identity should be realised, the consensual insistence on the importance of that realisation by political candidates is indicative that, as a generic process, identity realisation is likely to be of psychological importance to group members in the formation of their own opinions about the issues.

There are, however, two points which are important to clarify in order to set the scope and limits of the above claims. First, stressing the importance of an identity tie between people and their political representative is not to say that this tie always has to be framed in national terms. Rather, it can be evaluated on the basis of many different categories, from political or ideological to demographic (e.g. left vs. right, rural vs. urban). Second, the establishment of a shared identity is a necessary but not a sufficient condition to a successful claim of representativeness. Many other factors, such as agreement of opinions, may shape the relative degree to which particular ingroup members are seen as more or less prototypical of the group and thus more or less able to speak and act on its behalf (Hogg, 2001). In the same vein, the successful establishment of a shared identity does not necessarily imply a consensus of opinion and its absence a dissension. Rather, the claim is that the presence of absence of a shared identity frames how such (dis)agreements are construed. Disagreements with a particular would-be representative may not invalidate their overall capacity to represent "us", as long as the disagreements are not so fundamental as to put that shared membership in jeopardy (Sani & Reicher, 1998). Conversely, agreements with those seen as the outgroup are unlikely to be construed as implying that they are legitimately able to represent the ingroup. Rather, they are more likely to be seen as contingent facts (e.g. "our" opinion and "their" opinion happen to coincide on this particular point, but "their" opinion as a whole remain "theirs" and not "ours").

Conclusion: why does it matter? The epistemological and political consequences of views about political power

At this point a critic might perhaps object that even if political power is not limited to its objective tools, an emphasis on its dependence on identity-based social relationships is as partial as a focus on those tools. At one level, such an objection would be entirely valid. Since the objective tools of power obviously matter, a conceptual approach that defines political power in those terms may be perfectly appropriate whenever studying these tools in their own right constitutes the goal of empirical research. However, this should not prevent us from asking what is gained and what is lost by looking at political power in one way or the other. Beyond their immediate empirical purposes, our views about political power have larger consequences at both the epistemological and the political level (see Dowding, 2012).

In epistemological terms, the danger is that a selective focus initially conceived as a methodological choice may easily turn into a conceptual straightjacket that defines what has been left aside out of existence altogether. In particular, it can be argued along with Ricoeur that the existence of power-in-common and its key role in politics has too often been neglected, and that such neglect is not accidental. Power-in-common is therefore in dire need of scholarly attention, lest we compound a view of politics that is limited to its most visible aspects of domination and violence (Ricoeur, 1992). Neglecting the reality of power-in-common may also limit the study of political power to its institutionalised expressions, losing sight of the foundational basis as well as the source of legitimacy of those institutions.

Another advantage of an insistence on power-in-common and its relationship to identity is that it may contribute more generally to the development of a concept of social power that can cater for group-level analyses of power without negating individual agency. Indeed, recent advances within the Social Identity tradition suggest that the development of a shared, consensual identity is not only important for political power but forms the basis from which all forms of group power emerge (Drury et al., this volume; Reicher & Haslam, this volume). Mainly, this is because a shared identity creates both expectations of support and actual support by other group members. Actual support guarantees the coordination of social action so that the energies of individual actions are oriented towards the same purpose, whereas expectations of support mean that group members may act in the safe knowledge that their actions will be sanctioned by other members of the group, giving them the confidence (and the feelings of legitimacy) necessary to act in the first place. Together, both determine the capacity of group members to act effectively upon both the social and physical worlds.

Conceived in those terms, the role of the group in the determination of power does not negate the fact that agency belongs to people. It is group members who act, not collective entities or systems. However, whether or not the actions of group members can be characterised as powerful depends entirely on the system of social relations within which their actions take place. The system determines whether or not particular actions carry the consensual weight of the group, in the same way that it determines whether or not some group members can be said to speak/act on behalf of others. Thus what may appear to be the same acts based on outward characteristics can take on radically different meanings, from the action of a marginal extremist to a powerful symbol of the group's spirit.

Politically, the way in which we conceptualise (political) power also has crucial consequences. Indeed, as Lukes (2005) points out, to engage in disputes about the meaning of power "is itself to engage in politics" since "how we think about power may serve to reproduce and reinforce power structures and relations, or alternatively it may challenge and subvert them (…) To the extent that this is so, conceptual and methodological questions are inescapably political" (pp. 62–63). In that respect, one of the political advantages of viewing power in terms of its objective tools is that it can provide a healthy safeguard against the possible slip into a purely subjective or symbolic view of power, which may be used to delude others into believing that they have a say in political matters when they do not. However, the political dangers of seeing power as an essentially repressive or dominative force, which tends to go hand in hand with such a view, are equally important to consider. Principally, this is bound to contribute to a negative view of all forms of power. This can be seen in Lukes' quote, where because such an equation is made it is taken for granted that challenging and subverting power structures is to be considered universally good. Certainly this is often a politically important task, especially when it is directed against relations of domination and oppression. Nevertheless, powerlessness can be every bit as politically problematic as powerfulness, so that by equating political power with domination one may be throwing the baby away with the bath water.

In particular, where political power as power-in-common is lacking, the temptation to resolve political issues by non-political means such as violence or other forms of coercive control increases. It is the ultimate lesson of the BBC Prison Study (Reicher & Haslam, 2006b, this volume), and also one of the most heartfelt arguments of Arendt (1972, 2005), that situations of powerlessness constitute particularly fertile grounds for the establishment of tyrannical regimes, for in such conditions they can easily end up being perceived as a "solution" to powerlessness. In other words, the mistrust in political power carries with it the danger of nurturing "solutions" to political issues that attempt to do away with the necessity for all genuine political processes to be rooted in the power-in-common of the people (Sindic, 2013). Against that danger, it is not challenging power but rather multiplying the sites of and possibilities for power-in-common to flourish that becomes essential to maintaining and promoting a healthy democracy.

Looking at political power as group-based and as intrinsically linked to identity issues is of course but a small step in that process. Nevertheless, this can contribute to a more open evaluation of our structures of power by looking beyond the objective tools of power when we try to decide whether or not people are dominated, oppressed or empowered. By focusing on political power as power-in-common, one is also made more sensitive to the potentially disastrous effects of its absence, as well as better equipped to evaluate those effects. In the case of political representation and decision-making, one can, for instance, question the (often implicit) assumptions on the basis of which claims to legitimate representations are made. Where such a foundation in the collective support of people cannot be established, then those "in power" are in fact powerless; their "power", if it remains, has to base itself on other methods for securing the compliance and obedience of others.

Notes

1 For some separatist movements, the debate can also bear upon the question of whether the would-be separatist group can be considered to be a nation at all, and thereby to possess the right to self-determination that normally ensues from being awarded this status. In the context of the UK, however, Scottish, English, Welsh and Northern Irish are already formally recognised as different nationalities (of course, whether this implies radically different identities can be and is very much debated, as is the existence or absence of a common superordinate British identity that binds them together). The right of the Scots to self-determination has also been acknowledged by most opponents to independence, Scots or otherwise, so that what is at stake is merely (so to speak) whether or not that right should be expressed in establishing a separate government.

2 This is precisely why these particular definitions were chosen. It was more interesting to follow authors in the questioning of their own previous tools than limiting the discussion to a divergence in schools of thought.

3 Of course, one could easily point out that this is what elections are meant to establish without the need to invoke identity. However, elections only represent the formalisation, aimed at expressing group support, of a process that runs deeper. This is witnessed, for

instance, by the notion of "political capital" (e.g. winning elections with more votes than is necessary), which political actors themselves treat as empowering beyond the tools of office. By contrast, where political actors holding office lose the support of the electors, they also lose the legitimacy of the "power" to represent them; all that remains are the objective tools.

References

Allen, A. (1999) *The Power of Feminist Theory: Domination, Resistance, Solidarity*. Boulder, CO: Westview Press.

Anderson, B. (1991) *Imagined Communities: A Reflection on the Origin and the Spread of Nationalism* (rev. ed.). London: Verso.

Arendt, H. (1972) *Crises of the Republic*. New York: Harvest Books.

——(2005) *The Promise of Politics* (J. Kohn, Ed.). New York, NY: Schocken books.

Billig, M. (1976) *Social Psychology and Intergroup Relations*. London: Academic Press.

Billig, M. (1995) *Banal Nationalism*. London: Sage.

Brown, A., McCrone, D., Paterson, L. & Surridge, P. (1999) *The Scottish Electorate: The 1997 General Election and Beyond*. London: Macmillan.

Clegg, S. (1989) *Frameworks of Power*. London: Sage.

Dahl, R.A. (1957) The concept of power. *Behavioural Science*, 2, 201–215.

Dowding, K.M. (1996) *Power*. Minneapolis: University of Minnesota Press.

——(2012) Why should we care about the definition of power? *Journal of Political Power*, 5, 119–165.

Drury, J., Cocking, C., Beale, J., Hanson, C. & Rapley, F. (2005) The phenomenology of empowerment in collective action. *British Journal of Social Psychology*, 44, 309–328.

Fiske, S.T. & Dépret, E. (1996) Control, interdependence and power: Understanding social cognition in its social context. *European Review of Social Psychology*, 7, 31–61.

Foucault, M. (1995) *Discipline and Punish: The Birth of the Prison* (A. Sheridan, trans.). New York: Random House, Vintage books. (Original work published 1975.)

Guinote, A. & Vescio, T.K. (Eds) (2010) *The Social Psychology of Power*. New York: Guilford Press.

Haslam, A. (2001) *Psychology in Organizations: The Social Identity Approach*. London: Sage.

Haslam, S.A. & Reicher, S.D. (2006) Stressing the group: Social identity and the unfolding dynamics of responses to stress. *Journal of Applied Psychology*, 91, 1037–1052.

Haslam, S.A., Reicher, S.D. & Platow, M.J. (2011) *The New Psychology of Leadership: Identity, Influence and Power*. London: Psychology Press.

Haugaard, M. (1997) *The Constitution of Power*. Manchester: Manchester University Press.

Hindess, B. (1996) *Discourses of Power: From Hobbes to Foucault*. Oxford: Blackwell.

Hogg, M.A. (2001) A social identity theory of leadership. *Personality and Social Psychology Review*, 5, 184–200.

Lukes, S. (1977) *Essays in Social Theory*. London: Macmillan.

——(2005) *Power: A Radical View* (2nd ed.). London: Macmillan.

Mann, M. (1986) *The Sources of Social Power* (vol. 1). Cambridge: Cambridge University Press.

Morriss, P. (2002) *Power: A Philosophical Analysis* (2nd ed.). Manchester: Manchester University Press.

Parsons, T. (1967) *Sociological Theory and Modern Society*. New York: Free Press.

——(1969) On the concept of political power. In R. Bell, D. Edwards & R.H. Wagner (Eds), *Political Power* (pp. 251–284). New York: Free Press.

Pitkin, H.F. (1972) *Wittgenstein and Justice: On the Significance of Ludwig Wittgenstein for Social and Political Thought*. Berkeley, CA: University of California Press.

Reicher, S.D. & Haslam, S.A. (2006a) Tyranny revisited: Groups, psychological well-being and the health of societies. *The Psychologist*, 19, 146–150.

——(2006b) Rethinking the psychology of tyranny: The BBC Prison Study. *British Journal of Social Psychology*, 45, 1–40.

Reicher, S. & Hopkins, N. (2004) On the science of the art of leadership. In D. van Knippenberg & M. Hogg (Eds), *Identity, Leadership and Power* (pp. 197–209). Oxford: Blackwell.

Ricoeur, P. (1992) *Oneself as Another* (K. Blamey, trans.). Chicago, IL: University of Chicago Press. (Original work published 1990.)

Sachdev, I. & Bourhis, R.Y. (1985) Social categorization and power differentials in group relations. *European Journal of Social Psychology*, 15, 415–434.

——(1991) Power and status differentials in minority and majority group relations. *European Journal of Social Psychology*, 21, 1–24.

Sani, F. & Reicher, S. (1998) When consensus fails: An analysis of the schism within the Italian Communist Party (1991). *European Journal of Social Psychology*, 28, 623–645.

Simon, B. & Klandermans, B. (2001) Politicized collective identity. A social psychological analysis. *American Psychologist*, 56, 319–331.

Simon, B. & Oakes, P. (2006) Beyond dependence: An identity approach to social power and domination. *Human Relations*, 59, 105–139.

Sindic, D. (2010) *National Identity, Separatism, and Supra-nation Integration: Attitudes Towards Britain and Europe in Scotland*. Saarbrücken: VDM Verlag Müller.

——(2013) Arendt and the politics of theory and practice: Beyond ivory towers and philosopher-kings. *Theory and Psychology*, 23, 499–517.

Sindic, D. & Reicher, S.D. (2009) Our way of life is worth defending: Testing a model of attitudes towards superordinate group membership through a study of Scots' attitudes towards Britain. *European Journal of Social Psychology*, 39, 114–129.

Spears, R. & Smith, H.J. (2001) Experiments as politics. *Political Psychology*, 22, 309–330.

Tajfel, H. & Turner, J.C. (1979) An integrative theory of intergroup relatons. In S. Worchel & W.G. Austin (Eds), *Psychology of intergroup relations* (pp. 33–47). Monterey, CA: Brooks-Cole.

Taylor, C. (1989) *Sources of the self: The making of modern identity*. Cambridge: Cambridge University Press.

Turner, J.C. (1985) Social categorization and the self-concept: A social cognitive theory of group behaviour. In E.J. Lawler (Ed.), *Advances in Group Processes: Theory and Research* (Vol. 2, pp. 77–122). Greenwich, Conn.: JAI Press.

Turner, J.C. (1987) A self-categorization theory. In J.C. Turner, M.A. Hogg, P.J. Oakes, S.D. Reicher & M.S. Wetherell (Eds), *Rediscovering the Social Group* (pp. 1–88). Oxford: Blackwell.

Turner, J.C. (2005) Explaining the nature of power: A three-process theory. *European Journal of Social Psychology*, 35, 1–22.

Turner, J.C., Oakes, P.J., Haslam, S.A. & McGarty, C. (1994) Self and collective: Cognition and social context. *Personality and Social Psychology Bulletin*, 20, 454–463.

Wartenberg, T. (1990) *The Forms of Power: From Domination to Transformation.* Philadelphia: Temple University Press.

9

UNDERSTANDING INTERGROUP RELATIONS IN CONTEXT

Power and identity

John F. Dovidio

This chapter attempts to develop an integrated understanding of power and collective identity and how they shape intergroup relations in different contexts. Social psychology has a long history of pursuing issues of deep social consequence centred around issues of collective identity. LeBon's (1896) work on the capacity for extreme antisocial behaviour by people in groups emphasised the role of the development of a group mind. Cooley (1902), in *Human Nature and the Social Order*, emphasised that looking at people as individuals is no more natural than looking at them as groups, and that the life of individuals was inseparable from their membership in groups. The pioneering work on ethnocentrism by Sumner (1906), who was credited with coining the terms "ingroup" and "outgroup", has had a profound historical influence. Moreover, as Allport (1954) observed, these collective identities and the resulting intergroup relations are highly contextualised, shaped by history, economics and politics, as well as contemporary structures and institutions. Indeed, classic research on intergroup conflict by Sherif, Harvey, White, Hood and Sherif (1961), on obedience by Milgram (1974) and social roles by Zimbardo (1989) dramatically illustrated the profound effect of context on identity and, ultimately, on consequential forms of social behaviour.

By the late 1960s and early 1970s the paradigm had shifted. Tajfel's work on the minimal intergroup paradigm revolutionised how the field of social psychology understood intergroup relations (see Robinson, 1996). Whereas previous work considered the importance of distinguishing ingroups from outgroups (Allport, 1954) and whether groups were cooperatively or competitively interdependent (Sherif et al., 1961), Tajfel demonstrated that the mere classification of people into ingroups and outgroups in specific experimental conditions—that is, under even the most minimal conditions of group assignment—was sufficient to initiate intergroup bias. At the same time, the social-cognitive revolution, which described how basic cognitive processes for simplifying a complex and cognitively demanding environment affect social categorisation, produced an explosion of research on social stereotyping (see Hamilton, 1981; Fiedler, Freytag & Meiser, 2009).

Research on Social Identity Theory (Tajfel & Turner, 1979) and the related Self-Categorisation Theory (Turner, Hogg, Oakes, Reicher & Wetherell, 1987; see also Abrams & Hogg, 2010) emphasised how different identities become salient in different contexts, but work using the minimal intergroup paradigm attracted considerable attention to understanding intergroup relations in the absence of meaningful context. Similarly, social-cognitive work on social categorisation and stereotyping drew attention to common underlying processes across various forms of intergroup relations. This emphasis on intra-individual processes and eventually on neural and micro-level processes, drew social psychologists away from work on more macro-level influences such as the role of history, religion and economics on intergroup relations.

This volume, *Power and Identity*, pushes the pendulum back to a greater appreciation of the macro-level context in the social psychology of intergroup relations. It contextualises identity processes by examining both the role of group status, representing the ways groups are socially valued, and the role of power, involving the extent to which groups or individuals can affect social reality or influence others to do so (Boldry & Gaertner, 2006; Turner, 2005). Status and power are often intertwined since groups that are higher in status generally have greater access to power (Sindic & Condor, 2014). In turn, disparities in economic, political and social power produce different social realities, which substantially shape the everyday lives of members of advantaged and disadvantaged groups (Demoulin, Leyens, & Dovidio, 2009).

Feelings of power—about having it or not having it—affect the ways people think and act. With respect to social-cognitive processes, low power people must be attentive to the needs, desires, thoughts and feelings of high power people and groups, which control their outcomes. High power people, by contrast, do not have to devote as much attention to any individual low power person because their outcomes are not directly contingent on them. Thus, low power people are highly motivated to form accurate and individuated impressions of high power individuals and groups, whereas high power people may be less attentive to individual qualities of low power people and have a greater propensity to rely on group stereotypes to form impressions (Fiske, 2000).

Power is also central to social identity processes. A key premise of Social Identity Theory is that people's context-specific attention to their personal and social identities is driven by their motivation to feel positively about themselves. One way to achieve this end is to join social groups that elicit a positive identity, such as high status groups; another is to increase the perceived worthiness of the social groups to which one already belongs, for example by enhancing the perceived or actual status of one's group relative to another group. To the extent that people are motivated to regard themselves positively, they will also be motivated to achieve positive distinctiveness between their group and groups to which they do not belong (Tajfel & Turner, 1979). Thus, intergroup relations rarely involve groups of equal status. Even if groups are initially equivalent in status, group members are motivated to perceive or achieve higher status for their group. Such differences in status are, in turn, influenced by power differences, if only because the extent to which group members are able to achieve a positive identity depends on their existing capacity (i.e. power) to affect existing perceptions of social identities (Sindic & Condor, 2014).

Social status also affects the way people perceive the social context and their motivations regarding the status quo (Boldry & Gaertner, 2006). Whereas members of advantaged groups are likely to desire the stability of the social system that benefits them, members of disadvantaged groups are typically more motivated toward social change (Sidanius & Pratto, 1999; Tajfel & Turner, 1979; Wright, 2001). Group members may also use different strategies to satisfy their motivations regarding the status quo. For example, whereas members of advantaged groups may promote ideas that make the social hierarchy seem natural and legitimate (Jost, Banaji & Nosek, 2004; Sidanius & Pratto, 1999), members of disadvantaged groups, under certain conditions, may assemble and collectively challenge the status quo (van Zomeren, Postmes & Spears, 2008; Wright, 2001). Again, whether or not (dis)advantaged groups are successful in using these opposite strategies depends on their existing power. Conversely, changes in the social status quo may affect the relative power of groups (Sindic & Condor, 2014).

The chapters in this volume offer distinctly different perspectives on the intersections of power and identity, adopting different methodologies and levels of analysis. Collectively, these chapters reflect three key themes that inform research on intergroup relations in novel ways. One theme, triangulating from the broad global focus of these chapters, is that basic psychological processes, which psychologists often assume to be universal, are significantly shaped by historical events. These events, which may have occurred in the dim and distant past, continue to determine the contemporary nature of a group's social identity, its sense of power and its relations with other groups. A second theme is that group identity may play a different role in the psychological and social functioning of high and low power groups and their members. The third theme is that whereas the psychological literature has suggested clear and obvious distinctions between high and low status groups, social (dis)advantage does not automatically equate with power(lessness). For instance, low status groups may cloak their influence with the guise of powerlessness to produce change without arousing reactance or resistance. The next section presents a conceptual model that integrates these three themes, elaborates their interrelationships and identifies relevant processes with additional psychological research and theory.

Conceptual model

Figure 9.1 highlights key elements and insights from the chapters in this volume in the context of hypothesised processes, iterative effects, and social outcomes.

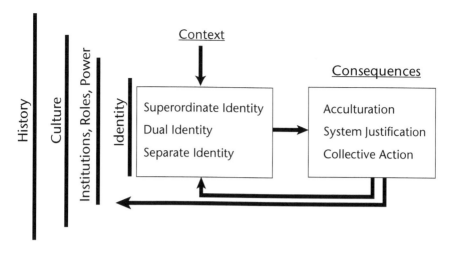

FIGURE 9.1 Context, power, and identity: How historical, cultural and structural processes affect reciprocal relations between power and identity.

As the contributors to this volume amply demonstrate, social and political events have a significant impact on group identity and ultimately on contemporary and future intergroup relations. In addition, several of the chapters consider the relationship between group identity and collective action, recognising the potential bi-directional nature of this relationship. Using Figure 9.1 as a guide, the next parts of this section summarise and synthesise elements of the chapters and other work, relating first to the influences among history, culture, institutions, roles and power, and then to the nature of group identity and reciprocal relations between identity and power.

History, culture, institutions, roles, and power

The effects of colonisation represent a recurring theme in this volume. Colonisation involves more than occupying a group's sovereign land. It also alters their longstanding social structure, the roles group members occupy, power relations between and within groups, and national, social and personal identity. These effects are more than material: colonisation alters the psychology of both colonised groups and colonisers, with enduring consequences.

As Chapter 2 by Xavier explains, colonisation was characterised by different models of dealing with the colonised that either stressed assimilation (the model mostly promoted by the Portuguese and the French) or cultural and racial difference (mostly promoted by the Dutch and the British). Both approaches are assertions of national and cultural power. Whereas emphasis on difference typically involves a direct expression of cultural superiority, assimilation is more indirect, providing incentives for adherence to the coloniser's values: "By transforming themselves, by adapting their identities to the ideal type designed by the coloniser—becoming

Christians, becoming like 'whites', becoming 'civilised'—many of the colonised could enter the world of social mobility." Despite the promise of equality associated with religious conversion to Christianity, as Xavier discusses, "neither the Jewish, nor the Indians, became truly 'Christian' and truly 'Portuguese'. Indeed, if it had been fully applied, this legal framework would have dissolved the difference between the rulers and the ruled, colonisers and colonised, compromising the very foundations of the political community." Thus, colonisation reinforced the standards of the colonisers while altering the values of colonised groups in ways that affirmed the position, wealth and well-being of the dominant group.

In Chapter 3, Sobral examines the development of Portuguese national identity, originating as a kingdom in the twelfth century. He explains that despite the substantial ethnic diversity in the region at the time, "state power defined a political core, established borders and progressively defined an economic, political, linguistic and cultural space" that were crucial in the definition of a national identity. This national identity was further strengthened by wars and conflicts with other countries. However, this process of developing a strong collective identity also involved distinguishing and targeting minorities within the country (e.g. Moors and Jews) to enforce the beliefs of the majority. This strong national identity both stimulated and justified colonisation in Africa, India and the Americas.

Although the chapters in this volume focus on relatively recent events, such as European colonisation in Africa and India, the more generalised theme identified earlier is that more distant and general historical circumstances can shape the basic fabric of cultures in profoundly different ways. Among the most extensively researched dimensions of cultural difference is the difference between individualism and collectivism (e.g. Hofstede, 1980, 1991). Most Western European, Northern European and North American countries are characterised as individualistic, whereas most East Asian countries represent collectivistic cultures. Cultural psychologists (e.g. Nisbett, 2003) have proposed that this general difference in cultural orientation—individual versus group orientations—may be traced to the difference in ecological conditions between ancient Greek and Chinese cultures, which are considered to be the origins of Western and Eastern cultures in general. Greek culture was trade-oriented, which emphasises individual choice and effort, whereas Chinese culture was agriculture-oriented, which required collective group work.

These different activity orientations may have been further reinforced by different philosophical traditions that shaped the values of each culture. The Protestant ethic (Weber, 1905/2008), which has been a dominant philosophical influence in the United States, emphasises personal responsibilities and diligence and encourages personal achievements, rationalising individual wealth. Meritocracy is also based on the Protestant ethic (Sidanius & Pratto, 1999) and is a particularly central cultural value in individual-oriented cultures, although meritocracy beliefs operate globally. Meritocracy is an ideology based on the belief that people earn their social status based on their individual talents and efforts. As a consequence, in individual-oriented cultures, such as the United States, the focus of cultural values is on each individual's personal characteristics, choices, efforts, responsibilities and achievements (Katz & Hass, 1988; Rokeach, 1973).

By contrast, Confucianism (Confucius, 551–478 BC) is a more group-oriented philosophy. Confucianism has been a major philosophical tradition in East Asia since about the fourth century, and Confucian values still permeate Asian societies. Confucianism emphasises "humanity in relations" rather than individual morality (Gardner & Seeley, 2001). Confucianism teaches not only how people deal with related others but also lifelong roles and duties associated with the status of the group or class to which people belong. In Confucian instruction, individuals are identified and perceived in general collective terms or roles (e.g. the king/head–vassals, parents–children, husbands–wives, or older–younger) rather than individual characteristics. That is, the self consists of several different roles involving interdependence with others (see Markus & Kitayama, 1991). It teaches that individuals' preferences are less important than the needs of the groups to which individuals belong (Gardner & Seeley, 2001).

As a consequence of their different histories, cultural values, institutions and role orientations, Western European/North American and East Asian populations differ systematically in self-concept (Markus & Kitayama, 1991), cognitive processes (Nisbett, Peng, Choi & Norenzayan, 2001), attribution (Choi, Nisbett & Norenzayan, 1999), motivation (Heine, Lehman, Markus & Kitayama, 1999), and perception (Masuda & Nisbett, 2001). As depicted in Figure 9.1, these forces profoundly determine contemporary identity and social relationships.

Historical oppression, such as colonisation, further alters group perspectives, adaptations and identities, as well as the nature of intergroup relations. Jones (2003), for instance, studied the role that the institution of slavery has had on African Americans. He identified how contemporary African American culture represents a blend of enduring elements of African cultural heritage combined with adaptations that African Americans developed to cope reactively with slavery and discrimination. His TRIOS theory (acronym for Time, Rhythm, Improvisation, Orality and Spirituality) represents the cultural capital that Africans brought with them to the New World (Jones, 2003). TRIOS is associated with characteristics that are useful for coping and adapting to threatening and uncertain contexts. These characteristics include flexible and creative responses to unexpected threats and challenges, using verbal and nonverbal communication to share information and knowledge, establish group boundaries and create group cohesion, adopting ways to be in synch with situations and contexts one is in, acute focus on the demands and opportunities of the immediate context, and drawing upon a spiritual belief in a power beyond oneself to make sense of one's predicament and create or sustain beliefs in alternative positive possibilities.

However, Jones (2003) notes that European American culture—the dominant American culture—ascribes greater value to planfulness, consistency, future-thinking, practicality and deliberative thought and action over the qualities of flexibility, resourcefulness, spirituality and improvisation developed in TRIOS. Thus, African Americans experience cultural racism, in which the values embedded in TRIOS are perceived as inferior to those that are the central cultural values advocated by European Americans. Consequently, even in the absence of discrimination based on skin colour today, African Americans may still be systematically disadvantaged by their historical traditions and social adaptations to oppression in the United States.

In addition, historical events affect the basic needs that members of low power and historically victimised groups and members of high power and historical perpetrator groups experience in their contemporary, seemingly interpersonal interactions. According to the Needs–Based Model of Reconciliation (Shnabel & Nadler, 2008; Shnabel, Nadler, Ullrich, Dovidio & Carmi, 2009), the two fundamental needs are for *acceptance* and *empowerment*. Because of the historical relations between the groups, members of minority groups feel like victims and experience an impaired sense of status and control. They therefore seek re-affirmation of their power and competence. Members of advantaged groups, influenced by feelings of collective responsibility and guilt for their group's transgressions, are motivated to re-establish the moral legitimacy of their group, and they therefore seek acceptance and social approval from members of disadvantaged groups (Shnabel et al., 2009). In turn, these different group-based needs shape the strategies that members of high and low power groups adopt in their intergroup encounters. In the United States, for example, African Americans and Latinos are motivated to be respected and consequently make particular efforts to manage the impressions of Whites so that they are seen as competent. Whites, in contrast, are motivated to be liked, and in these interactions they go out of their way to be ingratiating (Bergsieker, Shelton & Richeson, 2010).

Taken together, the findings presented in several chapters of this volume, along with the broader literature, reveal that intergroup encounters, which may seem to be immediate, interpersonal and decontextualised, are significantly determined by prior intergroup history, the roles and positions of power the groups currently occupy in society, and the group-based needs, motivations and identities that result. History and social structure frame even the most casual and limited encounters between members of different groups. The next section of this chapter focuses on the second half of Figure 9.1—on the ways that the immediate interaction context affects the salience of different collective identities and their consequences for support of the status quo or collective action for change.

Context, identity, and implications for action

Social categorisation forms the basis of the ways people think about themselves and others. When people think of themselves in terms of their group identity, they perceive themselves and other ingroup members in terms of the group prototype— the "cognitive representation of features that describe and prescribe attributes of the group" (Hogg & Terry, 2000, p. 123)—and see themselves as interchangeable representatives of that prototype. Group needs and goals take precedence over personal needs and goals, and people automatically evaluate other members of their ingroup more positively, feel psychologically closer to them, trust them more, and are more helpful and generous toward them (see Dovidio & Gaertner, 2010, for a review).

As outlined in Social Identity Theory (Tajfel & Turner, 1979), these processes motivate additional actions that further distinguish the ingroup from the outgroup. Because social identity (and consequently one's self-esteem) is commonly enhanced by emphasising the "positive distinctiveness" of one's group (Tajfel & Turner, 1979; see also Abrams & Hogg, 2010), group members often tend to value the defining characteristics of their group more than those of other groups. To maintain the positive distinctiveness of their group, people engage in ingroup favouritism and outgroup derogation, and they are inclined to compete with and discriminate against other groups to gain or maintain advantage for their group (Insko *et al.*, 2001). As a consequence, when interactions between groups take place in contexts that activate separate (we-they) group identities, intergroup interactions are typically tense and potentially conflictual.

However, social identity is malleable and sensitive to the immediate intergroup context; thus, in different situations different forms of collective identity can be activated. According to the Common Ingroup Identity Model (Gaertner & Dovidio, 2000, 2012), different types of intergroup interdependence (e.g. cooperation) and cognitive, perceptual, linguistic, affective and environmental factors can—either independently or in concert—alter individuals' cognitive representations in ways that lead people to reconceive of the way they think about the different groups, from an "us" versus "them" orientation to a more encompassing, superordinate "we" connection (Gaertner, Mann, Dovidio, Murrell & Pomare, 1990). Creating a common ingroup identity redirects positive beliefs, feelings, and behaviours, which are usually reserved for ingroup members, and extends them to former outgroup members.

Whereas much of the research on the Common Ingroup Identity Model has focused on the benefits of creating a single, common ingroup identity, the development of a shared identity does not necessarily require each group to forsake its original, less inclusive group identity. Depending on their degree of identification with the different categories and contextual factors that make particular identities salient, individuals may activate two or more of their multiple social identities simultaneously (Roccas & Brewer, 2002) or sequentially (Turner *et al.*, 1987). They may thus experience a dual identity (see Figure 9.1). Whereas common ingroup identity is related to the cultural ideology of colour-blindness, a dual identity is related to endorsement of a multicultural identity.

Of particular relevance to the current volume, although recategorisation both exclusively in terms of a common identity or as a dual identity improves intergroup attitudes for members of high and low status groups, they have different effects on collective action for change. Perhaps as a consequence (Hehman *et al.*, 2012), high and low status groups have different preferences for common identity and colour-blindness relative to a dual identity and multiculturalism. Internationally, citizens of host countries and ethnic majority groups prefer "one group" representations and colour-blindness; immigrants and ethnic minority group members more strongly endorse dual identity and multiculturalism (Ryan, Hunt, Weible, Peterson & Casas, 2007; Verkuyten, 2006).

Dovidio, Gaertner and Saguy (2009) further argued that these different preferred representations—common identity for members of high status groups and dual identity for members of low status groups—are functional for achieving the different goals of members of these groups. Focusing only on common superordinate identity distracts members of both low and high status groups from recognising group-based disparities—particularly relating to subtle, complex, or structural disadvantage—and from seeing them as unfair. As a consequence, it undermines action for change, either in terms of collective action by members of the low status/low power group (Saguy, Tausch, Dovidio & Pratto, 2009) or initiated by members of the high status/high power group to address injustice (Banfield & Dovidio, 2013; Saguy & Chernyak-Hai, 2012). That is, to the degree that factors that promote common identity (e.g. positive intergroup contact), assimilation, or colour-blindness reduce attention to structural inequality as they promote positive attitudes toward members of the outgroup, they may undermine the motivation of both minority and majority group members to engage in action for social change to achieve true equality. This is the potential "irony of harmony". As Xavier discusses in Chapter 2, assimilation of minority and colonised individuals and adherence to Portuguese standards offered colonised groups an illusion of mobility and acceptance without arousing unrest that jeopardised the advantages that the Portuguese enjoyed over the colonised population.

By contrast, making dual identity salient in a particular context promotes action for social change. For instance, past work has found that a dual identification of being both Turkish *and* German (Turkish-German) predicted collective politicisation among Turkish immigrants in Germany (Simon & Ruhs, 2008). Furthermore, when superordinate and subgroup identities are perceived to be oppositional, collective action is more likely to be confrontational (Simon, Reichert & Gabrow, 2013).

Although much of the research in social psychology emphasises new actions in opposition to current policy or practice, Gao's chapter (Chapter 4) reminds us that under some conditions a dual identity in which subgroup and superordinate identities are seen as complementary can promote more regularised action for change within an ongoing political system. As Gao explains, although Jordan has a central government, tribal identities remain salient across the country. These tribes are viewed as integral but discrete components of an overarching Jordanian identity. They operate as separate political units (instead of having a strong national political party system), recognised and accommodated by the central government. Thus, tribes represent a distinctive and valued subgroup identity, with strong symbolic value associated with ancestry and immediate expectations of mutual support, but in a way that is compatible with a superordinate Jordanian identity. The government of Jordan thus directly incorporates recognition of and responsiveness to citizens with different social identities within its ongoing political process.

The more common example, however, is the failure of groups in power to recognise and respond to social disadvantages experienced by members of specific subgroups. Successfully addressing group-based disparities requires being conscious of subgroup identities. This acknowledgement of identities permits recognition of group-based disparities and differences, while a common, inclusive identity promotes the positive connection to view differences as complementary resources and unfair disparities as a threat to the integrity of the larger group, motivating both members of high power and low power groups to restore justice (Tyler, 2005; Tyler & Blader, 2003; see Banfield & Dovidio, 2013; Glasford & Dovidio, 2011).

The elements of Figure 9.1 that relate to context, identity and action reflect the two recurring themes across chapters in this volume, that group identity may play a different role in the psychological and social functioning of members of high and low power groups and their members, and that social disadvantage does not automatically equate with powerlessness. Reicher and Haslam, in their analysis of the results of the BBC Prison Study in Chapter 7 (see also Reicher & Haslam, 2006), explain how a strong sense of group identity facilitates social action against seemingly higher power groups. They observe that "whatever the reasons why Prisoners formed a sense of *shared* identity and Guards did not, the consequences of this for their coordination, power and effectiveness were readily apparent. Indeed, possibly the clearest finding to emerge from the entire study was that shared identity created group power, while lack of shared identity undermined group power". They propose that group identity facilitated greater cooperation and coordination among Prisoners who began "to act with reference to the same collective beliefs and priorities" and with greater respect and trust for members of their group. Reicher and Haslam conclude that the "combination of these cognitive and relational transformations empowers group members to enact group beliefs and priorities even against the opposition of outgroups".

Albeit in very different ways, the chapters by Sindic (Chapter 8), by Klein, Allen, Bernard and Gervais (Chapter 5) and by Drury, Evripidou and van Zomeren (Chapter 6) all show persuasively how the traditional social psychological distinction between the powerful and the powerless—the former with control of outcomes over the latter—obscures the complex and reciprocal relationship between power and identity. According to Sindic, "the *power to* act and achieve anything may be crucially dependent on what can be termed *power with* others". Political power, which is the focus of his chapter, requires that people share and value a common identity and the "will to act and live together". It rests on people's conception of "we" as the political unit based on a shared identity. With respect to Figure 9.1, political power exists when members of different groups value a common identity. Conceiving the "we" as a different identity, such as a Scottish identity, represents a challenge to the legitimacy of political power and promotes separatism. Support for separatism is an assertion of power, not a reflection of powerlessness.

In Chapter 5, Klein, Allen, Bernard and Gervais illustrate how stereotypes, which are typically assumed to help legitimise the low status of disadvantaged groups and thereby to create or maintain their powerlessness, can also be used strategically by members of these groups to achieve power and influence. Stereotypes are typically conceived in psychology as limiting the opportunities of disadvantaged groups and arousing stereotype threat, which adversely affects the performance of members of low power groups even in the absence of immediate discrimination. However, the analysis by Klein and colleagues reveals that because high status groups may be vigilant to direct threats to their status and control, members of low status groups may use stereotype-consistent expressions and actions to convey messages that ultimately increase their group's power. People process stereotypic information with minimal effort, often automatically. Thus, as suggested by the diverse examples of the rhetoric of Congolese nationalist leader Patrice Lumumba and the political statement made by Amina Tyler, a young Tunisian woman who posted a topless photo on Facebook, co-opting stereotypic portrayals of one's group identity can be instrumental in instigating social change. Encrypted by stereotypic images, the seemingly powerless can broadcast highly influential political messages to coalesce support for collective protest and action.

Drury, Evripidou and van Zomeren further elaborate in Chapter 6 on the bidirectional effects of social identity on collective action, as depicted in Figure 9.1. Several models of collective action, such as the Dual-Pathway Model (Stürmer & Simon, 2004) and the Social Identity Model of Collective Action (SIMCA; van Zomeren et al., 2008), highlight the importance of perceptions of group efficacy—the belief that a problem can be solved through group effort—as a critical antecedent of collective action. The model that Drury and colleagues describe in their chapter, the Elaborated Social Identity Model (ESIM; Drury & Reicher, 2000), by contrast, considers collective efficacy as both a cause and a consequence of collective action. In their model, collective action changes social identity. Engaging in collective action changes the content of identity (for example, changing "who we are" from moderates to radicals) and expands who is included in the ingroup and the outgroup. This crystallisation of the distinction between the ingroup and the outgroup and enhanced perceptions of consensus, and hence expectations of mutual support among ingroup members, then *empowers* group members to express their radical beliefs and confront the outgroup. As further illustrated in Figure 9.1, this action strengthens and potentially changes ingroup identity, particularly if the collective action successfully alters social structure and power relations between the groups. The dynamic and iterative nature of these processes illustrates how groups can be radicalised and formerly low power groups can become empowered for action.

Implications and conclusion

Taken together, the chapters in this volume and other converging literature demonstrate the value of expanding the scope of psychological research on intergroup relations to incorporate historical, cultural and structural analyses—using qualitative as well as quantitative methods—to produce a more comprehensive understanding of the dynamics of intergroup relations. The current emphasis within social psychology on discovering basic processes of psychological functioning that can apply to a wide range of groups and situations has many advantages. Given the enormous range of historical effects and structural influences that determine the nature of relations between specific groups, a general process-oriented approach can elucidate common dynamics across contexts, and thus represent an efficient scholarly strategy. However, as the chapters in this volume attest, efficiency in approach does not necessarily produce a sufficient, comprehensive understanding of intergroup phenomena.

Too much emphasis on artificial groups or to decontextualised relations may substantially limit an understanding of how power and identity shape the dynamics of intergroup relations. Clearly, an approach that ignores important moderating factors jeopardises the generalisability of social psychological findings about intergroup relations. However, mainstream social psychology journals prioritise internal validity far above external validity. As Reicher and Haslam observed in their chapter, field research in social psychology has become increasingly rare. Moreover, the different geographic origins, cultural influences, social position and realities, religious values and acculturation experiences that participants bring with them to laboratory studies are rarely acknowledged, reported or analysed. The effects of these variables are, as the contributions to the present volume exemplify, systematic and profound. Too often these effects are ignored and relegated to error variance.

In addition, for most social psychology journals, the kinds of qualitative and detailed case study analyses represented in many of the chapters of the current volume are not methodologically appropriate. Although there has been a greater call for multi-level, multi-method perspectives in behavioural science, much of the work on intergroup relations occurs within separate methodological and theoretical disciplinary-based silos. The present volume thus makes a unique contribution by demonstrating how different disciplinary perspectives and methodologies can complement the strength of social psychology in discovering basic underlying processes by helping to put these processes back into their proper context.

Indeed, integrating the results of different disciplines—including history, philosophy, anthropology, sociology, political science and psychology—is challenging. The chapters in this volume demonstrate the complexity of intergroup relations, complications that are difficult for existing social psychological theories to encompass fully. The chapters reveal how intergroup relations evolve across time and geography, and show not only how power shapes the way people think of themselves, but also how people may reframe or re-design their social identity to regain power and achieve a sense of group autonomy and efficacy.

This broader perspective makes the dynamic nature of intergroup relations, the bi-directional effects between identity and power and the interconnection between identity and action, clearer than appears in the thin slices of group life typically observed within the walls of the psychology laboratory. Understanding the complexities of the intersections of identity and power raise new and productive questions—for example, about how grass-roots social movements arise, when action leads to radicalisation, how high and low power groups perceive history and how they are motivated by it, and how groups, depending on their power, selectively perpetuate aspects of history in functionally advantageous ways in framing contemporary intergroup relations. Theoretically and methodologically, these questions push the boundaries of traditional social psychology and its paradigms, but they also help to fulfil the unique potential of social psychology as a bridge between macro- and micro-levels of analysis and offer practical solutions for improving intergroup relations.

References

Abrams, D. & Hogg, M.A. (2010) Social identity and self-categorization. In J.F. Dovidio, M. Hewstone, P. Glick & V.M. Esses (Eds), *Handbook of prejudice, stereotyping, and discrimination* (pp. 179–193). London: Sage.

Allport, G.W. (1954) *The nature of prejudice*. Cambridge, MA: Addison-Wesley.

Banfield, J.C. & Dovidio, J.F. (2013) Whites' perceptions of discrimination against Blacks: The influence of common identity. *Journal of Experimental Social Psychology*, 49, 833–841.

Bergsieker, H.B., Shelton, J.N. & Richeson, J.A. (2010) To be liked versus respected: Divergent goals in interracial interaction. *Journal of Personality and Social Psychology*, 99, 248–264.

Boldry, J.G. & Gaertner, L. (2006) Separating status from power as an antecedent of intergroup perception. *Group Processes & Intergroup Relations*, 9, 377–400.

Choi, I., Nisbett, R.E. & Norenzayan, A. (1999) Causal attribution across cultures: Variation and universality. *Psychological Bulletin*, 125, 47–63.

Cooley, C. (1902) *Human nature and the social order*. New York: Charles Scribner's Sons.

Demoulin, S., Leyens, J-P. & Dovidio, J.F. (Eds) (2009) *Intergroup Misunderstandings: Impact of divergent social realities*. New York: Psychology Press.

Dovidio, J.F. & Gaertner, S.L. (2010) Intergroup bias. In S.T. Fiske, D.T. Gilbert & G. Lindzey (Eds), *Handbook of Social Psychology* (Vol. 2, pp. 1084–1121). New York: Wiley.

Dovidio, J.F., Gaertner, S.L. & Saguy, T. (2009) Commonality and the complexity of "we": Social attitudes and social change. *Personality and Social Psychology Review*, 13, 3–20.

Drury, J. & Reicher, S. (2000) Collective action and psychological change: The emergence of new social identities. *British Journal of Social Psychology*, 39, 579–604.

Fiedler, K., Freytag, P. & Meiser, T. (2009) Pseudocontingencies: An integrative account of an intriguing cognitive illusion. *Psychological Review*, 116, 187–206.

Fiske, S.T. (2000) Interdependence and the reduction of prejudice. In S. Oskamp (Ed.), *Reducing prejudice and discrimination* (pp. 115–135). Hillsdale, NJ: Erlbaum.

Gaertner, S.L. & Dovidio, J.F. (2000) *Reducing Intergroup Bias: the Common Ingroup Identity Model*. Philadelphia, PA: The Psychology Press.

——(2012) Reducing intergroup bias: The Common Ingroup Identity Model. In P.A.M. Van Lange, A.W. Kruglanski & E.T. Higgins (Eds), *Handbook of Theories of Social Psychology* (Vol. 2, pp. 439–457). Thousand Oaks, CA: Sage.

Gaertner, S.L., Mann, J.A., Dovidio, J.F., Murrell, A.J. & Pomare, M. (1990) How does cooperation reduce intergroup bias? *Journal of Personality and Social Psychology*, 59, 692–704.

Gardner, W.L. & Seeley, E.A. (2001) Confucius, "Jen," and the benevolent use of power: The interdependent self as psychological contract preventing exploitation. In A.Y. Lee-Chai & J.A. Bargh (Eds), *The use and abuse of power* (pp. 263–280). Philadelphia, PA: Psychology Press.

Glasford, D.E. & Dovidio, J.F. (2011) E pluribus unum: Dual identity and minority group members' motivation to engage in contact, as well as social change. *Journal of Experimental Social Psychology, 47*, 1021–1024.

Hamilton, D.L. (1981) Stereotyping and intergroup behavior: Some thoughts on the cognitive approach. In D.L. Hamilton (Ed.), *Cognitive processes in stereotyping and intergroup behavior* (pp. 333–353). Hillsdale, NJ: Erlbaum.

Hehman, E., Gaertner, S.L., Dovidio, J.F., Mania, E.W., Guerra, R., Wilson, D.C. & Friel, B.M. (2012) Group status drives majority and minority integration preferences. *Psychological Science*, 23, 46–52.

Heine, S.J., Lehman, D.R., Markus, H.R. & Kitayama, S. (1999) Is there a universal need for positive self-regard? *Psychological Review*, 106, 766–794.

Hofstede, G. (1980) *Culture's consequences: International differences in work-related values.* London: Sage.

——(1991) *Cultures and organizations: Software of the mind.* London: McGraw-Hill.

Hogg, M.A. & Terry, D.J. (2000) Social identity and self-categorization processes in organizational contexts. *The Academy of Management Review*, 25, 121–140.

Insko, C.A., Schopler, J., Gaertner, L., Wildschut, T., Kozar, R., Pinter, B., Finkel, E.J., Brazil, D.M., Cecil, C.L. & Montoya, M.R. (2001) Interindividual-intergroup discontinuity reduction through the anticipation of future interaction. *Journal of Personality and Social Psychology*, 80, 95–111.

Jones, J.M. (2003) TRIOS: A psychological theory of African legacy in American culture. *Journal of Social Issues*, 59, 217–241.

Jost, J.T., Banaji, M. & Nosek, B.A. (2004) A decade of System Justification Theory: Accumulated evidence of conscious and unconscious bolstering of the *status quo. Political Psychology*, 25, 881–919.

Katz, I. & Hass, R.G. (1988) Racial ambivalence and American value conflict: Correlational and priming studies of dual cognitive structures. *Journal of Personality and Social Psychology*, 55, 893–905.

LeBon, G. (1896) *The crowd: A study of the popular mind.* New York: Macmillan.

Markus, H.R. & Kitayama, S. (1991) Culture and the self: Implications for cognition, emotion and motivation. *Psychological Review*, 98, 224–253.

Masuda, T. & Nisbett, R.E. (2001) Attending holistically versus analytically: Comparing the context sensitivity of Japanese and Americans. *Journal of Personality and Social Psychology*, 81, 922–934.

Milgram, S. (1974) *Obedience to authority.* New York: Harper-Collins.

Nisbett, R.E. (2003) *The geography of thought: How Asians and Westerners think differently and why.* New York: The Free Press.

Nisbett, R.E., Peng, K., Choi, I. & Norenzayan, A. (2001) Culture and systems of thought: Holistic vs. analytic cognition. *Psychological Review*, 108, 291–310.

Reicher, S.D. & Haslam, S.A. (2006) Rethinking the psychology of tyranny: The BBC Prison Study. *British Journal of Social Psychology*, 45, 1–40.

Robinson, W.P. (Ed.) (1996) *Social groups and identities: Developing the legacy of Henri Tajfel.* Oxford, England: Butterworth-Heinemann.

Roccas, S. & Brewer, M. (2002) Social identity complexity. *Personality and Social Psychology Review*, 6, 88–106.

Rokeach, M. (1973) *The nature of human values*. New York: Free Press.

Ryan, C.S., Hunt, J.S., Weible, J.A., Peterson, C.R. & Casas, J.F. (2007) Multicultural and colorblind ideology, stereotypes, and ethnocentrism among Black and White Americans. *Group Processes and Intergroup Relations*, 10, 617–637.

Saguy, T. & Chernyak-Hai, L. (2012) Intergroup contact can undermine disadvantaged group members' attributions to discrimination. *Journal of Experimental Social Psychology*, 48, 714–720.

Saguy, T., Tausch, N., Dovidio, J.F. & Pratto, F. (2009) The irony of harmony: Intergroup contact can produce false expectations for equality. *Psychological Science*, 29, 114–121.

Sherif, M., Harvey, O.J., White, B.J., Hood, W.R. & Sherif, C.W. (1961) *Intergroup conflict and cooperation: The Robbers' Cave experiment*. Norman, OK: University of Oklahoma Book Exchange.

Shnabel, N. & Nadler, A. (2008) A needs-based model of reconciliation: Satisfying the differential emotional needs of victim and perpetrator as a key to promoting reconciliation. *Journal of Personality and Social Psychology*, 94, 116–132.

Shnabel, N., Nadler, A., Ullrich, J., Dovidio, J.F. & Carmi, D. (2009) Promoting reconciliation through the satisfaction of the emotional needs of victimized and perpetrating group members: The Needs-Based Model of Reconciliation. *Personality and Social Psychology Bulletin*, 35, 1021–1030.

Sidanius, J. & Pratto, F. (1999) *Social dominance: An intergroup theory of social hierarchy and oppression*. New York: University Press.

Simon, B., Reichert, F. & Grabow, O. (2013) When dual identity becomes a liability: Identity and political radicalism among migrants. *Psychological Science*, 24, 251–257.

Simon, B. & Ruhs, D. (2008) Identity and politicisation among Turkish migrants in Germany: The role of dual identification. *Journal of Personality and Social Psychology*, 95, 1354–1366.

Sindic, D. & Condor, S. (2014) Social Identity Theory and Self-Categorization Theory. In C. Kinvall, T. Capelos, H. Dekker & P. Nesbitt-Larking (Eds), *The Palgrave handbook of global political psychology*. London: Palgrave (in press).

Stürmer, S. & Simon, B. (2004) Collective action: Towards a dual pathway model. In W. Stroebe & M. Hewstone (Eds), *European review of social psychology* (pp. 59–99). Hove, UK: Psychology Press.

Sumner, W. (1906) *Folkways*. New York: Ginn.

Tajfel, H. & Turner, J.C. (1979) An integrative theory of intergroup conflict. In W.G. Austin & S. Worchel (Eds), *The social psychology of intergroup relations* (pp. 33–48). Monterey, CA: Brooks/Cole.

Turner, J.C. (2005) Explaining the nature of power: A three-process theory. *European Journal of Social Psychology*, 35, 1–22.

Turner, J.C., Hogg, M.A., Oakes, P.J., Reicher, S.D. & Wetherell, M.S. (1987) *Rediscovering the social group: A self-categorization theory*. Oxford, England: Basil Blackwell.

Tyler, T.R. (2005) Managing conflicts of interest within organizations: Does activating social values change the impact of self-interest on behavior? In D.A. Moore, D.M. Cain, G.Loewenstein & M.H. Bazerman (Eds), *Conflicts of interest: Challenges and solutions in business, law, medicine, and public policy* (pp. 13–35). New York: Cambridge University Press.

Tyler, T.R. & Blader, S.L. (2003) The Group Engagement Model: Procedural justice, social identity, and cooperative behavior. *Personality and Social Psychology Review*, 7, 349–361.

van Zomeren, M., Postmes, T. & Spears, R. (2008) Toward an integrative social identity model of collective action: A quantitative research synthesis of three socio-psychological perspectives. *Psychological Bulletin*, 134, 504–535.

Verkuyten, M. (2006) Multicultural recognition and ethnic minority rights: A social identity perspective. *European Review of Social Psychology*, 17, 148–184.

Weber, M. (1905/2008) *The Protestant ethic and the spirit of capitalism.* Digireads.com publishing.

Wright, S.C. (2001) Strategic collective action: Social psychology and social change. In R. Brown & S.L. Gaertner (Eds), *Blackwell handbook of social psychology: Intergroup processes* (pp. 223–256). Oxford, England: Blackwell.

Zimbardo, P. (1989) *Quiet rage: The Stanford prison study video.* Stanford, CA: Stanford University.

INDEX

Printed by PGSTL